LINCOLN THE UNKNOWN

DALE CARNEGIE

★

Lincoln
THE UNKNOWN

DALE CARNEGIE & ASSOCIATES, INC.
HAUPPAUGE, NEW YORK

To
MY FATHER AND MOTHER

HOW THIS BOOK WAS WRITTEN—
AND WHY

ONE SPRING DAY, some years ago, I was breakfasting in the Hotel Dysart, London; and, as usual, I was trying to winnow a bit of American news from the columns of the "Morning Post." Ordinarily I found none, but on that fortunate morning I made a strike rich and unexpected.

The late T. P. O'Connor, reputed "Father of the House of Commons," conducted in those days a column in the "Morning Post" entitled "Men and Memories." On that particular morning, and for several mornings following, "Tay Pay's" column was devoted to Abraham Lincoln—not to his political activities but to the personal side of his career: to his sorrows, his repeated failures, his poverty, his great love for Ann Rutledge, and his tragic marriage to Mary Todd.

I read the series with profound interest—and surprise. I had spent the first twenty years of my life in the Middle West, not far from the Lincoln country; and, in addition to that, I had always been keenly interested in United States history. I should have said that of course I knew Lincoln's life-story; but I soon discovered that I didn't. The fact is that I, an American, had had to come to London and read a series of articles written by an Irishman, in an English newspaper, before I realized that the story of Lincoln's career was one of the most fascinating tales in all the annals of mankind.

Was this lamentable ignorance peculiar to me? I wondered.

But I didn't wonder long, for I soon discussed the subject with a number of my fellow-countrymen, and I discovered that they were in the same boat, that about all they knew about Lincoln was this: that he had been born in a log cabin, had walked miles to borrow books and then read them at night, stretched out on the floor in front of the fireplace; that he split rails, became a lawyer, told funny stories, said that a man's legs ought to be long enough to reach the ground, was called "Honest Abe," debated with Judge Douglas, was elected President of the United States, wore a silk hat, freed the slaves, spoke at Gettysburg, declared that he wished he knew what brand of whisky Grant drank so he could send a barrel of it to his other generals, and was shot by Booth in a theater in Washington.

Aroused by these articles in the "Morning Post," I went over to the British Museum library and read a number of Lincoln books; and the more I read, the more fascinated I became. Finally I caught on fire and I determined to write a book about Lincoln, myself. I knew that I had not the urge, temperament, training, or ability necessary to produce a learned treatise for the benefit of scholars and historians. Besides, I felt there was little need for another book of that kind, for many excellent ones are already in existence. However, after reading many Lincoln volumes, I did feel that there was a genuine need for a short biography that would tell the most interesting facts about his career briefly and tersely for the average busy and hurried citizen of to-day. I have tried to write such a book.

I began the work in Europe, and labored over it for a year there and then for two years in New York. Finally I tore up all that I had written and tossed it into the wastebasket. I then went out to Illinois, to write of Lincoln on the very ground where he himself had dreamed and toiled. For months I lived among people whose fathers had helped Lincoln survey land and build fences and drive hogs to market. For months I delved among old books and letters and speeches and half-forgotten newspapers and musty court records, trying to understand Lincoln.

I spent one summer in the little town of Petersburg. I went there because it is only a mile away from the restored village of New Salem, where Lincoln spent the happiest and most formative years of his life. There he ran a mill and a grocery store, studied law, worked as a blacksmith, refereed cock-fights and horse-races, fell in love, and had his heart broken.

Even in the heydey of its glory New Salem never had more than a hundred inhabitants, and its entire existence covered a span of about ten years. Shortly after Lincoln left the village it was abandoned; bats and swallows nested in the decaying cabins, and for more than half a century cows grazed over the spot.

A few years ago, however, the State of Illinois secured the site, made it a public park, and built replicas of the log cabins that had stood there a hundred years before. So to-day the deserted village of New Salem looks much as it did in Lincoln's time.

The same white oaks under which Lincoln studied and wrestled and made love are still standing. Every morning I used to take my typewriter and motor up there from Petersburg, and half of the chapters of this book were written under those trees. What a lovely spot in which to work! In front of me flowed the winding Sangamon, and all about me the woods and the hay-fields were musical with the call of the bob-white; and through the trees flashed the color of the blue jay, the yellowhammer, and the redbird. I felt Lincoln there.

I often used to go there alone on summer nights when the whip-poor-wills were crying in the woods along the banks of the Sangamon, when the moonlight outlined Rutledge's tavern against the sky; and it stirred me to realize that on just such nights, about a hundred years ago, young Abe Lincoln and Ann Rutledge had walked over this same ground arm in arm in the moonlight, listening to the night-birds and dreaming ecstatic dreams that were destined never to come true. Yet I am convinced that Lincoln found here at New Salem the only supreme happiness that he ever knew.

When I came to write the chapter dealing with the death of Lincoln's sweetheart, I put a little folding table and a typewriter in a car and drove out over country roads and through a hog lot and a cow pasture until I reached the quiet, secluded spot where Ann Rutledge lies buried. It is utterly abandoned now, and overgrown. To get near her grave, it was necessary to mow down the weeds and brush and vines. And there, where Lincoln came to weep, was set down the story of his grief.

Many of the chapters were written in Springfield. Some in the sitting-room of the old home where Lincoln lived for sixteen unhappy years, some at the desk where he composed his first inaugural address, and others above the spot where he came to court and quarrel with Mary Todd.

★

PART ONE

★

1

THERE WAS a woman in Harrodsburg—it was called Fort Harrod in those days—named Ann McGinty. The old histories record that Ann and her husband brought the first hogs into Kentucky, the first ducks and the first spinning-wheel; and they also declare that she was the first woman ever to make butter out there in the dark and bloody wilderness. But her real claim to fame rests upon the fact that she performed an economic and textile miracle. Cotton could be neither grown nor purchased there in the mysterious Indian country, and timber-wolves slaughtered the sheep. So it was well-nigh impossible to find any substance from which clothes could be made. Then the ingenious Ann McGinty found a way of spinning thread and making "McGinty cloth" from two substances that were both plentiful and cheap—nettle lint and buffalo wool.

It was a tremendous discovery, and housewives traveled as far as a hundred and fifty miles to sit in her cabin and learn the new art. And as they spun and wove they talked. And they didn't always talk about nettle lint and buffalo wool. Frequently the conversation degenerated into gossip, and Ann McGinty's cabin soon became the community's acknowledged clearing-house for scandal.

In those days fornication was an indictable offense, and bastardy was a misdemeanor. And evidently there were few other activities in life that gave Ann's shriveled soul more deep and abiding satisfaction than uncovering the story of some suf-

13

fering girl's error, and then running to the Grand Jury with the news. The records of the Court of Quarter Sessions in Fort Harrod repeatedly tell the pathetic story of some unfortunate girl indicted for fornication "on information of Ann McGinty." Seventeen cases were tried at Harrodsburg in the spring of 1783, and eight were for fornication.

Among these indictments, there is one brought by the Grand Jury on November 24, 1789, and reading as follows:

"Lucy Hanks for fornication."

This wasn't Lucy's first offense. The first had been years before, back in Virginia.

That was a long time ago, and the old records are meager: they give only a few bare facts and no setting for the facts. From them and from other sources, however, a probable story can be reconstructed. The essential elements, at any rate, are well established.

The Virginia home of the Hanks family had been on a narrow strip of land bounded on one side by the Rappahannock River, on the other by the Potomac. On this same narrow strip of land dwelt the Washingtons and the Lees, the Carters and the Fauntleroys, and many another snuff-and-silk-breeches family. These aristocrats attended services at Christ Church, and so did the poor and illiterate families of the neighborhood such as the Hankses.

Lucy Hanks was present, as usual, on the second Sunday in November, 1781, when General Washington caused a great craning of necks by bringing General La Fayette to church, as his guest. Every one was eager to see the distinguished Frenchman who, only a month before, had helped Washington capture the army of Lord Cornwallis at Yorktown.

After the last hymn had been sung that morning and the benediction pronounced, the parishioners marched by in single file, shaking hands with the two military heroes.

But La Fayette had a predilection for other things besides military tactics and affairs of state. He took a profound interest in beautiful young ladies; and it was his custom, on being introduced to one that appealed to him, to pay her the compliment of a kiss. On this particular morning he kissed seven girls in front of Christ Church; and in doing so he caused more comment than had the third chapter of the Gospel according to

St. Luke, which had been read so sonorously by the rector. One of the seven fortunate girls that he kissed was Lucy Hanks.

This kiss started a chain of events that did as much to modify the future of the United States as did all the battles La Fayette fought for us. Perhaps more.

There was a bachelor in the congregation that morning—a rich, aristocratic bachelor who for a long time had known vaguely of the Hanks family, an illiterate, poverty-stricken tribe that moved in a world far below his. But this morning—of course it may have been pure imagination—he thought that La Fayette put just a trifle more ardor and enthusiasm into the kiss he gave Lucy Hanks than in those he bestowed upon the other girls.

This planter looked up to the French general, both as a military genius and as a connoisseur of beautiful women. So he fell to dreaming now of Lucy Hanks. And when he stopped to think of it, he knew that some of the world's most celebrated beauties had been bred in circumstances as poor as Lucy's— some in circumstances even more humble. There was Lady Hamilton, for example; and Madame DuBarry, the illegitimate child of a poverty-stricken dressmaker. DuBarry herself was almost illiterate, yet she all but ruled France under Louis XV. They were comforting, these historical precedents; and they helped to dignify the bachelor's desires.

This was Sunday. He turned the matter over in his mind all day Monday; and on Tuesday morning he rode over to the dirt-floor cabin that the Hanks tribe occupied and hired Lucy to be a servant in the farm-house on his plantation.

He already owned a number of slaves, and he didn't need another servant. Nevertheless he hired Lucy, gave her some light tasks about the house, and didn't ask her to associate with the slaves.

It was the custom of many of the wealthy families of Virginia at that time to educate their sons in England. Lucy's employer had attended Oxford, and he had brought back to America a collection of books that he cherished. One day he drifted into the library and found Lucy seated, dust-cloth in hand, poring over the illustrations in a history book.

That was an odd thing for a servant to be doing. But, instead of censuring her, he closed the library door and sat down and read her the captions underneath the pictures, and told her something of what they meant.

She listened with very evident interest; and finally, to his surprise, she confessed that she wanted to learn to read and write.

Just how astonishing that aspiration was in a servant-girl in the year of our Lord 1781, it is difficult now to understand. Virginia at that time did not have any free schools; not half the property-owners of the State could sign their names to a deed, and virtually all of the women made their marks when transferring land.

Yet here was a servant-girl aspiring to read and write. The best people in Virginia would have called it dangerous, if not revolutionary. But the idea appealed to Lucy's employer, and he volunteered to be her tutor. That evening, after supper, he called her into the library and began teaching her the letters of the alphabet. A few evenings later he put his hand over hers as it grasped the quill, and showed her how to form the letters. For a long time after that he taught her, and to his credit let it be recorded that he did a very good job. There is one specimen of her handwriting still in existence, and it shows that she wrote with a bold, self-confident flourish. There are spirit and personality and character in her handwriting; and she not only used the word "approbation," but spelled it correctly. That was no little achievement at a time when the orthography of men like George Washington was not always flawless.

And when the reading and spelling lessons were finished for the evening Lucy and her tutor sat side by side in the library, looking at the dancing flames in the fireplace, and watching the moon rise over the rim of the forest.

She fell in love with him, and trusted him; but she trusted him too far. . . . Then came weeks of anxiety. She couldn't eat. She hardly slept. She worried a haggard look into her face. When she could no longer deny the truth even to herself she told him. For a moment he considered marrying her. But only for a moment. Family. Friends. Social position. Complications. Unpleasant scenes. . . . No. Besides, he was begining to tire of her. So he gave her some money and sent her away.

As the months went by people pointed at Lucy and shunned her.

One Sunday morning she created a sensation by shamelessly bringing her baby to church. The good women of the congregation were indignant, and one stood up in the meeting-house and demanded that "that slut be sent away."

That was enough. Lucy's father did not mean to have his

daughter insulted any longer. So the Hanks tribe loaded their few earthly possessions into a wagon and traveled out over the Wilderness Road, through the Cumberland Gap, and settled at Fort Harrod, Kentucky. No one knew them there: they could lie more effectively about the father of Lucy's child.

But in Fort Harrod Lucy was quite as pretty, quite as attractive to men as she had been back in Virginia. She was sought after, and flattered. She fell in love again. This time it was a little easier to stray. Somebody found it out. Somebody told somebody else. Then it was repeated at Ann McGinty's. And, as we have already recorded, the Grand Jury indicted Lucy for fornication. But the sheriff knew Lucy wasn't the kind of woman to have the law upon; so he stuck the summons in his pocket, and went off deer-hunting and left her alone.

That was in November. In March the court met again. And when it met, a certain woman appeared with further gossip and slander about Lucy and demanded that the hussy be haled into court and made to answer to the charges against her. So another summons was issued; but high-spirited Lucy tore it up and flung it into the face of the man who served it. In May the court would convene again; and Lucy would doubtless have been forced into court at that time, had not a remarkable young man appeared on the scene.

His name was Henry Sparrow. He rode into town, tied his horse in front of her cabin, and went in.

"Lucy," he probably said to her, "I don't give a damn about what these women are saying about you. I love you and want you to be my wife." At any rate, he did ask her to marry him.

However, she was not willing to marry immediately. She was not willing to have the gossips of the town say that Sparrow had been forced into matrimony.

"We'll wait a year, Henry," she insisted. "During that time I want to prove to every one that I can live a decent life. If at the end of that time, you still want me, come; I'll be waiting for you."

Henry Sparrow took out the license at once, April 26, 1790, and nothing more was heard of the summons. Almost a year later they were married.

That set the Ann McGinty crowd to shaking their heads and wagging their tongues: the marriage wouldn't last long, Lucy would be up to her old tricks again. Henry Sparrow heard this talk. Every one heard it. He wanted to shield Lucy. So he suggested that they move farther West and begin life all over again in kindlier surroundings. She refused that customary means of escape. She wasn't bad, she said; and she held her head high as she said it. She wasn't going to run away. She was determined to settle down there in Fort Harrod and fight it out.

And she did. She reared eight children and redeemed her name in the very community where it had once been a signal for coarse jests.

In time two of her sons became preachers; and one of her grandsons, the son of her illegitimate daughter, became President of the United States. His name was Abraham Lincoln.

I have told this story to show Lincoln's more immediate ancestry. He himself set great store by his well-bred Virginia grandfather.

William H. Herndon was Lincoln's law partner for twenty-one years. He probably knew Lincoln better than any other man who ever lived. Fortunately, he wrote a three-volume biography of Lincoln that appeared in 1888. It is one of the most important of the multitude of works on Lincoln. I quote now from pages 3 and 4 of Volume I:

On the subject of his ancestry and origin I only remember one time when Mr. Lincoln ever referred to it. It was about 1850, when he and I were driving in his one-horse buggy to the court in Menard county, Illinois. The suit we were going to try was one in which we were likely, either directly or collaterally, to touch upon the subject of hereditary traits. During the ride he spoke, for the first time in my hearing, of his mother, dwelling on her characteristics, and mentioning or enumerating what qualities he inherited from her. He said, among other things, that she was the illegitimate daughter of Lucy Hanks and a well-bred Virginia farmer or planter; and he argued that from this last source came his power of analysis, his logic, his mental activity, his ambition, and all the qualities that distinguished him from the other members and descendants of the Hanks family. His theory in discussing the matter of hereditary traits has been, that, for certain reasons, illegitimate children are oftentimes sturdier and brighter than those born in lawful wedlock; and in his case, he believed that his better nature and finer qualities came from this broad-minded, unknown Virginian. The revelation—painful as it was—called up the recollection of his mother, and, as the buggy jolted over the road, he added ruefully, "God bless my mother; all that I am or ever hope to be I owe to her," and immediately lapsed into silence. Our interchange of ideas ceased, and we rode on for some time without exchanging a word. He was sad and absorbed. Burying himself in thought, and musing no doubt over the disclosure he had just made, he drew round him a barrier which I feared to penetrate. His words and melancholy tone made a deep impression on me. It was an experience I can never forget.

2

Lincoln's mother, Nancy Hanks, was brought up by her aunt and uncle, and probably had no schooling at all. We know she could not write, for she made her mark when signing a deed.

She lived deep in the somber woods and made few friends; and, when she was twenty-two, she married one of the most illiterate and lowly men in all Kentucky—a dull, ignorant day-laborer and deer-hunter. His name was Thomas Lincoln, but the people in the backwoods and canebrake settlements where he lived called him "Linkhorn."

Thomas Lincoln was a rover, a drifter, a ne'er-do-well, floating about from one place to another, taking any kind of job he could get when hunger drove him to it. He worked on roads, cut brush, trapped bear, cleared land, plowed corn, built log cabins; and the old records show that on three different occasions he was employed to guard prisoners, with a shot-gun. In 1805 Hardin County, Kentucky, paid him six cents an hour for catching and whipping recalcitrant slaves.

He had no money sense whatever: he lived for fourteen years on one farm in Indiana, and during that period he was unable to save and pay as much as ten dollars a year on his land. At a time when he was so poor that his wife had to pin her dresses together with wild thorns, he went to a store in Elizabethtown, Kentucky, and bought a pair of silk suspenders for himself—and bought them on credit. Shortly after that, at an auction sale, he paid three dollars for a sword. Probably he wore his silk suspenders and carried his sword even when going barefoot.

Shortly after his marriage he moved to town and tried to make a living as a carpenter. He got a job building a mill, but he did not square his timbers or cut them the right length. So his employer sharply refused to pay him for his bungling efforts, and three lawsuits followed.

Tom Lincoln had come from the woods, and, dull as he was, he soon realized now that he belonged to the woods. He took his wife back to a poor, stony farm on the edge of the forest, and never again did he have the temerity to forsake the soil for the village.

Not far from Elizabethtown there was a vast stretch of treeless land known as "the barrens." For generations the Indians had started fires there and burned away the forests and brush and undergrowth, so that the coarse prairie-grass could grow in the sun, and the buffaloes would come there to wallow and graze.

In December, 1808, Tom Lincoln purchased a farm on "the barrens" for sixty-six and two thirds cents per acre. There was a hunter's hut on it, a crude sort of cabin surrounded with wild crab-apple trees; and half a mile away flowed the South Fork of Nolin Creek, where the dogwood blossomed in the spring. In the summertime, hawks circled lazily in the blue overhead, and the tall grasses surged in the wind like an illimitable sea of green. Few people had had the poor judgment to settle there. So in the wintertime it was one of the most lonely and desolate regions in all Kentucky.

And it was in a hunter's hut on the edge of these lonely barrens, deep in the winter of 1809, that Abraham Lincoln came into the world. He was born on a Sunday morning—born on a bed of poles covered with corn husks. It was storming outside, and the February wind blew the snow through the cracks between the logs and drifted it across the bearskin that covered Nancy Hanks and her baby. She was destined to die nine years later, at the age of thirty-five, worn out by the strain and hardships of pioneer life. She never knew much of happiness. Wherever she lived, she was hounded by gossip about her illegitimate birth. What a pity she could not have looked into the future that morning, and seen the marble temple that a grateful people have now erected on the spot which she then consecrated with her suffering!

The paper money in circulation at that time, in the wilderness, was often of very doubtful value. Much of it was worthless. So hogs, venison hams, whisky, coon-skins, bear-hides, and farm produce were much used as mediums of exchange. Even preachers sometimes took whisky as part pay for their services. In the autumn of 1816, when Abraham was seven years old, old Tom Lincoln bartered his Kentucky farm for about four hundred gallons of corn whisky, and moved his family into the gloom and solitude of the wild and desolate forests of Indiana. Their nearest neighbor was a bear-hunter; and all about them the trees and brush and grape-vines and undergrowth were so thick that a man had to cut and hack his way through it. This was the spot, "Rite in the Brush," as Dennis Hanks described it, where Abraham Lincoln was to spend the next fourteen years of his life.

The first snow of winter was already falling when the family arrived; and Tom Lincoln hastily built what was then known as "a three-faced camp." To-day it would be called a shed. It had no floor, no door, no windows—nothing but three sides and a roof of poles and brush. The fourth side was entirely open to wind and snow and sleet and cold. Nowadays an up-to-date farmer in Indiana wouldn't winter his cattle or hogs in such a crude shelter, but Tom Lincoln felt it was good enough for himself and his family all during the long winter of 1816–17, one of the severest and most violent winters in our history.

Nancy Hanks and her children slept there that winter like dogs, curled up on a heap of leaves and bearskins dumped on the dirt floor in a corner of the shed.

As for food, they had no butter, no milk, no eggs, no fruit, no vegetables, not even potatoes. They lived chiefly on wild game and nuts.

Tom Lincoln tried to raise hogs, but the bears were so hungry that they seized the hogs and ate them alive.

For years, there in Indiana, Abraham Lincoln endured more terrible poverty than did thousands of the slaves whom he would one day liberate.

Dentists were almost unknown in that region, and the nearest doctor was thirty-five miles away; so when Nancy Lincoln had a toothache, probably old Tom Lincoln did what the other pioneers did; he whittled out a hickory peg, set the end of it against the complaining molar, and hit the peg a hard blow with a rock.

From the earliest times in the Middle West the pioneers suffered from a mysterious malady known as the "milk sick." It was fatal to cattle, sheep, and horses, and sometimes carried off entire communities of people. No one knew what caused it, and for a hundred years it baffled the medical profession. It was not until the beginning of the present century that science showed that the poisoning was due to animals eating a plant known as white snakeroot. The poison was transmitted to humans through the milk of cows. White snakeroot thrives in wooded pastures and deeply shaded ravines, and to this day it continues to take its toll of human life. Every year the Department of Agriculture of the State of Illinois posts placards in the county court-houses, warning farmers that if they do not eradicate this plant, they may die.

In the autumn of 1818 this dreadful scourge came to the Buckhorn Valley of Indiana, wiping out many families. Nancy Lincoln helped nurse the wife of Peter Brooner, the bear-hunter, whose cabin was only half a mile away. Mrs. Brooner died, and Nancy herself suddenly felt ill. Her head swam, and sharp pains shot through her abdomen. Vomiting severely, she was carried home to her wretched pallet of leaves and skins. Her hands and feet were cold, but her vitals seemed to be on fire. She kept calling for water. Water. Water. More water.

Tom Lincoln had a profound faith in signs and omens; so, on the second night of her illness, when a dog howled long and piteously outside the cabin, he abandoned all hope and said she was going to die.

Finally Nancy was unable even to raise her head from the pillow, and she could not talk above a whisper. Beckoning Abraham and his sister to her, she tried to speak. They bent over to catch her words: she pleaded with them to be good to each other, to live as she had taught them, and to worship God.

These were her last words, for her throat and entire intestinal tract were already in the first stages of paralysis. She sank into a prolonged coma, and finally died on the seventh day of her illness, October 5, 1818.

Tom Lincoln put two copper pennies on her eyelids, to hold them shut; and then went out into the forest and felled a tree and cut it into rough, uneven boards and fastened these together with wooden pegs; and in this crude coffin he placed the tired, worn body of the sad-faced daughter of Lucy Hanks.

Two years before, he had brought her into this settlement on a sled; and now, again on a sled, he hauled her body to the summit of a thickly wooded hill, a quarter of a mile away, and buried her without service or ceremony.

So perished the mother of Abraham Lincoln. We shall probably never know what she looked like or what manner of woman she was, for she spent most of her short life in the gloomy forests, and made only a faint impression upon the few people who crossed her path.

Shortly after Lincoln's death one of his biographers set out to get some information about the President's mother. She had been dead then for half a century. He interviewed the few people living who had ever seen her, but their memories were as vague as a faded dream. They were unable to agree even as to her physical appearance. One described her as a "heavy built, squatty woman," but another said she had a "spare, delicate form." One man thought she had black eyes, another described them as hazel, another was sure they were bluish green. Dennis Hanks, her cousin, who had lived under the same roof with her for fifteen years, wrote that she had "lite hair." After further reflection, he reversed himself and said her hair was black.

For sixty years after her death there was not so much as a stone to mark her resting-place, so that to-day only the approximate position of her grave is known. She is buried beside her aunt and uncle, who reared her; but it is impossible to say which of the three graves is hers.

A short time before Nancy's death Tom Lincoln had built a new cabin. It had four sides, but no floor, no windows, no door. A dirty bearskin hung over the entrance, and the interior was dark and foul. Tom Lincoln spent most of his time hunting in the woods, leaving his two motherless children to run the place. Sarah did the cooking, while Abraham kept the fire going and carried water from the spring a mile away. Having no knives and forks, they ate with their fingers, and with fingers that were seldom clean, for water was hard to get and they had no soap. Nancy had probably made her own soft lye soap, but the small supply that she left at her death had long since vanished, and the children didn't know how to make more; and Tom Lincoln wouldn't make it. So they lived on in their poverty and dirt.

During the long, cold winter months they made no attempt to wash their bodies; and few, if any, attempts to wash their soiled and ragged garments. Their beds of leaves and skins grew filthy. No sunlight warmed and purified the cabin. The only light they had was from the fireplace or from hog fat. We know from accurate descriptions of other cabins on the frontier what the womanless Lincoln cabin must have been like. It smelled. It was infested with fleas, crawling with vermin.

After a year of this squalor even old Tom Lincoln could stand it no longer; he decided to get a new wife who would clean up.

Thirteen years before he had proposed to a woman in Kentucky named Sarah Bush. She had refused him then and married the jailer of Hardin County, but the jailer had since died and left her with three children and some debts. Tom Lincoln felt that the time was auspicious now for renewing his proposal; so he went to the creek, washed up, scrubbed his grimy hands and face with sand, strapped on his sword, and started back through the deep, dark woods to Kentucky.

When he reached Elizabethtown he bought another pair of silk suspenders, and marched whistling down the street.

That was in 1819. Things were happening, and people were talking of progress. A steamship had crossed the Atlantic Ocean!

Wнem Lincoln was fifteen he knew his alphabet and could read a little but with difficulty. He could not write at all. That autumn—1824—a wandering backwoods pedagogue drifted into the settlement along Pigeon Creek and started a school. Lincoln and his sister walked four miles through the forests, night and morning, to study under the new teacher, Azel Dorsey. Dorsey kept what was known as a "blab" school; the children studied aloud. In that way the teacher believed he could tell whether or not they were applying themselves. He marched about the room, switch in hand, giving a cut to those who were silent. With such a premium on vociferousness, each pupil strove to out-blab the others. The uproar could often be heard a quarter of a mile away.

While attending this school Lincoln wore a cap of squirrel-skin, and breeches made from the hide of a deer. The breeches failed by a considerable stretch to meet the top of his shoes, leaving several inches of sharp, blue shinbone exposed to the wind and snow.

The school was held in a crude cabin barely high enough for the teacher to stand up in. There were no windows; a log had been left out at each side, and the opening covered with greased paper to let in the light. The floor and seats were made of split logs.

Lincoln's reading lessons were chapters from the Bible; and in his writing exercises he took the chirography of Washington and Jefferson as his models. His handwriting resembled theirs. It was unusually clear and distinct. People commented on it, and the illiterate neighbors walked for miles to have Abraham write their letters.

He was finding a real tang and zest, now, in learning. The hours at school were all too short, he carried his studies home. Paper was scarce and high, so he wrote on a board with a charcoal stick. Sometimes he ciphered on the flat sides of the hewn logs that formed the cabin walls. Whenever a bare surface became covered with figures and writing he shaved them off with a drawing-knife and began anew.

Too poor to buy an arithmetic, he borrowed one and copied it on sheets of paper about the size of an ordinary letter-head. Then he sewed them together with twine, and so had a home-made arithmetic of his own. At the time of his death his step-mother still had portions of this book.

Now he began to exhibit a trait which sharply distinguished him from the rest of the backwoods scholars. He wanted to write out his opinions on various topics; at times he even broke into verse. And he took his verse and prose composition to William Wood, a neighbor, for criticism. He memorized and recited his rhymes, and his essays attracted attention. A lawyer was so impressed with his article on national politics that he sent it away and had it published. A newspaper in Ohio featured an article he wrote on temperance.

But this was later. His first composition here in school was inspired by the cruel sports of his playmates. They used to catch terrapins and put burning coals on their backs. Lincoln pleaded with them to stop it, and ran and kicked off the coals with his bare feet. His first essay was a plea for mercy to animals. Already the boy was showing that deep sympathy for the suffering which was to be so characteristic of the man.

Five years later he attended another school irregularly—"by littles," as he phrased it.

Thus ended all his formal attempts at education, with a total of not more than twelve months of schooling.

When he went to Congress in 1847 and filled out a biographical blank, he came to the question, "What has been your education?" He answered it with one word: "Defective."

After he was nominated for the Presidency he said: "When I came of age, I did not know much. Still, somehow, I could read, write, and cipher to the rule of three; but that was all.

I have not been to school since. The little advance I now have upon this store of education, I have picked up from time to time under the pressure of necessity."

And who had been his teachers? Wandering, benighted pedagogues who had faith in witches and believed that the world was flat. Yet, during these broken and irregular periods, he had developed one of the most valuable assets any man can have, even from a university education: a love of knowledge and a thirst for learning.

The ability to read opened up a new and magic world for him, a world he had never dreamed of before. It changed him. It broadened his horizon and gave him vision; and, for a quarter of a century, reading remained the dominant passion of his life. His stepmother had brought a little library of five volumes with her: the Bible, Æsop's Fables, "Robinson Crusoe," "The Pilgrim's Progress," and "Sinbad the Sailor." The boy pored over these priceless treasures. He kept the Bible and Æsop's Fables within easy reach and read them so often that they profoundly affected his style, his manner of talking, his method of presenting arguments.

But these books weren't enough. He longed for more things to read, but he had no money. So he began to borrow books, newspapers, anything in print. Walking down to the Ohio River, he borrowed a copy of the Revised Laws of Indiana from a lawyer. Then, for the first time, he read the Declaration of Independence and the Constitution of the United States.

He borrowed two or three biographies from a neighboring farmer for whom he had often grubbed stumps and hoed corn. One was the Life of Washington by Parson Weems. It fascinated Lincoln, and he read it at night as long as he could see; and, when he went to sleep, he stuck it in a crack between the logs so that he could begin it again as soon as daylight filtered into the hut. One night a storm blew up, and the book was soaked. The owner refused to take it back, so Lincoln had to cut and shock fodder for three days to pay for it.

But in all his book-borrowing expeditions, he never made a richer find than "Scott's Lessons." This book gave him instruction in public speaking, and introduced him to the renowned speeches of Cicero and Demosthenes and those of Shakespeare's characters.

With "Scott's Lessons" open in his hand, he would walk back and forth under the trees, declaiming Hamlet's instructions to the players, and repeating Antony's oration over the dead body of Cæsar: "Friends, Romans, countrymen, lend me your ears; I come to bury Cæsar, not to praise him."

When he came across a passage that appealed especially to him, he would chalk it down on a board if he had no paper. Finally he made a crude scrap-book. In this he wrote all his favorites, using a buzzard's quill for a pen and pokeberry juice for ink. He carried the scrap-book with him and studied it until he could repeat many long poems and speeches by heart.

When he went out in the field to work his book went with him. While the horses rested at the end of the corn row he sat on the top rail of a fence and studied. At noontime, instead of sitting down and eating with the rest of the family, he took a corn-dodger in one hand and a book in the other and, hoisting his feet higher than his head, lost himself in the lines of print.

When court was in session Lincoln would often walk fifteen miles to the river towns to hear the lawyers argue. Later, when he was out working in the fields with other men, he would now and then drop the grub-hoe or hay-fork, mount a fence, and repeat the speeches he had heard the lawyers make down at Rockport or Boonville. At other times he mimicked the shouting hard-shell Baptist preachers who held forth in the Little Pigeon Creek church on Sundays.

Abe often carried "Quinn's Jests," a joke-book, to the fields; and when he sat astride a log and read parts of it aloud, the woods resounded with the loud guffaws of his audience; but the weeds throve in the corn rows and the wheat yellowed in the fields.

The farmers who were hiring Lincoln complained that he was lazy, "awful lazy." He admitted it. "My father taught me to work," he said, "but he never taught me to love it."

Old Tom Lincoln issued peremptory orders: all this foolishness had to stop. But it didn't stop; Abe kept on telling his jokes and making his speeches. One day—in the presence of others —the old man struck him a blow in the face and knocked him down. The boy wept, but he said nothing. There was already growing up between father and son an estrangement that would last for the rest of their lives. Although Lincoln looked after his father financially in his old age, yet when the old man lay on his death-bed, in 1851, the son did not go to see him, "If we met now," he said, "it is doubtful whether it would not be more painful than pleasant."

In the winter of 1830 the "milk sick" came again, spreading death once more through the Buckhorn Valley of Indiana.

Filled with fear and discouragement, the roving and migratory Tom Lincoln disposed of his hogs and corn, sold his stump-infested farm for eighty dollars, made a cumbersome wagon— the first he had ever owned—loaded his family and furniture into it, gave Abe the whip, yelled at the oxen, and started out for a valley in Illinois which the Indians called the Sangamon, "the land of plenty to eat."

For two weeks the oxen crept slowly forward as the heavy wagon creaked and groaned over the hills and through the deep forests of Indiana and out across the bleak, desolate, uninhabited prairies of Illinois, carpeted then with withered yellow grass that grew six feet tall under the summer sun.

At Vincennes Lincoln saw a printing-press for the first time; he was then twenty-one.

At Decatur the emigrants camped in the court-house square; and, twenty-six years later, Lincoln pointed out the exact spot where the wagon had stood.

"I didn't know then that I had sense enough to be a lawyer," he said.

Herndon tells us:

Mr. Lincoln once described this journey to me. He said the ground had not yet yielded up the frosts of winter; that during the day the roads would thaw out on the surface and at night freeze over again, thus making travelling, especially with oxen, painfully slow and tiresome. There were, of course, no bridges, and the party were consequently driven to ford the streams, unless by a circuitous route they could avoid them. In the early part of the day the latter were also frozen slightly, and the oxen would break through a square yard of thin ice at every step. Among other things which the party brought with them was a pet dog, which trotted along after the wagon. One day the little fellow fell behind and failed to catch up till after they had crossed the stream. Missing him they looked back, and there, on the opposite bank, he stood, whining and jumping about in great distress. The water was running over the broken edges of the ice, and the poor animal was afraid to cross. It would not pay to turn the oxen and wagon back and ford the stream again in order to recover a dog, and so the majority, in their anxiety to move forward, decided to go on without him. "But I could not endure the idea of abandoning even a dog," related Lincoln. "Pulling off shoes and socks I waded across the stream and triumphantly returned with the shivering animal under my arm. His frantic leaps of joy and other evidences of a dog's gratitude amply repaid me for all the exposure I had undergone."

While the oxen were pulling the Lincolns across the prairies Congress was debating with deep and ominous emotion the question of whether or not a State had a right to withdraw from the Union; and during that debate Daniel Webster arose in the United States Senate and, in his deep, golden, bell-like voice, delivered a speech which Lincoln afterward regarded "as the grandest specimen of American oratory." It is known as "Webster's Reply to Hayne" and ends with the memorable words which Lincoln later adopted as his own political religion: "Liberty and Union, now and forever, one and inseparable!"

This cyclonic issue of secession was to be settled a third of a century later, not by the mighty Webster, the gifted Clay, or the famous Calhoun, but by an awkward, penniless, obscure driver of oxen who was now heading for Illinois, wearing a coonskin cap and buckskin trousers, and singing with ribald gusto:

> "Hail Columbia, happy land,
> If you ain't drunk, then I'll be damned."

4

THE LINCOLNS SETTLED near Decatur, Illinois, on a stretch of timber land running along a bluff overlooking the Sangamon River.

Abe helped to fell trees, erect a cabin, cut brush, clear the land, break fifteen acres of sod with a yoke of oxen, plant it to corn, split rails, and fence the property in.

The next year he worked as a hired man in the neighborhood, doing odd jobs for farmers: plowing, pitching hay, mauling rails, butchering hogs.

The first winter Abe Lincoln spent in Illinois was one of the coldest the State had known. Snow drifted fifteen feet deep on the prairies; cattle died, the deer and wild turkey were almost exterminated, and even people were frozen to death.

During this winter Lincoln agreed to split a thousand rails for a pair of trousers made from brown jean cloth dyed with white-walnut bark. He had to travel three miles each day to work. Once, while crossing the Sangamon, his canoe was upset, he was thrown into the icy water, and before he could reach the nearest house, Major Warnick's, his feet froze. For a month he was unable to walk, and so he spent that time lying in front of the fireplace at Major Warnick's telling stories, and reading a volume of the Statutes of Illinois.

Prior to this, Lincoln had courted the major's daughter, but the major frowned on the idea. What? A daughter of his, a Warnick, married to this gawky, uneducated rail-splitter? A man without land, without cash, and without prospects? Never!

True, Lincoln didn't own any land; and that wasn't all—he didn't want to own any. He had spent twenty-two years on farms, and he had had enough of pioneer farming. He hated the grinding toil, the lonely monotony of the life. Longing for distinction, as well as for contact with other social beings, he wanted a job where he could meet people and gather a crowd around him and keep them roaring at his stories.

While living back in Indiana Abe had once helped float a flatboat down the river to New Orleans, and what fun he had had! Novelty. Excitement. Adventure. One night while the boat was tied up to the shore at the plantation of Madame Duchesne, a gang of Negroes, armed with knives and clubs, climbed aboard. They meant to kill the crew, throw their bodies into the river, and float the cargo down to the thieves' headquarters at New Orleans.

Lincoln seized a club, and with his long, powerful arms knocked three of the marauders into the river, then chased the others ashore; but, in the fight, one of the Negroes slashed Lincoln's forehead with a knife and left over his right eye a scar that he carried to his grave.

No, Tom Lincoln could not hold the boy Abe to a pioneer farm.

Having seen New Orleans once, Abe now got himself another river job. For fifty cents a day and a bonus he and his stepbrother and second cousin cut down trees, hewed logs, floated them to a sawmill, built a flatboat eighty feet long, loaded it with bacon, corn, and hogs, and floated it down the Mississippi.

Lincoln did the cooking for the crew, steered the boat, told stories, played seven-up, and sang in a loud voice:

> "The turbaned Turk that scorns the world
> And struts about with his whiskers curled
> For no other man but himself to see."

This trip down the river made a profound and lasting impression upon Lincoln. Herndon says:

> In New Orleans, for the first time Lincoln beheld the true horrors of human slavery. He saw *"negroes in chains —whipped and scourged."* Against this inhumanity his sense of right and justice rebelled, and his mind and con-

science were awakened to a realization of what he had often heard and read. No doubt, as one of his companions has said, "Slavery ran the iron into him then and there." One morning in their rambles over the city the trio passed a slave auction. A vigorous and comely mulatto girl was being sold. She underwent a thorough examination at the hands of the bidders; they pinched her flesh and made her trot up and down the room like a horse, to show how she moved, and in order, as the auctioneer said, that "bidders might satisfy themselves" whether the article they were offering to buy was sound or not. The whole thing was so revolting that Lincoln moved away from the scene with a deep feeling of "unconquerable hate." Bidding his companions follow him he said, *"By God, boys, let's get away from this. If ever I get a chance to hit that thing* [meaning slavery], *I'll hit it hard."*

Lincoln became very popular with Denton Offut, the man who hired him to go to New Orleans. Offut liked his jokes and stories and honesty. He employed the young man to go back to Illinois, fell trees, and build a log-cabin grocery store in New Salem, a tiny village composed of fifteen or twenty cabins perched on a bluff high above the winding Sangamon. Here Lincoln clerked in the store and also ran a grist and sawmill, and here he lived for six years—years that had a tremendous influence on his future.

The village had a wild, pugnacious, hell-raising gang of ruffians called the Clary's Grove Boys, a crowd who boasted that they could drink more whisky, swear more profanely, wrestle better, and hit harder than any other group in all Illinois.

At heart they weren't a bad lot. They were loyal, frank, generous, and sympathetic, but they loved to show off. So when the loud-mouthed Denton Offut came to town and proclaimed the physical prowess of his grocery clerk, Abe Lincoln, the Clary's Grove Boys were delighted. They would show this upstart a thing or two.

But the showing was all the other way, for this young giant won their foot-races and jumping contests; and with his extraordinarily long arms he could throw a maul or toss a cannon-ball farther than any of them. Besides, he could tell the kind of funny stories they could understand; and he kept them laughing for hours at his back-woods tales.

He reached the high-water mark of his career in New Salem, as far as the Clary's Grove Boys were concerned, on the day all the town gathered under the white-oak trees to see him wrestle with their leader, Jack Armstrong. When Lincoln laid Armstrong out, he had arrived, he had achieved the ultimate. From that time on the Clary's Grove Boys gave him their friendship and crowned him with their allegiance. They appointed him judge of their horse-races and referee of their cock-fights. And when Lincoln was out of work and had no home, they took him into their cabins and fed him.

Lincoln found here in New Salem an opportunity he had been seeking for years, an opportunity to conquer his fears and learn to speak in public. Back in Indiana the only chance that he had had at this sort of thing had been in talking to little groups of laborers in the fields. But here in New Salem there was an organized "literary society" that met every Saturday night in the dining-room of the Rutledge tavern. Lincoln joined it with alacrity and took a leading part on its program, telling stories, reading verses that he had written himself, making extemporaneous talks on such subjects as the navigation of the Sangamon River, and debating the various questions of the day.

This activity was priceless. It widened his mental horizon and awakened his ambition. He discovered that he had an unusual ability to influence other men by his speech. That knowledge developed his courage and self-confidence as nothing else had ever done.

In a few months Offut's store failed and Lincoln was out of a job. An election was coming on, the State was seething with politics, and so he proposed to cash in on his ability to speak.

With the aid of Mentor Graham, the local school-teacher, he toiled for weeks over his first address to the public, in which he announced that he was a candidate for the State Legislature. He stated that he favored "internal improvements . . . the navigation of the Sangamon . . . better education . . . justice," and so on.

In closing he said:

"I was born and have ever remained in the most humble walks of life. I have no wealthy or popular relatives or friends to recommend me." And he concluded with this pathetic sentence: "But if the good people in their wisdom shall see fit to keep me in the background, I have been too familiar with disappointments to be very much chagrined."

A few days later a horseman dashed into New Salem with the startling news that the great Sac Indian chief, Black Hawk, was on the war-path with his braves, burning homes, capturing women, massacring settlers, and spreading red terror along Rock River.

In a panic Governor Reynolds was calling for volunteers; and Lincoln, "out of work, penniless, a candidate for office," joined the forces for thirty days, was elected captain, and tried to drill the Clary's Grove Boys, who shouted back at his commands, "Go to the devil."

Herndon says Lincoln always regarded his participation in the Black Hawk War "as a sort of holiday affair and chicken-stealing expedition." It was just about that.

Later, in the course of a speech in Congress, Lincoln declared that he didn't attack any redskins, but that he made "charges upon the wild onions." He said he didn't see any Indians, but that he had "a good many bloody struggles with the mosquitoes."

Returning from the war, "Captain Lincoln" plunged again into his political campaign, going from cabin to cabin, shaking hands, telling stories, agreeing with every one, and making speeches whenever and wherever he could find a crowd.

When the election came he was defeated, although he received all but three of the two hundred and eight votes cast in New Salem.

Two years later he ran again, was elected, and had to borrow money to buy a suit of clothes to wear to the legislature.

He was reëlected in 1836, 1838, and 1840.

There was living in New Salem at that time a ne'er-do-well whose wife had to take in boarders while he fished and played the fiddle and recited poetry. Most of the people in town looked down upon Jack Kelso as a failure. But Lincoln liked him, chummed with him, and was greatly influenced by him. Before he met Kelso, Shakspere and Burns had meant little to Lincoln; they had been merely names, and vague names at that. But now as he sat listening to Jack Kelso reading "Hamlet" and reciting "Macbeth," Lincoln realized for the first time what symphonies could be played with the English language. What a thing of infinite beauty it could be! What a whirlwind of sense and emotion!

Shakspere awed him, but Bobby Burns won his love and sympathy. He felt even a kinship with Burns. Burns had been poor like Lincoln. Burns had been born in a cabin no better than the one that had seen Abe's birth. Burns too had been a plowboy. But a plowboy to whom the plowing up of the nest of a field-mouse was a tiny tragedy, an event worthy of being caught up and immortalized in a poem. Through the poetry of Burns and Shakspere, a whole new world of meaning and feeling and loveliness opened up to Abraham Lincoln.

But to him the most astounding thing of all was this: neither Shakspere nor Burns had gone to college. Neither of them had had much more schooling and education than he.

At times he dared to think that perhaps he too, the unschooled son of illiterate Tom Lincoln, might be fitted for finer things. Perhaps it would not be necessary for him to go on forever selling groceries or working as a blacksmith.

From that time on Burns and Shakspere were his favorite authors. He read more of Shakspere than of all other authors put together, and this reading left its imprint upon his style. Even after he reached the White House, when the burdens and worries of the Civil War were chiseling deep furrows in his face, he devoted much time to Shakspere. Busy as he was, he discussed the plays with Shaksperian authorities, and carried on a correspondence regarding certain passages. The week he was shot, he read "Macbeth" aloud for two hours to a circle of friends.

The influence of Jack Kelso, the shiftless New Salem fisherman, had reached to the White House. . . .

The founder of New Salem and the keeper of the tavern was a Southerner named James Rutledge, and he had a most attractive daughter, Ann. She was only nineteen when Lincoln met her—a beautiful girl with blue eyes and auburn hair. Despite the fact that she was already engaged to the richest merchant in town, Lincoln fell in love with her.

Ann had already promised to become the wife of John McNeil, but it was understood that they were not to be married until she had had two years of college.

Lincoln had not been in New Salem very long when a strange thing happened. McNeil sold his store and said that he was returning to New York State to bring his mother and father and family back to Illinois. But before leaving town he confessed something to Ann Rutledge that almost stunned her. However, she was young and she loved him, and she believed his story.

A few days later, he set out from Salem, waving good-by to Ann and promising to write often.

Lincoln was postmaster of the village then. The mail arrived by stage-coach twice a week, and there was very little of it, for it cost from six and a quarter cents to twenty-five to send a letter, depending on the distance it must travel. Lincoln carried the letters about in his hat. When people met him they would ask if he had any mail for them, and he would pull off his hat and look through his collection to see what he had.

Twice each week Ann Rutledge inquired for a letter. Three months passed before the first one arrived. McNeil explained that he had not written sooner because he had been taken sick with a fever while crossing Ohio, and had been in bed for three weeks—part of the time unconscious.

Three more months passed before the next letter came; and when it arrived it was almost worse than no letter at all. It was cold and vague. He said that his father was very ill, that he was being harassed by his father's creditors, and that he did not know when he would be back.

After that Ann watched the mail for months, hoping for more letters which never came. Had he ever really loved her at all? She had begun now to doubt it.

Lincoln, seeing her distress, volunteered to try to find McNeil.

"No," she said, "he knows where I am, and if he doesn't care enough to write to me I am sure I do not care enough to have you try to find him."

Then she told her father of the extraordinary confession that McNeil had made before he left. He had admitted that he had been living under an assumed name for years. His real name was not McNeil, as every one in New Salem believed, but McNamar.

Why had he practised this deception? His father, he explained, had failed in business, back in New York State, and had become heavily involved in debts. He, being the eldest son, had, without disclosing his destination, come West to make money. He feared that if he used his right name, his family might learn of his whereabouts and follow him, and he would be obliged to support them all. He didn't want to be hampered by any such burden while struggling to make a start. It might delay his progress for years. So he took an assumed name. But now that he had accumulated property he was going to bring his parents to Illinois and let them share his prosperity.

When the story got abroad in the village it created a sensation. People called it a damn lie and branded him as an impostor. The situation looked bad and gossip made the worst of it. He was—well, there was no telling what he was. Perhaps he was already married. Maybe he was hiding from two or three wives. Who knew? Maybe he had robbed a bank. Maybe he had murdered somebody. Maybe he was this. Maybe he was that. He had deserted Ann Rutledge, and she ought to thank God for it.

Such was New Salem's verdict. Lincoln said nothing, but he thought much.

At last the chance for which he had hoped and prayed had come.

★ ★ ★

5

★ ★ ★

THE RUTLEDGE TAVERN was a rough, weather-beaten affair with nothing whatever to distinguish it from a thousand other log cabins along the frontier. A stranger would not have given it a second glance; but Lincoln could not keep his eyes off it now, nor his heart out of it. To him, it filled the earth and towered to the sky, and he never crossed the threshold of it without a quickening of his heart.

Borrowing a copy of Shakspere's plays from Jack Kelso, he stretched himself out on top of the store counter, and, turning over the pages, he read these lines again and again:

> But, soft! what light through yonder window breaks?
> It is the east, and Juliet is the sun.

He closed the book. He could not read. He could not think. He lay there for an hour, dreaming, living over in memory all the lovely things Ann had said the night before. He lived now for only one thing—for the hours that he spent with her.

Quilting parties were popular in those days, and Ann was invariably invited to these affairs, where her slender fingers plied the needle with unusual swiftness and art. Lincoln used to ride with her in the morning to the place where the quilting was to be held, and call for her again in the evening. Once he boldly went into the house—a place where men seldom ventured on such occasions—and sat down beside her. Her heart throbbed, and a flood of color rose to her face. In her excitement she made irregular and uncertain stitches, and the older and more composed women noticed it. They smiled. The owner kept this quilt for years, and after Lincoln became President she proudly displayed it to visitors and pointed out the irregular stitches made by his sweetheart.

On summer evenings Lincoln and Ann strolled together along the banks of the Sangamon, where whippoorwills called in the trees and fireflies wove golden threads through the night.

In the autumn they drifted through the woods when the oaks were flaming with color and hickory-nuts were pattering to the ground. In the winter, after the snow had fallen, they walked through the forest, when—

> Every oak and ash and walnut
> Wore ermine too dear for an earl
> And the poorest twig on the elm tree
> Was ridged inch-deep with pearl.

For both of them, now, life had taken on a sacred tenderness, a new and strangely beautiful meaning. When Lincoln but stood and looked down into Ann's blue eyes her heart sang within her; and at the mere touch of her hands he caught his breath and was amazed to discover that there was so much felicity in all the world. . . .

A short time before this, Lincoln had gone into business with a drunkard, a preacher's son, named Berry. The little village of New Salem was dying, all its stores were gasping for breath. But neither Lincoln nor Berry could see what was happening, so they bought the wrecks of three of these log-cabin groceries, consolidated them, and started an establishment of their own.

One day a mover who was driving out to Iowa halted his covered wagon in front of the Lincoln & Berry store. The roads were soft, his horses were tired, and the mover decided to lighten his load. So he sold Lincoln a barrel of household plunder. Lincoln didn't want the plunder, but he felt sorry for the horses; he paid the mover fifty cents, and without examining the barrel rolled it into the back room of the store.

A fortnight later he emptied the contents of the barrel out on the floor, idly curious to see what he had bought. There, at the bottom of the rubbish, he found a complete edition of Blackstone's Commentaries on Law; and started to read. The farmers were busy in their fields, and customers were few and far between, so he had plenty of time. And the more he read, the more interested he became. Never before had he been so absorbed in a book. He read until he had devoured all four volumes.

Then he made a momentous decision: he would be a lawyer. He would be the kind of man Ann Rutledge would be proud to marry. She approved his plans, and they were to be married as soon as he completed his law studies and established himself in the profession.

After finishing Blackstone he set out across the prairies for Springfield, twenty miles away, to borrow other law-books from an attorney he had met in the Black Hawk War. On his way home he carried an open book in one hand, studying as he walked. When he struck a knotty passage, he shuffled to a standstill, and concentrated on it until he had mastered the sense.

He kept on studying, until he had conquered twenty or thirty pages, kept on until dusk fell and he could no longer see to read. . . . The stars came out, he was hungry, he hastened his pace.

He pored over his books now incessantly, having heart for little else. By day he lay on his back, reading in the shade of an elm that grew beside the store, his bare feet angling up against the trunk of the tree. By night he read in the cooper's shop, kindling a light from the waste material lying about. Frequently he read aloud to himself, now and then closing the book and writing down the sense of what he had just read, revising, rephrasing it until it became clear enough for a child to comprehend.

Wherever Lincoln went now—on his rambles along the river, on his walks through the woods, on his way to labor in the fields—wherever he went, a volume of Chitty or Blackstone was under his arm. Once a farmer, who had hired him to cut firewood, came around the corner of the barn in the middle of the afternoon and found Lincoln sitting barefooted on top of the woodpile, studying law.

Mentor Graham told Lincoln that if he aspired to get ahead in politics and law he must know grammar.

"Where can I borrow one?" Lincoln asked.

Graham said that John Vance, a farmer living six miles out in the country, had a copy of Kirkham's Grammar; and Lincoln arose immediately, put on his hat, and was off after the book.

He astonished Graham with the speed with which he mastered Kirkham's rules. Thirty years later this schoolmaster said he had taught more than five thousand students, but that Lincoln was the "most studious, diligent, straightforward young man in the pursuit of knowledge and literature" he had ever met.

"I have known him," said Mentor Graham, "to study for hours the best way of three to express an idea."

Having mastered Kirkham's Grammar, Lincoln devoured next Gibbon's "Decline and Fall of the Roman Empire," Rollin's "Ancient History," a volume on American military biography, lives of Jefferson, Clay, and Webster, and Tom Paine's "Age of Reason."

Dressed in "blue cotton roundabout coat, stoga shoes, and pale-blue casinet pantaloons which failed to make the connection with either coat or socks, coming about three inches below the former and an inch or two above the latter," this extraordinary young man drifted about New Salem, reading, studying, dreaming, telling stories, and making "a host of friends wherever he went."

The late Albert J. Beveridge, the outstanding Lincoln scholar of his time, says in his monumental biography:

"Not only did his wit, kindliness and knowledge attract the people, but his strange clothes and uncouth awkwardness advertised him, the shortness of his trousers causing particular remark and amusement. Soon the name of 'Abe Lincoln' became a household word."

Finally the grocery firm of Lincoln & Berry failed. This was to be expected, for, with Lincoln absorbed in his books and Berry half groggy with whisky, the end was inevitable. Without a dollar left to pay for his meals and lodging now, Lincoln had to do any kind of manual labor he could find: he cut brush, pitched hay, built fences, shucked corn, labored in a sawmill, and worked for a while as a blacksmith.

Then, with the aid of Mentor Graham, he plunged into the intricacies of trigonometry and logarithms, prepared himself to be a surveyor, bought a horse and compass on credit, cut a grape-vine to be used as a chain, and started out surveying town lots for thirty-seven and a half cents apiece.

In the meantime the Rutledge tavern also had failed, and Lincoln's sweetheart had had to go to work as a servant in a farmer's kitchen. Lincoln soon got a job plowing corn on the same farm. In the evening he stood in the kitchen wiping the dishes which Ann washed. He was filled with a vast happiness at the very thought of being near her. Never again was he to experience such rapture and such content. Shortly before his death he confessed to a friend that he had been happier as a barefoot farm laborer back in Illinois than he had ever been in the White House.

But the ecstasy of the lovers was as short as it was intense. In August, 1835, Ann fell ill. At first there was no pain, nothing but great fatigue and weariness. She tried to carry on her work as usual, but one morning she was unable to get out of bed. That day the fever came, and her brother rode over to New Salem for Dr. Allen. He pronounced it typhoid. Her body seemed to be burning, but her feet were so cold that they had to be warmed with hot stones. She kept begging vainly for water. Medical science now knows that she should have been packed in ice and given all the water she could drink, but Dr. Allen didn't know that.

Dreadful weeks dragged by. Finally Ann was so exhausted that she could no longer raise even her hands from the sheets. Dr. Allen ordered absolute rest, visitors were forbidden, and that night when Lincoln came even he was not permitted to see her. But the next day and the following day she kept murmuring his name and calling for him so pitifully that he was sent for. When he arrived, he went to her bedside immediately, the door was closed, and they were left alone. This was the last hour of the lovers together.

The next day Ann lost consciousness and remained unconscious until her death.

The weeks that followed were the most terrible period of Lincoln's life. He couldn't sleep. He wouldn't eat. He repeatedly said that he didn't want to live, and he threatened to kill himself. His friends became alarmed, took his pocket-knife away, and watched to keep him from throwing himself into the river. He avoided people, and when he met them he didn't speak, didn't even seem to see them, but appeared to be staring into another world, hardly conscious of the existence of this.

Day after day he walked five miles to the Concord Cemetery, where Ann was buried. Sometimes he sat there so long that his friends grew anxious, and went and brought him home. When the storms came, he wept, saying that he couldn't bear to think of the rain beating down upon her grave.

Once he was found stumbling along the Sangamon, mumbling incoherent sentences. People feared he was losing his mind.

So Dr. Allen was sent for. Realizing what was wrong, he said Lincoln must be given some kind of work, some activity to occupy his mind.

A mile to the north of town lived one of Lincoln's closest friends, Bowling Greene. He took Lincoln to his home, and assumed complete charge of him. It was a quiet, secluded spot. Behind the house oak-covered bluffs rose and rolled back to the west. In front the flat bottom-lands stretched away to the Sangamon River, framed in trees. Nancy Greene kept Lincoln busy cutting wood, digging potatoes, picking apples, milking the cows, holding the yarn for her as she spun.

The weeks grew into months, and the months into years, but Lincoln continued to grieve. In 1837, two years after Ann's death, he said to a fellow-member of the State Legislature:

"Although I seem to others to enjoy life rapturously at times, yet when I am alone I am so depressed that I am afraid to trust myself to carry a pocket-knife."

From the day of Ann's death he was a changed individual. The melancholy that then settled upon him lifted at times for short intervals; but it grew steadily worse, until he became the saddest man in all Illinois.

Herndon, later his law partner, said:

"If Lincoln ever had a happy day in twenty years, I never knew of it. . . . Melancholy dripped from him as he walked."

From this time to the end of his life, Lincoln had a fondness, almost an obsession, for poems dealing with sorrow and death. He would often sit for hours without saying a word, lost in reverie, the very picture of dejection, and then would suddenly break forth with these lines from "The Last Leaf":

> The mossy marbles rest
> On the lips that he has prest
>   In their bloom;
> And the names he loved to hear
> Have been carved for many a year
>   On the tomb.

Shortly after Ann's death, he memorized a poem "Mortality" and beginning, "Oh, why should the spirit of mortal be proud?"

It became his favorite. He often repeated it to himself when he thought no one else was listening; repeated it to people in the country hotels of Illinois; repeated it in public addresses; repeated it to guests in the White House; wrote copies of it for his friends; and said:

"I would give all I am worth, and go in debt, to be able to write like that."

He loved the last two stanzas best:

> Yea! hope and despondency, pleasure and pain,
> Are mingled together in sunshine and rain;
> And the smile and the tear and the song and the dirge
> Still follow each other, like surge upon surge.

> 'Tis the wink of an eye, 'tis the draught of a breath,
> From the blossom of health to the paleness of death,
> From the gilded saloon to the bier and the shroud,—
> Oh, why should the spirit of mortal be proud?

The old Concord Cemetery, where Ann Rutledge was buried, is a peaceful acre in the midst of a quiet farm, surrounded on three sides by wheat-fields and on the fourth by a blue-grass pasture where cattle feed and sheep graze. The cemetery itself is overgrown now with brush and vines, and is seldom visited by man. In the springtime the quails make their nests in it and the silence of the place is broken only by the bleating of sheep and the call of the bob-white.

For more than half a century the body of Ann Rutledge lay there in peace. But in 1890 a local undertaker started a new cemetery in Petersburg, four miles away. Petersburg already had a beautiful and commodious burying-ground known as the Rose Hill Cemetery; so selling lots in the new one was slow and difficult. Consequently, the greedy undertaker, in an unholy moment, conceived the gruesome scheme of violating the grave of Lincoln's sweetheart, bringing her dust to his cemetery, and using its presence there as an argument to boost sales.

So "on or about the fifteenth of May, 1890"—to quote the exact words of his shocking confession—he opened her grave. And what did he find? We know, for there is a quiet old lady still living in Petersburg who told the story to the author of this volume, and made an affidavit to its veracity. She is the daughter of McGrady Rutledge, who was a first cousin of Ann Rutledge. McGrady Rutledge often worked with Lincoln in the fields, helped him as a surveyor, ate with him and shared his bed with him, and probably knew more about Lincoln's love for Ann than any other third person has ever known.

On a quiet summer evening this old lady sat in a rocking-chair on her porch and told the author: "I have often heard Pa say that after Ann's death Mr. Lincoln would walk five miles out to Ann's grave and stay there so long that Pa would get worried and fear something would happen to him, and go and bring him home. . . . Yes, Pa was with the undertaker when Ann's grave was opened, and I have often heard him tell that the only trace they could find of Ann's body was four pearl buttons from her dress."

So the undertaker scooped up the four pearl buttons, and some dirt and interred them in his new Oakland Cemetery at Petersburg—and then advertised that Ann Rutledge was buried there.

And now, in the summer months, thousands of pilgrims motor there to dream over what purports to be her grave; I have seen them stand with bowed heads and shed tears above the four pearl buttons. Over those four buttons there stands a beautiful granite monument bearing this verse from Edgar Lee Masters' "Spoon River Anthology":

> Out of me unworthy and unknown
> The vibrations of deathless music:
> "With malice toward none, with charity for all."
> Out of me the forgiveness of millions toward millions,
> And the beneficent face of a nation
> Shining with justice and truth.
> I am Ann Rutledge who sleep beneath these weeds,
> Beloved in life of Abraham Lincoln,
> Wedded to him, not through union,
> But through separation.
> Bloom forever, O Republic,
> From the dust of my bosom!

But Ann's sacred dust remains in the old Concord Cemetery. The rapacious undertaker could not carry it away—she and her memories are still there. Where the bob-white calls and the wild rose blows, there is the spot that Abraham Lincoln hallowed with his tears, there is the spot where he said his heart lay buried, there would Ann Rutledge wish to be.

★　★　★

6

★　★　★

In March, 1837, two years after Ann's death, Lincoln turned his back on New Salem and rode into Springfield on a borrowed horse, to begin what he called his "experiment as a lawyer."

He carried in his saddle-bag all his earthly possessions. The only things he owned were several law-books and some extra shirts and some underwear. He also carried an old blue sock stuffed with six-and-a-quarter-cent and twelve-and-a-half-cent pieces—money that he had collected for postage before the post-office "winked out" back in New Salem. During this first year in Springfield, Lincoln needed cash often, and he needed it badly. He could have spent this money and paid the Government out of his own pocket, but he would have felt that that was dishonest. So when the post-office auditor finally came around for a settlement, Lincoln turned over to him not only the exact amount, but the exact coins he had taken in as post-master during the preceding year or two.

The morning that Lincoln rode into Springfield, he not only had no cash reserves of his own; but, to make matters worse, he was eleven hundred dollars in debt. He and Berry had lost that amount in their ill-fated grocery venture back in New Salem. Then Berry had drunk himself to death and left Lincoln to shoulder the obligations alone.

To be sure, Lincoln didn't have to pay; he could have pleaded divided responsibility and the failure of the business and have found a legal loophole of escape.

But that wasn't Lincoln's way. Instead, he went to his creditors and promised to pay them every dollar with interest, if they would only give him time. They all agreed, except one, Peter Van Bergen. He brought suit immediately, obtained a judgment, and had Lincoln's horse and surveying instruments sold at public auction. The others waited, however, and Lincoln scraped and saved and denied himself for fourteen years in order to keep faith with them. Even as late as 1848, when he was a member of Congress, he sent part of his salary home to pay off the last remnant of this old grocery debt.

The morning that Lincoln arrived in Springfield, he tied his horse in front of Joshua F. Speed's general store at the northwest corner of the public square; and here is the remainder of the story told in Speed's own words:

He had ridden into town on a borrowed horse, and engaged from the only cabinet-maker in the village a single bedstead. He came into my store, set his saddle-bags on the counter, and enquired what the furniture for a single bedstead would cost. I took slate and pencil, made a calculation, and found the sum for furniture complete would amount to seventeen dollars in all. Said he: "It is probably cheap enough; but I want to say that, cheap as it is, I have not the money to pay. But if you will credit me until Christmas and my experiment here as a lawyer is a success, I will pay you then. If I fail in that I will probably never pay you at all." The tone of his voice was so melancholy that I felt for him. I looked up at him and I thought then, as I think now, that I never saw so gloomy and melancholy a face in my life. I said to him, "So small a debt seems to affect you so deeply, I think I can suggest a plan by which you will be able to attain your end without incurring any debt. I have a very large room and a very large double bed in it, which you are perfectly welcome to share with me if you choose." "Where is your room?" he asked. "Upstairs," said I, pointing to the stairs leading from the store to my room. Without saying a word he took his saddle-bags on his arm, went upstairs, set them down on the floor, came down again, and with a face beaming with pleasure and smiles, exclaimed, "Well, Speed, I'm moved."

And so, for the next five and a half years, Lincoln slept in the bed with Speed, over the store, without paying any rent at all.

Another friend, William Butler, took Lincoln into his home and not only boarded him for five years, but bought many of his clothes for him.

Lincoln probably paid Butler a little something when, as, and if he could; but there was no specific charge. The whole thing was a haphazard arrangement between friends.

And Lincoln thanked God that it was, for if it hadn't been for the help of Butler and Speed, he could never have made a go of the law.

He went into partnership with another attorney, named Stuart. Stuart devoted most of his time to politics, and saddled the office routine on Lincoln. But there wasn't much routine to saddle, and there wasn't much of an office. The furnishings consisted of "a small, dirty bed, a buffalo robe, a chair, a bench" and a sort of bookcase containing a few legal volumes.

The office records show that during the first six months the firm took in only five fees: one was for two dollars and a half, two were for five dollars each, one was a ten-dollar fee, and they had to take an overcoat as part payment in another case.

Lincoln became so discouraged that he stopped one day at Page Eaton's carpenter shop in Springfield and confessed that he had a notion to abandon law and go to work as a carpenter. A few years before that, while studying law back in New Salem, Lincoln had seriously thought of giving up his books and becoming a blacksmith.

That first year in Springfield was a lonely one for Lincoln. About the only people he met were the men who forgathered of an evening, in the back of Speed's store, to argue politics and kill time. Lincoln wouldn't go to church on Sundays, because, as he said, he wouldn't know how to act in fine churches like those in Springfield.

Only one woman spoke to him during that first year, and he wrote to a friend that she wouldn't have spoken "if she could have avoided it."

But in 1839 a woman came to town who not only spoke to him, but courted him and determined to marry him. Her name was Mary Todd.

Somebody asked Lincoln once why the Todds spelled their name as they did, and he replied that he reckoned that one "d" was good enough for God, but that the Todds had to have two.

The Todds boasted of a genealogical chart extending back to the sixth century. Mary Todd's grandfathers and great-grandfathers and great-uncles had been generals and governors, and one had been Secretary of the Navy. She, herself, had been educated in a snobbish French school in Lexington, Kentucky, conducted by Madame Victorie Charlotte Le Clere Mentelle and her husband—two French aristocrats who had fled from Paris during the Revolution in order to save their necks from the guillotine. They had drilled Mary to speak French with a Parisian accent, and had taught her to dance the cotillion and the Circassian Circle as the silken courtiers had danced them at Versailles.

Mary was possessed of a high and haughty manner, an exalted opinion of her own superiority, and an abiding conviction that she would one day marry a man who would become President of the United States. Incredible as it seems, she not only believed that, but she openly boasted of it. It sounded silly, and people laughed and said things; but nothing could shake her conviction and nothing could stop her boasting.

Her own sister, speaking of Mary, said she "loved glitter, show, pomp and power," and was "the most ambitious woman I ever knew."

Unfortunately, Mary had a temper that was frequently out of control; so one day in 1839, she quarreled with her stepmother, slammed the front door, and walked out of her father's home in a rage and came to live with her married sister in Springfield.

If she was determined to marry a future President, she had certainly chosen the right place, for there wasn't another spot in all the world where her prospects would have been brighter than there in Springfield, Illinois. At that time it was a dirty little frontier village, sprawling out over the treeless prairie, with no pavements, no lights, no sidewalks, no sewers. Cattle roamed about the town at will, hogs wallowed in the mud-holes of the principal streets, and piles of rotton manure filled the air with a stench. The total population of the town was only fifteen hundred; but two young men who were destined to be candidates for the Presidency in 1860 lived there in Springfield in 1839—Stephen A. Douglas, candidate for the Northern wing of the Democratic party, and Abraham Lincoln for the Republicans.

Both of them met Mary Todd, both courted her at the same time, both held her in their arms, and she once stated that both of them had proposed.

When asked which suitor she intended to marry, Mary always answered, according to her sister's report, "Him who has the best prospects of being President."

And that was tantamount to saying Douglas, for, just then, Douglas's political prospects seemed a hundred times brighter than Lincoln's. Although Douglas was only twenty-six, he had already been nicknamed "the Little Giant," and he was already Secretary of the State, while Lincoln was only a struggling lawyer living in an attic over Speed's store and hardly able to pay a board bill.

Douglas was destined to become one of the mightiest political forces in the United States years and years before Abe Lincoln was even heard of outside his own State. In fact, two years before Lincoln became President, about the only thing that the average American knew about him was that he had once debated with the brilliant and powerful Stephen A. Douglas.

Mary's relatives all thought she cared more for Douglas than she did for Lincoln, and she probably did. Douglas was far more of a ladies' man; he had more personal charm, better prospects, better manners, and better social standing.

Besides, he had a deep golden voice, a wavy black pompadour, he waltzed superbly, and he paid Mary Todd lovely little compliments.

He was her beau-ideal of a man; and she looked in her mirror, whispering to herself, "Mary Todd Douglas." It sounded beautiful, and she dreamed dreams and saw herself waltzing with him in the White House. . . .

While Douglas was courting her he had a fight one day, right in the public square in Springfield, with a newspaper editor— the husband of one of Mary's dearest friends.

Probably she told him what she thought of that.

And probably she told him also what she thought of his getting drunk at a public banquet, climbing on top of a table and waltzing back and forth, shouting, singing, and kicking wineglasses and roast turkey, whisky bottles and gravy dishes onto the floor.

And if he took another girl to a dance while he was paying her attention, she made a disagreeable scene.

The courtship came to nothing. Senator Beveridge says:

Although it was afterwards given out that Douglas had proposed to Mary and was refused because of his bad "morals," that statement was obviously protective propaganda usual in such cases; for the shrewd, alert and, even then, worldly-wise Douglas never asked Miss Todd to marry him.

Immeasurably disappointed, she tried to arouse Douglas's jealousy by giving her ardent attention to one of his bitter political opponents, Abraham Lincoln. But that didn't bring back Douglas, and she laid her plans to capture Lincoln.

Mrs. Edwards, Mary Todd's sister, afterward described the courtship in this fashion:

I have often happened in the room where they were sitting, and Mary invariably led the conversation. Mr. Lincoln would sit at her side and listen. He scarcely said a word, but gazed on her as if irresistibly drawn toward her by some superior and unseen power. He was charmed with her wit, and fascinated by her quick sagacity. But he could not maintain himself in a continued conversation with a lady reared as Mary was.

In July of that year the great gathering of Whigs which had been talked of for months swarmed down upon Springfield and overwhelmed the town. They came from hundreds of miles around, with banners waving and bands playing. The Chicago delegation dragged half-way across the State a government yawl rigged as a two-masted ship. Music was playing on the ship, girls dancing, cannon belching into the air.

The Democrats had spoken of the Whig candidate, William Henry Harrison, as an old woman who lived in a log cabin and drank hard cider. So the Whigs mounted a log cabin on wheels and drew it through the streets of Springfield, behind thirty yoke of oxen. A hickory tree swayed beside the cabin; coons were playing in the tree; a barrel of hard cider was on tap by the door.

At night, under the light of flaming torches, Lincoln made a political speech.

At one meeting his party, the Whigs, had been accused of being aristocratic and wearing fine clothes while pleading for the votes of the plain people, Lincoln replied:

"I came to Illinois as a poor, strange, friendless, uneducated boy, and started working on a flatboat for eight dollars a month, and I had only one pair of breeches to my back, and they were buckskin. When buckskin gets wet and dried by the sun, it shrinks; and my breeches kept shrinking until they left several inches of my legs bare between the lower part of my breeches and the top of my socks. And while I was growing taller, the breeches were getting wet and becoming shorter and tighter until they left a blue streak around my legs that can be seen to this day. Now, if you call that being a fancily dressed aristocrat, I must plead guilty to the charge."

The audience whistled and shouted and shrieked its approval.

When Lincoln and Mary reached the Edwards house, she told him how proud she was of him, that he was a great speaker, and that some day he would be President.

He looked down at her, standing beside him in the moonlight, and her manner told him everything. Reaching over, he took her in his arms and kissed her tenderly. . . .

The wedding-day was set for the first of January, 1841.

That was only six months away, but many a storm was to brew and blow before then.

7

MARY TODD and Abraham Lincoln hadn't been engaged very long before she wanted to make him over. She didn't like the way he dressed. She often contrasted him with her father. Almost every morning for a dozen years she had seen Robert Todd walking down the streets of Lexington, carrying a gold-headed cane, clad in a blue broadcloth coat, and wearing white linen trousers strapped under his boots. But Lincoln in hot weather didn't wear a coat at all; and what was worse, sometimes he didn't wear even a collar. Usually he had only one gallus holding up his trousers, and when a button came off he whittled a peg and pinned things together with that.

Such crudeness irritated Mary Todd, and she told him so. But, unfortunately, she didn't use any tact or diplomacy or sweetness in her telling.

Though at Madame Victorie Charlotte Le Clere Mentelle's school back in Lexington she had been taught to dance the cotillion, she had been taught nothing about the fine art of handling people. So she took the surest way, the quickest way to annihilate a man's love: she nagged. She made Lincoln so uncomfortable that he wanted to avoid her. Instead of coming to see her two or three nights a week now, as he had formerly done, he sometimes let ten days drift by without calling; and she wrote him complaining letters, censuring him for his neglect.

Presently Matilda Edwards came to town. Matilda was a tall, stately, charming blonde, a cousin of Ninian W. Edwards, Mary

Todd's brother-in-law. She too took up her residence in the spacious Edwards mansion. And when Lincoln called to see Mary, Matilda contrived to be very much in evidence. She couldn't speak French with a Parisian accent or dance the Circassian Circle, but she knew how to handle men, and Lincoln grew very fond of her. When she swept into the room, Lincoln was so interested in watching her that he sometimes ceased to listen to what Mary Todd was saying. That made Mary indignant. Once he took Mary to a ball; but he didn't care for dancing, so he let her dance with other men while he sat in a corner talking to Matilda.

Mary accused him of being in love with Matilda, and he didn't deny it; she broke down and wept, and demanded that he cease even looking at Matilda.

What had once been a promising love-affair had now degenerated into a thing of strife and dissension and fault-finding.

Lincoln now saw that he and Mary were opposites in every way: in training, in background, in temperament, in tastes, in mental outlook. They irritated each other constantly, and Lincoln realized that their engagement ought to be broken, that their marriage would be disastrous.

Mary's sister and brother-in-law both arrived at a similar conclusion. They urged Mary to abandon all thought of marrying Lincoln, warning her over and over that they were strikingly unfit for each other, and that they could never be happy.

But Mary refused to listen.

Lincoln, after weeks of trying to screw up his courage to tell her the painful truth, came into Speed's store one night, walked back to the fireplace, drew a letter out of his pocket, and asked Speed to read it. Speed relates:

> The letter was addressed to Mary Todd, and in it he made a plain statement of his feelings, telling her that he had thought the matter over calmly and with great deliberation, and now felt that he did not love her sufficiently to warrant her in marrying him. This letter he desired me to deliver. Upon my declining to do so he threatened to intrust it to some other person's hand. I reminded him that the moment he placed the letter in Miss Todd's hand, she would have the advantage over him. "Words are forgotten," I said, "misunderstood, unnoticed in a private conversation, but once put your words in writing and they

stand a living and eternal monument against you." There-
upon I threw the unfortunate letter in the fire.

So we shall never know precisely what Lincoln said to her;
but "we can form a good idea of what he wrote to Mary Todd,"
says Senator Beveridge "by again reading his final letter to
Miss Owens."

The story of Lincoln's affair with Miss Owens can be told
briefly. It had occurred four years earlier. She was a sister of
Mrs. Bennett Abell, whom Lincoln knew in New Salem. In the
autumn of 1836 Mrs. Abell returned to Kentucky to visit her
family, saying that she would bring her sister back to Illinois
with her if Lincoln would agree to marry her.

Lincoln had seen the sister three years before, and he said
all right; and presto! the sister appeared. She had a beautiful
face, refinement, education, and wealth; but Lincoln didn't want
to marry her. He thought "she was a trifle too willing." Besides,
she was a year older than he, and short and very corpulent—
"a fair match for Falstaff," as Lincoln put it.

"I was not at all pleased with her," said Lincoln, "but what
could I do?"

Mrs. Abell "was very anxious," to have Lincoln stick to his
promise.

But he wasn't. He admits he was "continually repenting the
rashness" which had led him to make it, and dreaded the
thought of marrying her as "an Irishman does the halter."

So he wrote to Miss Owens, frankly and tactfully telling her
how he felt and trying to get out of the engagement.

Here is one of his letters. It was written in Springfield on
May 7, 1837, and I believe it gives us a very good idea of what
he wrote to Mary Todd.

Friend Mary:

I have commenced two letters to send you before this,
both of which displeased me before I got half done, and so
I tore them up. The first I thought wasn't serious enough,
and the second was on the other extreme. I shall send this,
turn out as it may.

This thing of living in Springfield is rather a dull business after all—at least it is so to me. I am quite as lone-
some here as [I] ever was anywhere in my life. I have been
spoken to by but one woman since I've been here, and
should not have been by her if she could have avoided it.

I've never been to church yet, and probably shall not be soon. I stay away because I am conscious I should not know how to behave myself. I am often thinking of what we said of your coming to live at Springfield. I am afraid you would not be satisfied. There is a great deal of flourishing about in carriages here, which it would be your doom to see without sharing in it. You would have to be poor without the means of hiding your poverty. Do you believe you could bear that patiently? Whatever woman may cast her lot with mine, should anyone ever do so, it is my intention to do all in my power to make her happy and contented, and there is nothing I can imagine that would make me more unhappy than to fail in the effort. I know I should be much happier with you than the way I am, provided I saw no signs of discontent in you.

What you have said to me may have been in jest or I may have misunderstood it. If so, then let it be forgotten; if otherwise I much wish you would think seriously before you decide. For my part I have already decided. What I have said I will most positively abide by, provided you wish it. My opinion is you had better not do it. You have not been accustomed to hardship, and it may be more severe than you imagine. I know you are capable of thinking correctly on any subject; and if you deliberate maturely upon this before you decide, then I am willing to abide your decision.

You must write me a good long letter after you get this. You have nothing else to do, and though it might not seem interesting to you after you have written it, it would be a good deal of company in this busy wilderness. Tell your sister I don't want to hear any more about selling out and moving. That gives me the hypo whenever I think of it.

Yours, etc.
LINCOLN.

So much for Lincoln's affair with Mary Owens. To return to his affair with Mary Todd: Speed tossed into the fire the letter which Lincoln had written to Miss Todd, and, turning to his friend and room-mate, said:

"Now, if you have the courage of manhood, go see Mary yourself; tell her, if you do not love her, the facts, and that you will not marry her. Be careful not to say too much, and then leave at your earliest opportunity."

"Thus admonished," Speed relates, "he buttoned his coat, and with a rather determined look started out to perform the serious duty for which I had just given him explicit directions."

Herndon says:

That night Speed did not go upstairs to bed with us, but under pretense of wanting to read, remained in the store below. He was waiting for Lincoln's return. Ten o'clock passed, and still the interview with Miss Todd had not ended. At length, shortly after eleven, he came stalking in. Speed was satisfied, from the length of Lincoln's stay, that his directions had not been followed.

"Well, old fellow, did you do as I told you and as you promised?" were Speed's first words.

"Yes, I did," responded Lincoln, thoughtfully, "and when I told Mary I did not love her, she burst into tears and almost springing from her chair and wringing her hands as if in agony, said something about the deceiver being himself deceived." Then he stopped.

"What else did you say?" inquired Speed, drawing the facts from him.

"To tell you the truth, Speed, it was too much for me. I found the tears trickling down my own cheeks. I caught her in my arms and kissed her."

"And that's how you broke the engagement," sneered Speed. "You not only acted the fool, but your conduct was tantamount to a renewal of the engagement, and in decency you cannot back down now."

"Well," drawled Lincoln, "if I am in again, so be it. It's done, and I shall abide by it."

Weeks rolled on, and the marriage date drew near. Seamstresses were at work upon Mary Todd's trousseau. The Edwards mansion was freshly painted, the living-rooms were redecorated, the rugs renovated, and the furniture polished and shifted.

But, in the meantime, a dreadful thing was happening to Abraham Lincoln. One is at a loss to know how to describe it. Profound mental depression is not like grief of the normal type; it is a dangerous illness affecting both mind and body.

Lincoln was sinking day by day, now, into just such a state.

His mind came very near being unbalanced; and it is doubtful whether he ever fully recovered from the effects of these awful weeks of unspeakable torture. Although he had definitely agreed to the marriage, his whole soul rebelled against it. Without realizing it, he was seeking a way of escape. He sat for hours in the room above the store, with no desire to go to his office or to attend the meetings of the legislature of which he was a member. Sometimes he arose at three o'clock in the morning, went down below, lighted a fire in the fireplace, and sat staring at it until daybreak. He ate less, and began to lose weight. He was irritable, avoided people, and would talk to no one.

He had begun now to recoil with horror from his approaching marriage. His mind seemed to be whirling through a dark abyss, and he feared that he was losing his reason. He wrote a long letter to Dr. Daniel Drake of Cincinnati, the most eminent physician in the West, the head of the medical department of the College of Cincinnati, describing his case and asking the physician to recommend a course of treatment. But Dr. Drake replied that it would be impossible for him to do so without a personal examination.

The marriage was set for January 1, 1841. The day dawned bright and clear, and the aristocracy of Springfield flourished about in sleighs, making their New Year's calls. Out of nostrils of horses issued breaths of steam, and the tinkle of tiny bells filled the air.

At the Edwards mansion the bustle and hurry of final preparation went on apace. Delivery boys hastened to the back door with this article and that that had been ordered at the last minute. A special chef had been hired for the occasion. The dinner was to be cooked, not in an old iron oven on the hearth, but in a new invention that had just been installed—a cooking stove.

The early evening of New Year's Day descended on the town, candles glowed softly, holly wreaths hung in the windows. The Edwards house was hushed with excitement, vibrant with expectation.

At six-thirty happy guests began to arrive. At six forty-five came the minister, the ritual of the Church under his arm. The rooms were banked with plants, colorful with flowers. Huge fires crackled and blazed on the hearths. The place resounded with pleasant and friendly chatter.

The clock struck seven. . . . Seven-thirty. Lincoln had not arrived. . . . He was late.

Minutes passed. . . . Slowly, inexorably, the grandfather's clock in the hallway ticked off a quarter of an hour. Half an hour. . . . Still there was no bridegroom. Going to the front door, Mrs. Edwards stared nervously down the driveway. What was wrong? Could he . . . ? No! Unthinkable! Impossible!

The family withdrew. . . . Whisperings. . . . A hurried consultation.

In the next room, Mary Todd, bedecked with bridal veil, attired in silken gown, waited . . . waited . . . nervously toying with the flowers in her hair. She walked to the window constantly. She peered down the street. She couldn't keep her eyes off the clock. The palms of her hands grew wet, perspiration gathered on her brow. Another awful hour passed. He had promised . . . Surely . . .

At nine-thirty, one by one, the guests withdrew, softly, wonderingly, and with embarrassment.

When the last one had disappeared the bride-to-be tore her veil from her head, snatched the flowers from her hair, rushed sobbing up the stairway, and flung herself on the bed. She was rent with grief. Oh, God! what would people say? She would be laughed at. Pitied. Disgraced. Ashamed to walk the streets. Great waves of bitterness, of violence, swept over her. One moment, she longed to have Lincoln there to take her in his arms. The next, she longed to kill him for the hurt, for the humiliation, he had heaped upon her.

Where was Lincoln? Had he met with foul play? Had there been an accident? Had he run away? Had he committed suicide? No one knew.

At midnight men came with lanterns, and searching parties set out. Some explored his favorite haunts in town, others searched the roads leading out into the country.

★ ★ ★

8

★ ★ ★

THE SEARCH continued all through the night, and shortly after daybreak Lincoln was found sitting in his office, talking incoherently. His friends feared he was losing his mind. Mary Todd's relatives declared that he was already insane. That was the way they explained his failure to show up at the wedding.

Dr. Henry was called immediately. Lincoln threatened to commit suicide, so the doctor ordered Speed and Butler to watch over him constantly. His knife was taken from him now and kept from him just as it had been after the death of Ann Rutledge.

Dr. Henry, wanting to keep his mind occupied, urged Lincoln to attend the sessions of the State Legislature. As the floor leader for the Whigs, he ought to have been there constantly. But the records show that he was present but four times in three weeks —and even then only for an hour or two. On January 19 John J. Hardin announced his illness to the House.

Three weeks after he had fled from his wedding Lincoln wrote to his law partner the saddest letter of his life:

> I am now the most miserable man living. If what I feel were equally distributed to the whole human family, there would not be one cheerful face on earth. Whether I shall ever be any better, I cannot tell. I awfully forbode that I shall not. To remain as I am is impossible. I must die or be better, it seems to me.

As the late Dr. William E. Barton says in his well-known biography of Lincoln, this letter "can mean nothing else than that Abraham Lincoln was mentally distraught . . . that he had grave fears for his own sanity."

He thought constantly of death, now, and longed for it and wrote a poem on suicide and had it published in the "Sangamo Journal."

Speed feared that he was going to die; so Lincoln was taken to the home of Speed's mother, near Louisville. Here he was given a Bible and assigned a quiet bedroom looking out over a brook meandering through meadows to the forest a mile away. Each morning a slave brought Lincoln his coffee in bed.

Mrs. Edwards, Mary's sister, says that Mary, "to set herself right and to free Mr. Lincoln's mind, wrote a letter to Mr. Lincoln, stating that she would release him from his engagement." But in releasing him, according to Mr. Edwards, "she left Lincoln the privilege of renewing it if he wished."

But that was the last thing in the world that he wished. He never wanted to see her again. Even a year after Lincoln had fled from his wedding, his good friend James Matheny "thought Lincoln would commit suicide."

For almost two years after the "fatal first of January," 1841, Lincoln ignored Mary Todd completely, hoping that she would forget him, praying that she would interest herself in some other man. But she did not, for her pride was at stake, her precious self-respect. She was determined to prove to herself and to those who had scorned and pitied her that she *could* and *would marry Abraham Lincoln.*

And he was *equally determined not to marry her.*

In fact, he was so determined that he proposed within a year to another girl. He was thirty-two at the time, the girl he proposed to was half that age. She was Sarah Rickard, the little sister of Mrs. Butler, at whose house Lincoln had been boarding for four years.

Lincoln pleaded his case with her, arguing that since his name was Abraham and hers Sarah it was evident that they were meant for one another.

But she refused him, because, as she later confessed in writing to a friend:

I was young, only sixteen years old and I had not thought much about matrimony. . . . I allway liked him as a friend but you Know his peculiar manner and his General deportment would not be likely to fascinate a Young Girl just entering into the society world. . . . He seemed allmost like an older Brother being as it were one of my sister's family.

Lincoln frequently wrote editorials for the local Whig paper, "The Springfield Journal"; and the editor, Simeon Francis, was one of his closest friends. Francis's wife, unfortunately, had never learned the fine art of minding her own business. Childless, over forty, she was the self-appointed match-maker of Springfield.

Early in October, 1842, she wrote Lincoln, asking him to call at her home the following afternoon. That was a strange request, and he went, wondering what it could mean. When he arrived, he was ushered into the parlor; and there, to his astonishment, he saw Mary Todd sitting before him.

What Lincoln and Mary Todd said, and how they said it, and what they did, that is not recorded. But of course the poor, tender-hearted fellow hadn't a chance to escape. If she cried— and of course she did—he probably delivered himself into her hands at once, and abjectly apologized for having gotten out of her hands.

They met often after that, but always secretly and behind closed doors in the Francis home.

At first Mary didn't let even her sister know that Lincoln was seeing her again.

Finally, when her sister did find out, she asked Mary "why she was so secretive."

And Mary replied "evasively that after all that had occurred, it was best to keep the courtship from all eyes and ears. Men and women of the world were uncertain and slippery, Mary continued, and if misfortune befell the engagement, all knowledge of it would be hidden from the world."

In other words, to put it bluntly, having learned a little lesson, she resolved to keep even the courtship secret, this time, until she was positive that Lincoln would marry her.

What technique did Miss Todd now employ?

James Matheny declared that Lincoln often told him "that he was driven into the marriage, and that Miss Todd told him he was in honor bound to marry her."

Herndon ought to have known if anybody did, and he said:

> To me it has always seemed plain that Mr. Lincoln married Mary Todd to save his honor, and in doing that he sacrificed his domestic peace. He had searched himself subjectively, introspectively, thoroughly: he knew he did not love her, but he had promised to marry her. The hideous thought came up like a nightmare. . . . At last he stood face to face with the great conflict between honor and domestic peace. He chose the former, and with it years of self-torture, sacrificial pangs, and the loss forever of a happy home.

Before he was willing to proceed, he wrote Speed, who had gone back to Kentucky, asking him if he had found happiness in his marriage.

"Please answer quickly," Lincoln urged, "as I am impatient to know."

Speed replied that he was far happier than he had ever expected to be.

So the next afternoon, Friday, November 4, 1842, Lincoln, reluctantly and with an aching heart, asked Mary Todd to be his wife.

She wanted to have the ceremony performed that very night. He hesitated, surprised, and a little frightened at the celerity with which events were moving. Knowing she was superstitious, he pointed out that the day was Friday. But, remembering what had happened before, she feared nothing now so much as delay. She was unwilling to wait even twenty-four hours. Besides, it was her birthday, her twenty-fourth birthday, so they hurried to Chatterton's jewelry store, bought a wedding-ring, and had these words engraved inside it: "Love is eternal."

Late that afternoon Lincoln asked James Matheny to be his best man, saying, "Jim, I shall have to marry that girl."

While Lincoln was putting on his best clothes that evening at Butler's house, and blacking his boots, Butler's little boy rushed in and asked him where he was going.

Lincoln replied: "To hell, I suppose."

In despair, Mary Todd had given away the trousseau that she had had made for the first wedding date, so that now she had to be married in a simple white muslin dress.

All arrangements were carried through with nervous haste.

Mrs. Edwards says she had only two hours' notice of the marriage and that the frosting on the wedding-cake which she hurriedly baked for the occasion was too warm to cut well when it was served.

As the Rev. Charles Dresser, clad in his clerical vestments, read the impressive Episcopal service, Lincoln seemed far from cheerful and happy. His best man testified that he "looked and acted as if he were going to the slaughter."

The only comment that Lincoln ever made in writing about his marriage was a postscript to a business letter that he wrote to Samuel Marshall about a week after the event. This letter is now in the possession of the Chicago Historical Society.

"Nothing new here," writes Lincoln, "except my marriage which to me is a matter of profound wonder."

★

PART TWO

★

9

WHILE I WAS writing this book, out in New Salem, Illinois, my good friend Henry Pond, a local attorney, said to me a number of times:

"You ought to go and see Uncle Jimmy Miles, for one of his uncles, Herndon, was Lincoln's law partner, and one of his aunts ran a boarding-house where Mr. and Mrs. Lincoln lived for a while."

That sounded like an interesting lead; so Mr. Pond and I climbed into his car one Sunday afternoon in July, and drove out to the Miles farm near New Salem—a farm where Lincoln used to stop and swap stories for a drink of cider while walking to Springfield to borrow law-books.

When we arrived, Uncle Jimmy dragged a trio of rocking-chairs out into the shade of a huge maple tree in the front yard; and there, while young turkeys and little ducks ran noisily through the grass about us, we talked for hours; and Uncle Jimmy related an illuminating and pathetic incident about Lincoln that has never been put into print heretofore. The story is this:

Mr. Miles's Aunt Catherine married a physician named Jacob M. Early. About a year after Lincoln arrived in Springfield— during the night of March 11, 1838, to be exact—an unknown man on horseback rode up to Dr. Early's house, knocked, called the physician to the door, emptied both barrels of a shot-gun into his body, then leaped upon a horse and dashed away.

Small as Springfield was at the time, no one was ever charged with the murder, and the killing remains a mystery to this day.

Dr. Early left a very small estate; so his widow was obliged to take in boarders to support herself; and, shortly after their marriage, Mr. and Mrs. Abraham Lincoln came to Mrs. Early's home to live.

Uncle Jimmy Miles told me that he had often heard his aunt, Dr. Early's widow, relate the following incident: One morning Mr. and Mrs. Lincoln were having breakfast when Lincoln did something that aroused the fiery temper of his wife. What, no one remembers now. But Mrs. Lincoln, in a rage, dashed a cup of hot coffee into her husband's face. And she did it in front of the other boarders.

Saying nothing, Lincoln sat there in humiliation and silence while Mrs. Early came with a wet towel and wiped off his face and clothes. That incident was probably typical of the married life of the Lincolns for the next quarter of a century.

Springfield had eleven attorneys, and they couldn't all make a living there; so they used to ride horseback from one county-seat to another, following Judge David Davis while he was holding court in the various places throughout the Eighth Judicial District. The other attorneys always managed to get back to Springfield each Saturday and spend the week-end with their families.

But Lincoln didn't. He dreaded to go home, and for three months in the spring, and again for three months in the autumn, he remained out on the circuit and never went near Springfield.

He kept this up year after year. Living conditions in the country hotels were often wretched; but wretched as they were, he preferred them to his own home and Mrs. Lincoln's constant nagging and wild outbursts of temper. "She vexed and harassed the soul out of him"—that was what the neighbors said; and the neighbors knew, for they saw her, and they couldn't help hearing her.

Mrs. Lincoln's "loud shrill voice," says Senator Beveridge, "could be heard across the street, and her incessant outbursts of wrath were audible to all who lived near the house. Frequently her anger was displayed by other means than words, and accounts of her violence are numerous and unimpeachable."

"She led her husband a wild and merry dance," says Herndon.

And Herndon felt he knew why "she unchained the bitterness of a disappointed and outraged nature."

It was her desire for vengeance. "He had crushed her proud womanly spirit," suggests Herndon, and "she felt degraded in the eyes of the world: Love fled at the approach of revenge."

She was always complaining, always criticizing her husband; nothing about him was ever right: He was stoopshouldered, he walked awkwardly and lifted his feet straight up and down like an Indian. She complained that there was no spring to his step, no grace to his movements; and she mimicked his gait and nagged at him to walk with his toes pointed down, as she had been taught at Madame Mentelle's.

She didn't like the way his huge ears stood out at right angles from his head. She even told him that his nose wasn't straight, that his lower lip stuck out, that he looked consumptive, that his feet and hands were too large, his head too small.

His shocking indifference to his personal appearance grated on her sensitive nature, and made her woefully unhappy. "Mrs. Lincoln," says Herndon, "was not a wildcat without cause." Sometimes her husband walked down the street with one trouser leg stuffed inside his boot-top and the other dangling on the outside. His boots were seldom blackened or greased. His collar often needed changing, his coat frequently needed brushing.

James Gourly, who lived next door to the Lincolns for years, wrote: "Mr. Lincoln used to come to our house, his feet encased in a pair of loose slippers, and with an old faded pair of trousers fastened with one suspender"—or "gallis" as Lincoln himself called it.

In warm weather he made extended trips "wearing a dirty linen duster for a coat, on the back of which the perspiration had splotched wide stains that resembled a map of the continent."

A young lawyer who once saw Lincoln in a country hotel, getting ready for bed, and clad "in a home made yellow flannel night shirt" that reached "halfway between his knees and his ankles," exclaimed, "He was the ungodliest figure I ever saw."

He never owned a razor in his life, and he didn't visit a barber as frequently as Mrs. Lincoln thought he should.

He neglected to groom his coarse, bushy hair, that stood out all over his head like horsehair. That irritated Mary Todd beyond words, and when she combed it, it was soon mussed again, by his bank-book, letters, and legal papers, which he carried in the top of his hat.

One day he was having his picture taken in Chicago, and the

photographer urged him to "slick up" a bit. He replied that "a portrait of a slicked-up Lincoln wouldn't be recognized down in Springfield."

His table manners were large and free. He didn't hold his knife right, and he didn't even lay it on his plate right. He had no skill whatever in the art of eating fish with a fork and a crust of bread. Sometimes he tilted the meat platter and raked or slid a pork chop off onto his plate. Mrs. Lincoln raised "merry war" with him because he persisted in using his own knife for the butter; and once when he put chicken bones on the side dish on which his lettuce had been served, she almost fainted.

She complained and scolded because he didn't stand up when ladies came into the room; because he didn't jump around to take their wraps, and didn't see callers to the door when they left.

He loved to read lying down. As soon as he came home from the office, he took off his coat and shoes and collar and dropped his one "gallis" from his shoulder, turned a chair upside down in the hallway, padded its sloping back with a pillow, propped his head and shoulders against it, and stretched out on the floor.

In that position he would lie and read for hours—usually the newspapers. Sometimes he read what he considered a very humorous story about an earthquake, from a book entitled "Flush Times in Alabama." Often, very often, he read poetry. And whatever he read, he read aloud. He had gotten the habit from the "blab" schools back in Indiana. He also felt that by reading aloud he could impress a thing on his sense of hearing as well as his sense of sight, and so remember it longer.

Sometimes he would lie on the floor and close his eyes and quote Shakspere or Byron or Poe; for example:

> "For the moon never beams without bringing me dreams
>   Of the beautiful Annabel Lee,
> And the stars never rise, but I feel the bright eyes
>   Of the beautiful Annabel Lee."

A lady—a relative—who lived with the Lincolns two years says that one evening Lincoln was lying down in the hall, reading, when company came. Without waiting for the servant to answer the door, he got up in his shirtsleeves, ushered the callers into the parlor, and said he would "trot the women folks out."

Mrs. Lincoln from an adjoining room witnessed the ladies' entrance, and overheard her husband's jocose expression. Her indignation was so instantaneous she made the situation exceedingly interesting for him, and he was glad to retreat from the mansion. He did not return until very late at night, and then slipped quietly in at a rear door.

Mrs. Lincoln was violently jealous, and she had little use for Joshua Speed. He had been her husband's intimate friend, and she suspected that he might have influenced Lincoln to run away from his wedding. Before his marriage, Lincoln had been in the habit of ending his letters to Speed with "Love to Fanny." But, after the marriage, Mrs. Lincoln demanded that that greeting be tempered down to "Regards to Mrs. Speed."

Lincoln never forgot a favor. That was one of his outstanding characteristics; so, as a little gesture of appreciation, he had promised that the first boy would be named Joshua Speed Lincoln. But when Mary Todd heard it she burst out in a storm. It was *her* child, and *she* was going to name it! And, what was more, the name was *not* going to be Joshua Speed! It was going to be Robert Todd, after her own father . . . and so on and so on.

It is hardly necessary to add that the boy *was* named Robert Todd. He was the only one of the four Lincoln children to reach maturity. Eddie died in 1850 at Springfield —age 4. Willie died in the White House—age 12. Tad died in Chicago in 1871—age 18. Robert Todd Lincoln died in Manchester, Vermont, July 26, 1926—age 83.

Mrs. Lincoln complained because the yard was without flowers, shrubs, or color. So Lincoln set out a few roses, but he took no interest in them and they soon perished of neglect. She urged him to plant a garden, and one spring he did, but the weeds overran it.

Though he was not much given to physical exertion, he did feed and curry "Old Buck"; he also "fed and milked his own cow and sawed his own wood." And he continued to do this, even after he was elected President, until he left Springfield.

However, John Hanks, Lincoln's second cousin, once remarked that "Abe was not good at any kind of work except dreamin'." And Mary Lincoln agreed with him.

Lincoln was absent-minded, often sank into curious spells of abstraction, and appeared to be entirely oblivious of the earth and everything that was on it. On Sundays, he would put one of his babies into a little wagon and haul the child up and down the rough sidewalk in front of his house. Sometimes the little chap happened to roll overboard. But Lincoln pulled steadily ahead, his eyes fixed on the ground, unconscious of the loud lamentations behind him. He never knew what had happened until Mrs. Lincoln thrust her head out at the door and yelled at him in a shrill, angry voice.

Sometimes he came into the house after a day at the office and looked at her and apparently didn't see her and didn't even speak. He was seldom interested in food; after she had prepared a meal, she frequently had hard work to get him into the dining-room. She called, but he seemed not to hear. He would sit down at the table and stare off dreamily into space, and forget to eat until she reminded him of it.

After dinner he sometimes stared into the fireplace for half an hour at a time, saying nothing. The boys literally crawled all over him and pulled his hair and talked to him, but he seemed unconscious of their existence. Then suddenly he would come to and tell a joke or recite one of his favorite verses:

"Oh, why should the spirit of mortal be proud?
Like a swift-fleeting meteor, a fast-flying cloud,
A flash of the lightning, a break of the wave,
He passes from life to his rest in the grave."

Mrs. Lincoln criticized him for never correcting the children. But he so adored them that "he was blind and deaf to their faults." "He never neglected to praise them for any of their good acts," said Mrs. Lincoln, "and declared: 'It is my pleasure that my children are free and happy, and unrestrained by parental tyranny. Love is the chain whereby to bind a child to its parents.' "

The liberties he allowed his children at times appear extraordinary. For example, once when he was playing chess with a judge of the Supreme Court, Robert came and told his father it was time to go to dinner. Lincoln replied, "Yes, yes." But, being very fond of the game, he quite forgot that he had been called, and played on.

Again the boy appeared, with another urgent message from Mrs. Lincoln. Again Lincoln promised to come, again he forgot.

A third time Robert arrived with a summons, a third time Lincoln promised, and a third time he played on. Then, suddenly, the boy drew back and violently kicked the chess-board higher than the players' heads, scattering the chessmen in every direction.

"Well, Judge," Lincoln said with a smile, "I reckon we'll have to finish this game some other time."

Lincoln apparently never even thought of correcting his son.

The Lincoln boys used to hide behind a hedge in the evening and stick a lath through the fence. As there were no street lights, passers-by would run into the lath and their hats would be knocked off. Once, in the darkness, the boys knocked off their father's hat by mistake. He didn't censure them, but merely told them that they ought to be careful, for they might make somebody mad.

Lincoln did not belong to any church, and avoided religious discussions even with his best friends. However, he once told Herndon that his religious code was like that of an old man named Glenn, in Indiana, whom he had heard speak at a church meeting, and who said: "When I do good, I feel good, when I do bad I feel bad, and that's my religion."

On Sunday mornings, as the children grew older, he usually took them out for a stroll, but once he left them at home and went to the First Presbyterian Church with Mrs. Lincoln. Half an hour later Tad came into the house and, missing his father, ran down the street and dashed into the church during the sermon. His hair was awry, his shoes unbuttoned, his stockings sagging down, and his face and hands were grimy with the black soil of Illinois. Mrs. Lincoln, herself elegantly attired, was shocked and embarrassed; but Lincoln calmly stretched out one of his long arms and lovingly drew Tad to him and held the boy's head close against his breast.

Sometimes on Sunday morning, Lincoln took the boys downtown to his office. There they were permitted to run wild. "They soon gutted the shelves of books," says Herndon, "rifled the drawers and riddled boxes, battered the point of my gold pen . . . threw the pencils into the spittoon, turned over the inkstands on the papers, scattered letters over the office and danced on them."

And Lincoln "never reproved them or gave them a fatherly frown. He was the most indulgent parent I have ever known," Herndon concludes.

Mrs. Lincoln seldom went to the office; but when she did, she was shocked. She had reason to be: the place had no order, no system, things were piled about everywhere. Lincoln tied up one bundle of papers and labeled it thus: "When you can't find it anywhere else, look in here."

As speed said, Lincoln's habits were "regularly irregular."

On one wall loomed a huge black stain, marking the place where one law student had hurled an inkstand at another one's head—and missed.

The office was seldom swept and almost never scrubbed. Some garden seeds that were lying on top of the bookcase had started to sprout and grow there, in the dust and dirt.

10

IN MOST RESPECTS, there wasn't a more economical housewife in all Springfield than Mary Lincoln. She was extravagant chiefly in matters having to do with showing off. She bought a carriage when the Lincolns could ill afford it and paid a neighbor's boy twenty-five cents an afternoon for driving her about town to make social calls. The place was a mere village, and she could have walked or hired a vehicle. But no, that would have been beneath her. And no matter how poor they were, she could always find money for clothes costing more than she could afford.

In 1844, the Lincolns paid fifteen hundred dollars for the home of the Rev. Charles Dresser who, two years before, had performed their marriage ceremony. The house had a living-room, kitchen, parlor, bedrooms; and, in the back yard, there was a woodpile, an outhouse, and a barn where Lincoln kept his cow and Old Buck.

At first the place seemed to Mary Lincoln an earthly paradise; and it was, in comparison with the bleak, bare rooms of the boarding-house she had just left. Besides, she had the new-found joy and pride of ownership. But its perfections soon began to fade, and she was forever finding fault with the home. Her sister lived in a huge two-story house, and this one was only a story and a half high. She once told Lincoln that no man who ever amounted to much lived in a story-and-a-half house.

Usually, when she asked him for anything, he never inquired

whether it was necessary. "You know what you want," he would say, "so go and get it." But in this instance, he rebelled: the family was small, and the house was entirely adequate. Besides, he was a poor man: he had only five hundred dollars when they were married, and he had not added much to it since. He knew that they couldn't afford to enlarge the house; and she knew it also; but she kept on urging and complaining. Finally, in order to quiet her, he had a contractor estimate the cost, and Lincoln told him to make it high. He did, and Lincoln showed her the figures. She gasped, and he imagined that settled the matter.

But he was too hopeful, for the next time he went away on the circuit she called in another carpenter, got a lower estimate, and ordered the work done at once.

When Lincoln returned to Springfield and walked down Eighth Street, he hardly recognized his own house. Meeting a friend, he inquired with mock seriousness, "Stranger, can you tell me where Mr. Lincoln lives?"

His income from the law was not large; and he often had, as he put it, "hard scratching" to meet his bills. And now he had come home to find a large and unnecessary carpenter bill added to his burdens.

It saddened him, and he said so.

Mrs. Lincoln answered him in the only way that she knew how to react to a criticism—with an attack. She told him testily that he had no money sense, that he didn't know how to manage, that he didn't charge enough for his services.

That was one of her favorite grievances, and many people would have backed her stand on that. The other attorneys were constantly irritated and annoyed by Lincoln's trifling charges, declaring that he was impoverishing the whole bar.

As late as 1853, when Lincoln was forty-four years old and only eight years away from the White House, he handled four cases in the McLean Circuit Court for a total charge of thirty dollars.

Many of his clients, he said, were as poor as he, and he didn't have the heart to charge them much.

Once a man sent him twenty-five dollars; and Lincoln returned ten, saying he had been too liberal.

In another instance, he prevented a swindler from getting hold of ten thousand dollars' worth of property owned by a demented girl. Lincoln won the case in fifteen minutes. An hour later, his associate, Ward Lamon, came to divide their fee of two hundred and fifty dollars. Lincoln rebuked him sternly. Lamon protested that the fee had been settled in advance, that the girl's brother was entirely satisfied to pay it.

"That may be," Lincoln retorted, "but I am not satisfied. That money comes out of the pocket of a poor, demented girl; and I would rather starve than swindle her in this manner. You return half this money at least, or I'll not take a cent of it as my share."

In another instance, a pension agent had charged the widow of a Revolutionary soldier half the four hundred dollars to which her pension amounted, for getting her claim allowed. The old woman was bent with age, and in poverty. Lincoln had her sue the pension agent, won the case for her, and charged her nothing. Besides, he paid her hotel bill and gave her money to buy a ticket home.

One day the Widow Armstrong came to Lincoln in great trouble. Her son Duff was charged with having murdered a man in a drunken brawl, and she pleaded with Abe to come and save the boy. Lincoln had known the Armstrongs back in New Salem. In fact, he had rocked Duff to sleep when he was a baby in the cradle. The Armstrongs had been a wild, rough lot; but Lincoln liked them. Jack Armstrong, Duff's father, had been the leader of the Clary's Grove Boys, and the renowned athlete whom Lincoln vanquished in a wrestling-match that has gone down in history.

Old Jack was dead now. Lincoln gladly went before the jury and made one of the most moving and appealing addresses of his career, and saved the boy from the gallows.

All the widowed mother had in the world was forty acres of land, which she offered to turn over to Lincoln.

"Aunt Hannah," he said, "you took me in years ago when I was poor and homeless, and you fed me and mended my clothes, and I shan't charge you a cent now."

Sometimes he urged his clients to settle out of court, and charged them nothing whatever for his advice. In one instance, he refused to take a judgment against a man, saying, "I am really sorry for him—poor and a cripple as he is."

Such kindness and consideration, beautiful though it was, didn't bring in cash; so Mary Lincoln scolded and fretted. Her husband wasn't getting on in the world, while other lawyers were growing wealthy with their fees and investments. Judge

David Davis, for example, and Logan. Yes, and Stephen A. Douglas. By investing in Chicago real estate, Douglas had amassed a fortune and even become a philanthropist, giving Chicago University ten acres of valuable land upon which to erect its buildings. Besides, he was now one of the most famous political leaders in the nation.

How often Mary Lincoln thought of him, and how keenly she wished she had married him! As Mrs. Douglas she would be a social leader in Washington, wear Paris clothes, enjoy trips to Europe, dine with queens, and some day live in the White House. So she probably pictured herself in vain day-dreams.

What was her future as Lincoln's wife? He would go on like this to the end: riding the circuit for six months out of the year, leaving her alone at home, lavishing no love on her, and giving her no attention. . . . How different, how poignantly different, the realities of life were from the romantic visions she had once dreamed at Madame Mentelle's in the long ago!

★ ★ ★

11

★ ★ ★

Iɴ ᴍᴏꜱᴛ ʀᴇꜱᴘᴇᴄᴛꜱ, as has been said, Mrs. Lincoln was economical, and took pride in the fact. She purchased supplies carefully and the table was set sparingly, very sparingly; there were just barely enough scraps left to feed the cats. The Lincolns had no dog.

She bought bottle after bottle of perfume, broke the seals, sampled them, and returned them, contending that they were inferior, that they had been misrepresented. She did this so often that the local druggist refused to honor her orders for more. His account-book may still be seen in Springfield with the penciled notations: "Perfume returned by Mrs. Lincoln."

She frequently had trouble with the tradespeople. For example, she felt that Myers, the iceman, was cheating her with short weights; so she turned on him and berated him in such a shrill, loud voice that neighbors half a block away ran to their doors to look and listen.

This was the second time she had made this accusation, and he swore that he would see her sizzling in hell before he would sell her another piece of ice.

He meant it, and he stopped his deliveries. That was awkward. She had to have ice, and he was the only man in town who supplied it; so, for once in her life, Mary Lincoln humbled herself. But she didn't do it personally: she paid a neighbor a quarter to go downtown and salve over the wound and coax Myers to resume his deliveries.

One of Lincoln's friends started a little newspaper called "The Springfield Republican." He canvassed the town, and Lincoln subscribed for it. When the first copy was delivered at the door, Mary Todd was enraged. What! Another worthless paper? More money thrown away when she was trying so hard to save every penny! She lectured and scolded; and, in order to pacify her, Lincoln said that he had not ordered the paper to be delivered. That was literally true. He had merely said he would pay for a subscription. He hadn't specifically said he wanted it delivered. A lawyer's finesse!

That evening, unknown to her husband, Mary Todd wrote a fiery letter, telling the editor what she thought of his paper, and demanding that it be discontinued.

She was so insulting that the editor answered her publicly in a column of the paper, and then wrote Lincoln, demanding an explanation. Lincoln was so distressed by the publicity that he was positively ill. In humiliation, he wrote the editor, saying it was all a mistake, trying to explain as best he could.

Once Lincoln wanted to invite his stepmother to spend Christmas at his home, but Mary Todd objected. She despised the old folks, and held Tom Lincoln and the Hanks tribe in profound contempt. She was ashamed of them, and Lincoln feared that even if they came to the house she wouldn't admit them. For twenty-three years his stepmother lived seventy miles away from Springfield, and he went to visit her, but she never saw the inside of his home.

The only relative of his that ever visited him after his marriage was a distant cousin, Harriet Hanks, a sensible girl with a pleasing disposition. Lincoln was very fond of her and invited her to live at his home while she attended school in Springfield. Mrs. Lincoln not only made a servant of her but tried to turn her into a veritable household drudge. Lincoln rebelled at this, refused to countenance such rank injustice, and the whole thing resulted in a distressing scene.

She had incessant trouble with her "hired girls." One or two explosions of her fiery wrath, and they packed up and left, an unending stream of them. They despised her and warned their friends; so the Lincoln home was soon on the maids' black-list.

She fumed and fussed and wrote letters about the "wild Irish" she had to employ. But all Irish became "wild" when they tried to work for her. She openly boasted that if she outlived her husband, she would spend the rest of her days in a

Southern State. The people with whom she had been brought up, back in Lexington, did not put up with any impudence from their servants. If a Negro did not mind, he was sent forthwith to the whipping-post in the public square, to be flogged. One of the Todds' neighbors flogged six of his Negroes until they died.

"Long Jake" was a well-known character in Springfield at that time. He had a span of mules and an old dilapidated wagon, and he ran what he vaingloriously described as an "express service." His niece, unfortunately, went to work for Mrs. Lincoln. A few days later, the servant and mistress quarreled; the girl threw off her apron, packed her trunk, and walked out of the house, slamming the door behind her.

That afternoon, Long Jake drove his mules down to the corner of Eighth and Jackson streets and told Mrs. Lincoln that he had come for his niece's baggage. Mrs. Lincoln flew into a rage, abused him and his niece in bitter language, and threatened to strike him if he entered her house. Indignant, he rushed down to Lincoln's office and demanded that the poor man make his wife apologize.

Lincoln listened to his story, and then said sadly:

"I regret to hear this, but let me ask you in all candor, can't you endure for a few moments what I have had as my daily portion for the last fifteen years?"

The interview ended in Long Jake's extending his sympathy to Lincoln and apologizing for having troubled him.

Once Mrs. Lincoln kept a maid for more than two years, and the neighbors marveled; they could not understand it. The explanation was very simple: Lincoln had made a secret bargain with this one. When she first came, he took her aside and told her very frankly what she would have to endure; that he was sorry, but it couldn't be helped. The girl must ignore it. Lincoln promised her an extra dollar a week, himself, if she would do so.

The outbursts went on as usual; but with her secret moral and monetary backing, Maria persisted. After Mrs. Lincoln had given her a tongue-lashing, Lincoln would watch his chance and steal out into the kitchen while the maid was alone and pat her on the shoulder, admonishing her:

"That's right. Keep up your courage, Maria. Stay with her. Stay with her."

This servant afterward married, and her husband fought

under Grant. When Lee surrendered, Maria hurried to Washington to obtain her husband's immediate release, for she and her children were in want. Lincoln was glad to see her, and sat down and talked to her about old times. He wanted to invite her to stay for dinner, but Mary Todd wouldn't hear of it. He gave her a basket of fruit and money to buy clothes, and told her to call again the next day and he would provide her with a pass through the lines. But she didn't call, for that night he was assassinated.

And so Mrs. Lincoln stormed on through the years, leaving in her wake a train of heartaches and hatred. At times she behaved as if insane.

There was something a trifle queer about the Todd family; and since Mary's parents were cousins, perhaps this queer streak had been accentuated by inbreeding. Some people—among others, her own physician—feared she was suffering from an incipient mental disease.

Lincoln bore it all with Christ-like patience, and seldom censured her. But his friends weren't so docile.

Herndon denounced her as a "wildcat" and a "she wolf."

Turner King, one of Lincoln's warmest admirers, described her as "a hellion, a she devil," and declared that he had seen her drive Lincoln out of the house time after time.

John Hay, as secretary to the President in Washington, called her a short, ugly name that it is best not to print.

The pastor of the Methodist Church in Springfield lived near the Lincoln house. He and Lincoln were friends; and his wife testified that the Lincolns "were very unhappy in their domestic life, and that *Mrs. Lincoln was seen frequently to drive him from the house with a broomstick.*"

James Gourley, who lived next door for sixteen years, declared that Mrs. Lincoln "had the devil in her," that she had hallucinations and carried on like a crazy woman, weeping and wailing until she could be heard all over the neighborhood, demanding that some one guard the premises, swearing that some rough character was going to attack her.

Her outbursts of wrath grew more frequent, more fiery, with the passing of time. Lincoln's friends felt deeply sorry for him. He had no home life, and he never invited even his most intimate companions to dine with him—not even men like Herndon and Judge Davis. He was afraid of what might happen. He himself avoided Mary as much as possible, spending his evenings spinning yarns with the other attorneys down at the law library or telling stories to a crowd of men in Diller's drugstore.

Sometimes he was seen wandering alone, late at night, through unfrequented streets, his head on his chest, gloomy and funereal. Sometimes he said, "I hate to go home." A friend, knowing what was wrong, would take him to his house for the night.

No one knew more than Herndon about the tragic home life of the Lincolns; and this is what Herndon had to say on pages 430-434 of the third volume of his Lincoln biography:

Mr. Lincoln never had a confidant, and therefore never unbosomed himself to others. He never spoke of his trials to me or, so far as I knew, to any of his friends. It was a great burden to carry, but he bore it sadly enough and without a murmur. I could always realize when he was in distress, without being told. He was not exactly an early riser, that is, he never usually appeared at the office till about nine o'clock in the morning. I usually preceded him an hour. Sometimes, however, he would come down as early as seven o'clock—in fact, on one occasion I remember he came down before daylight. If, on arriving at the office, I found him in, I knew instantly that a breeze had sprung up over the domestic sea, and that the waters were troubled. He would either be lying on the lounge looking skyward, or doubled up in a chair with his feet resting on the sill of a back window. He would not look up on my entering, and only answered my "Good morning" with a grunt. I at once busied myself with pen and paper, or ran through the leaves of some book; but the evidence of his melancholy and distress was so plain, and his silence so significant, that I would grow restless myself, and finding some excuse to go to the court-house or elsewhere, would leave the room.

The door of the office opening into a narrow hallway was half glass, with a curtain on it working on brass rings strung on wire. As I passed out on these occasions I would draw the curtain across the glass, and before I reached the bottom of the stairs I could hear the key turn in the lock, and Lincoln was alone in his gloom. An hour in the clerk's office at the court-house, an hour longer in a neighboring store having passed, I would return. By that time either a client had dropped in and Lincoln was propounding the law, or else the cloud of despondency had passed away, and he was busy in the recital of an Indiana story to whistle off the recollections of the morning's gloom. Noon having arrived I would depart homeward for my dinner. Returning within an hour, I would find him still in the office,— although his home stood but a few squares away,—lunching on a slice of cheese and a handful of crackers which, in my absence, he had brought up from a store below. Separating for the day at five or six o'clock in the evening, I would still leave him behind, either sitting on a box at the foot of the stairway, entertaining a few loungers, or killing time in the same way on the court-house steps. A light in the office after dark attested his presence there till late along in the night, when, after all the world had gone to sleep, the tall form of the man destined to be the nation's President could have seen strolling along in the shadows of trees and buildings, and quietly slipping in through the door of a modest frame house, which it pleased the world, in a conventional way, to call his home.

Some persons may insist that this picture is too highly colored. If so, I can only answer, they do not know the facts.

Once Mrs. Lincoln attacked her husband so savagely, and kept it up so long, that even he—"with malice toward none; with charity for all"—even he lost his self-control, and seizing her by the arm, he forced her across the kitchen and pushed her toward the door, saying: "You're ruining my life. You're making a hell of this home. Now, damn you, you get out of it."

★ ★ ★

12

★ ★ ★

IF LINCOLN had married Ann Rutledge, in all probability
he would have been happy, but he would not have been President. He was slow in thought and movement, and she was not
the type that would have driven him to achieve political distinction. But Mary Todd, obsessed with an undying determina-
tion to live in the White House, was no sooner married to Lincoln than she had him out running for the Whig nomination for
Congress.

The battle was a fierce one; and, incredible as it seems, his
political enemies accused him of being an infidel because he belonged to no church, and denounced him as a tool of wealth
and aristocracy because he had affiliated himself through marriage with the haughty Todd and Edwards families. Ridiculous
as the charges were, Lincoln realized that they might hurt him
politically. So he answered his critics: "Only one of my relatives
has ever visited me since I came to Springfield, and that one,
before he got out of town, was accused of stealing a jew's-harp.
Now, if that is being a member of a proud, aristocratic family,
then I am guilty of the offense."

When the election came, Lincoln was defeated. It was the
first political setback of his career.

Two years later he ran again and won. Mary Lincoln was
ecstatic; believing that his political triumphs had just begun,
she ordered a new evening gown and polished up her French
verbs. As soon as her husband reached the capital, she addressed her letters to "The Honorable A. Lincoln." But he put
a stop to that at once.

She wanted to live in Washington, too, she longed to bask in the social prestige that she was sure awaited her. But when she came East to join him, she found things vastly different from what she had anticipated. Lincoln was so poor that he had had to borrow money from Stephen A. Douglas to pay his expenses until he got his first salary check from the Government; so Mr. and Mrs. Lincoln stopped at Mrs. Spriggs's boarding-house in Duff Green's Row. The street in front of Mrs. Spriggs's establishment was unpaved, the sidewalk was made of ashes and gravel, the rooms were bleak, and there was no plumbing. In her back yard Mrs. Spriggs had an outhouse, a goose-pen, and a garden; and, as the neighbors' hogs were constantly breaking in to eat her vegetables, her little boy had to run out at intervals with a club to drive the animals away.

The city of Washington did not trouble in those days to collect the garbage; so Mrs. Spriggs dumped her refuse in the back alley, and depended upon the cows, pigs, and geese that wandered about the streets at will, to come and devour it.

Mrs. Lincoln found the door to the exclusive society of Washington shut tightly against her. She was ignored, and left alone to sit in her bleak boarding-house bedroom, with her spoiled children and a headache—listening to Mrs. Spriggs's boy, shouting to drive the hogs out of the cabbage-patch.

Disappointing as that was, it was nothing in comparison with the political disaster that lurked around the corner. When Lincoln entered Congress, the country had been waging a war against Mexico for twenty months—a shameful war of aggression, deliberately provoked by the slave power in Congress in order that the nation might acquire more territory where slavery would flourish and from which pro-slavery senators would be elected.

America accomplished two things in that war. Texas had once belonged to Mexico and then seceded. We forced Mexico to renounce all of her claims to Texas; and, in addition, we deliberately robbed Mexico of half of all the territory she owned and carved it up into the States of New Mexico, Arizona, Nevada, and California.

Grant said it was one of the wickedest wars in all history, and that he could never forgive himself for having fought in it. A great many of the American soldiers rebelled and went over to the enemy; one famous battalion in Santa Anna's army was composed entirely of American deserters.

Lincoln stood up in Congress and did what many other

Whigs had already done: he attacked the President for having started "a war of rapine and murder, a war of robbery and dishonor," and declared that the God of heaven had "forgotten to defend the weak and innocent, and permitted the strong band of murderers and demons from hell to kill men, women, and children and lay waste and pillage the land of the just."

The capital paid no attention whatever to this speech, for Lincoln was unknown. But back in Springfield, it raised a hurricane. Illinois had sent six thousand men to fight, as they believed, for the holy cause of liberty; and now their representative was standing up in Congress and calling their soldiers demons from hell, and accusing them of murder. In a rage, excited partizans held public meetings and denounced Lincoln as "base" . . . "dastardly" . . . "infamous" . . . "a reasonable guerilla" . . . "a second Benedict Arnold."

At one meeting resolutions were adopted declaring that never until then had they "known disgrace so black." . . . "Such black odium and infamy heaped upon the living brave and illustrious dead can but excite the indignation of every true Illinoisan."

The hatred was so bitter that it smoldered for more than a decade; and when Lincoln was running for the Presidency thirteen years later these denunciations were again hurled at his head.

"I have committed political suicide," Lincoln confessed to his law partner.

He dreaded to go back home now and face his resentful constituents; so he tried to secure a position that would keep him in Washington, and maneuvered to secure an appointment as Commissioner of the Land Office, but he failed.

Then he tried to have himself named Governor of the Territory of Oregon, with the hope that he might be one of the first senators when it came into the Union, but he failed in that too.

So he returned to Springfield and his dirty law office. Once more he hitched up Old Buck to his ramshackle buggy, and again he started driving over the circuit of the Eighth Judicial District—one of the most dejected men in all Illinois.

He was determined now to forget all about politics, and devote himself to his profession. He realized that he had no method in his work, that he lacked mental discipline; and so, to train himself to reason more closely and to demonstrate a proposition, he bought a geometry and carried it with him as he rode the circuit.

Herndon records in his biography:

At the little country inns, we usually occupied the same bed. In most cases the beds were too short for Lincoln, and his feet would hang over the footboard, thus exposing a limited expanse of shin bone. Placing a candle on a chair at the head of the bed, he would read and study for hours. I have known him to study in this position until two o'clock in the morning. Meanwhile, I and others who chanced to occupy the same room would be safely and soundly asleep. On the circuit in this way he studied Euclid until he could with ease demonstrate all the propositions in the six books.

After he had mastered geometry, he studied algebra, then astronomy, then he prepared a lecture on the origin and growth of languages. But no other study interested him as did Shakspere. The literary tastes that Jack Kelso had nurtured in New Salem still persisted.

The most striking characteristic of Abraham Lincoln, from this time on to the end of his life, was a sadness so profound, a melancholy so deep that mere words can hardly convey its depths.

When Jesse Weik was helping Herndon prepare his immortal biography, he felt that surely the reports of Lincoln's sadness must be exaggerated. So he went and discussed this point at length with the men who had been associated with Lincoln for years—men such as Stuart, Whitney, Matheny, Swett, and Judge Davis.

Then Weik was firmly convinced "that men who never saw Lincoln could scarcely realize his tendency to melancholy," and Herndon, agreeing with him, went farther, making the statement from which I have already quoted: "If Lincoln ever had a happy day in twenty years, I never knew of it. A perpetual look of sadness was his most prominent feature. Melancholy dripped from him as he walked."

When he was riding the circuit he would frequently sleep in the same room with two or three other attorneys. They would be awakened early in the morning by the sound of his voice and find him sitting on the edge of the bed, mumbling incoherently to himself. Getting up, he would start a fire and sit for hours, staring into the blaze. Frequently, on such occasions, he would recite "Oh, why should the spirit of mortal be proud?"

Sometimes as he walked down the street, he was so deep in

despair that he took no notice of those who met him and spoke to him. Occasionally he shook hands with people without knowing what he was doing.

Jonathan Birch, who all but worshiped Lincoln's memory, says:

> When attending court at Bloomington, Lincoln would keep his hearers in the court room, office or on the street convulsed with laughter at one hour and the next hour be so deeply submerged in speculation that no one dared arouse him. . . . He would sit in a chair tilted against the wall, his feet on the lower rung, legs drawn up and knees level with his chin, hat tipped forward, hands clasped about knees, eyes infinitely sad, the very picture of dejection and gloom. Thus absorbed I have seen him sit for hours at a time, defying the interruption of even his closest friends.

Senator Beveridge, after studying Lincoln's career perhaps more exhaustively than any one else has ever done, came to the conclusion that "the dominant quality in Lincoln's life from 1849 to the end was a sadness so profound that the depths of it cannot be sounded or estimated by normal minds."

Yet Lincoln's inexhaustible humor, his amazing capacity for telling stories, were as striking and inseparable a part of his personality as his sadness.

At times Judge Davis even stopped court to listen to his boisterous humor.

"Crowds thronged about him, crowds of two hundred and three hundred," says Herndon, holding their sides and laughing the hours away.

One eye-witness declares that when Lincoln reached the "nub" of a good story, men "whooped" and rolled off their chairs.

Those who knew Lincoln intimately agreed that "his abysmal sadness" was caused by two things: his crushing political disappointments and his tragic marriage.

And so the poignant years of apparently permanent political oblivion dragged by—six of them—and then suddenly an event occurred that altered the whole course of Lincoln's life, and started him toward the White House.

The instigator and moving spirit behind this event was Mary Lincoln's old sweetheart, Stephen A. Douglas.

★ ★ ★

13

★ ★ ★

In 1854, a tremendous thing happened to Lincoln. It came about as a result of the repeal of the Missouri Compromise. The Missouri Compromise, in brief, was this: In 1819, Missouri had wanted to come into the Union as a slave State. The North had opposed its doing so and the situation became serious. Finally, the ablest public men of that day arranged what is now known as the Missouri Compromise. The South got what it wanted: the admission of Missouri as a slave State. The North got what it wanted: thereafter slavery was never to be permitted in the West anywhere north of the southern boundary of Missouri.

People thought that would stop the quarreling about slavery, and it did—for a while. But now, a third of a century later, Stephen A. Douglas secured the repeal of the Compromise, and made it possible for a new area lying west of the Mississippi and equal in size to the original thirteen States, to be blighted with the curse of slavery. He fought long and hard in Congress for the repeal. The struggle lasted for months. Once during the bitter debates in the House of Representatives, members leaped on top of their desks, knives flashed, and guns were drawn. But finally, after an impassioned plea by Douglas, lasting from midnight until almost dawn, the Senate passed his bill on March 4, 1854. It was a tremendous event. Messengers ran through the streets of the slumbering city of Washington, shouting the news. Cannon in the Navy Yard boomed to salute the dawn of a new era—a new era that was to be drenched in blood.

Why did Douglas do it? No one seems to know. Historians in skullcaps are still arguing about it. Of this much, however, we are certain: Douglas hoped to be elected President in 1856. He knew this repeal would help him in the South.

But what of the North?

"By God, I know it will raise a hell of a storm there," he declared.

He was right. It did. It raised a regular tornado that blew both the great parties into bits, and eventually whirled the nation into civil war.

Meetings of protest and indignation flared up spontaneously in hundreds of cities and villages and hamlets. Stephen Arnold Douglas was denounced as the "traitor Arnold." People said that he had been named after Benedict Arnold. He was branded as a modern Judas, and presented with thirty pieces of silver. He was given a rope and told to hang himself.

The churches leaped into the fight with a holy frenzy. Three thousand and fifty clergymen in New England wrote a protest "in the name of Almighty God and in His presence," and laid it before the Senate. Fiery and indignant editorials fed the flames of public indignation. In Chicago even the Democratic papers turned upon Douglas with vindictive fierceness.

Congress adjourned in August, and Douglas started home. Amazed at the sights that met his eyes, he declared afterward that he could have traveled all the way from Boston to Illinois by the light of burning effigies of himself hanging by the neck.

Daring and defiant, he announced that he was going to speak in Chicago. The hatred against him there, in his own home town, amounted to nothing less than fanaticism. The press assailed him, and wrathful ministers demanded that he never again be permitted to "pollute the pure air of Illinois with his perfidious breath." Men rushed to the hardware stores, and, by sundown, there wasn't another revolver left for sale in all the city. His enemies swore that he should never live to defend his infamous deeds.

The moment Douglas entered the city, boats in the harbor lowered their flags to half-mast; and bells in a score of churches tolled, mourning the death of Liberty.

The night that he spoke was one of the hottest Chicago had ever known. Perspiration rolled down the faces of men as they sat idling in their chairs. Women fainted as they struggled to get out to the shore of the lake where they could sleep on the cool sands. Horses fell in their harness and lay dying in the streets.

But notwithstanding the heat, thousands of excited men, guns in their pockets, flocked to hear Douglas. No hall in Chicago could hold the throng. They packed a public square, and hundreds stood on balconies and sat astride the roofs of near-by houses.

The very first sentence that Douglas uttered was greeted with groans and hisses. He continued to talk—or, at least, he continued to try—and the audience yelled and booed and sang insulting songs and called him names that are unprintable.

His excited partizans wanted to start a fight. Douglas begged them to be quiet. He would tame the mob. He kept on trying, but he kept on failing. When he denounced the "Chicago Tribune," the great gathering cheered the paper. When he threatened to stand there all night unless they let him speak, eight thousand voices sang: "We won't go home until morning. We won't go home until morning."

It was a Saturday night. Finally, after four hours of futility and insult, Douglas took out his watch and shouted at the howling, bellowing, milling mob: "It is now Sunday morning, I'll go to church. And you can go to hell."

Exhausted, he gave up and left the speaker's stand. The Little Giant had met humiliation and defeat for the first time in his life.

The next morning the papers told all about it; and down in Springfield, a proud, plump brunette, trembling on the brink of middle age, read it with peculiar satisfaction. Fifteen years before, she had dreamed of being Mrs. Douglas. For years she had watched him mount on wings until he had become the most popular and powerful leader in the nation, while her husband had gone down in humiliating defeat; and, deep in her heart, she resented it.

But now, thank God, the haughty Douglas was doomed. He had split his own party in his own State. And just before the election. This was Lincoln's chance. And Mary Lincoln knew it—his chance to win back the public favor that he had lost in 1848, his chance to reinstate himself politically, his chance to be elected to the United States Senate. True, Douglas still had four more years to serve. But his colleague was coming up for reëlection in a few months.

And who was his colleague? A swaggering, pugnacious Irishman named Shields. Mary Lincoln had an old score to settle with Shields, too. Back in 1842, largely because of insulting letters that she herself had written, Shields had challenged Lincoln to a duel; and the two of them, armed with cavalry swords and accompanied by their seconds, had met on a sand-bar in the Mississippi River, prepared to kill each other. But, at the last moment, friends interceded and prevented bloodshed. Since that time, Shields had gone up in politics, but Lincoln had gone down.

But now Lincoln had struck bottom, and had started to rebound. The repeal of the Missouri Compromise had, as he said, "aroused" him. He could no longer remain quiet. He was determined to strike with all the vigor and conviction of his soul.

So he began preparing his speech, working for weeks in the State library, consulting histories, mastering facts, classifying, clarifying, studying all the hot debates that had been thundered back and forth across the Senate chamber during the stormy passage of this bill.

On October 3 the State Fair opened at Springfield. Thousands of farmers poured into town; men bringing their prize hogs and horses, their cattle and corn; women fetching their jellies and jam, their pies and preserves. But these displays were all but forgotten in the excitement of another attraction. For weeks it had been advertised that Douglas was to speak the opening day of the fair, and political leaders from all parts of the State had thronged there to hear him.

That afternoon he spoke for more than three hours, going over his record, explaining, defending, attacking. He hotly denied that he was trying either "to legislate slavery into a territory or to exclude it therefrom." Let the people in a territory do whatever they pleased about slavery.

"Surely," he shouted, "if the people of Kansas and Nebraska are able to govern themselves, surely they are able to govern a few miserable Negroes."

Lincoln sat near the front, listening to every word, weighing every argument. When Douglas finished, Lincoln declared: "I'll hang his hide on the fence to-morrow."

The next morning handbills were scattered all over town and the fair-grounds, announcing that Lincoln would reply to Douglas. The public interest was intense, and before two o'clock every seat was occupied in the hall where the speaking was to take place. Presently Douglas appeared and sat on the platform. As usual, he was immaculately attired and faultlessly groomed.

Mary Lincoln was already in the audience. Before leaving the house that morning she had vigorously brushed Lincoln's coat, had laid out a fresh collar and carefully ironed his best tie. She was anxious to have him appear to advantage. But the day was hot, and Lincoln knew the air in the hall would be oppressive. So he strode onto the platform without a coat, without a vest, without a collar, without a tie. His long, brown, skinny neck rose out of the shirt that hung loosely on his gaunt frame. His hair was disordered, his boots rusty and unkempt. One single knitted "gallis" held up his short, ill-fitting trousers.

At the first sight of him, Mary Lincoln flushed with anger and embarrassment. She could have wept in her disappointment and despair.

No one dreamed of it at the time, but we know now that this homely man, whose wife was ashamed of him, was starting out that hot October afternoon on a career that was to give him a place among the immortals.

That afternoon, he made the first great speech of his life. If all the addresses that he had made previously were collected and placed in one book, and those that he made from that afternoon on were placed in another volume, you could hardly believe that the same man was the author of them all. It was a new Lincoln speaking that day—a Lincoln stirred to the depths by a mighty wrong, a Lincoln pleading for an oppressed race, a Lincoln touched and moved and lifted up by moral grandeur.

He reviewed the history of slavery, and gave five fiery reasons for hating it.

But with lofty tolerance, he declared: "I have no prejudice against the Southern people. They are just what we would be in their situation. If slavery did not now exist among them, they would not introduce it. If it did now exist among us, we should not instantly give it up.

"When Southern people tell us they are no more responsible for the origin of slavery than we are, I acknowledge the fact. When it is said that the institution exists, and that it is very difficult to get rid of it in any satisfactory way, I can understand and appreciate the saying. I surely will not blame them for not doing what I should not know how to do myself. If all earthly power were given me, I should not know what to do with the existing institution."

For more than three hours, with the perspiration rolling down his face, he continued to answer Douglas, revealing the senator's sophistry, showing the utter falseness of his position.

It was a profound speech, and it made a profound impression. Douglas winced and writhed under it. Time after time he rose to his feet and interrupted Lincoln.

The election wasn't far off. Progressive young Democrats were already bolting the ticket and attacking Douglas, and when the voters of Illinois cast their ballots, the Douglas Democrats were overwhelmed.

Senators were chosen in those days by the State legislatures; and the Illinois Legislature met in Springfield on February 8, 1855, for that purpose. Mrs. Lincoln had bought a new dress and hat for the occasion and her brother-in-law, Ninian W. Edwards, had with sanguine anticipation arranged for a reception to be given that night in Senator Lincoln's honor.

On the first ballot, Lincoln led all the other candidates, and came within six votes of victory. But he steadily lost after that; and on the tenth ballot he was definitely defeated, and Lyman W. Trumbull was elected.

Lyman Trumbull had married Julia Jayne, a young woman who had been bridesmaid at Mary Lincoln's wedding and probably had been the most intimate friend that Mrs. Lincoln ever had. Mary and Julia sat side by side in the balcony of the Hall of Representatives that afternoon, watching the senatorial election; and when the victory of Julia's husband was announced, Mrs. Lincoln turned in a temper and walked out of the building. Her anger was so fierce, and her jealousy was so galling, that from that day on, to the end of her life, she never again spoke to Julia Trumbull.

Saddened and depressed, Lincoln returned to his dingy law office with the ink-stain on the wall and the garden seeds sprouting in the dust on top of the bookcase.

A week later he hitched up Old Buck and once more started driving over the unsettled prairies, from one country courthouse to another. But his heart was no longer in the law. He talked now of little else but politics and slavery. He said that the thought of millions of people held in bondage continually made him miserable. His periods of melancholy returned now more frequently than ever; and they were more prolonged and more profound.

One night he was sharing a bed with another lawyer in a country tavern. His companion awoke at dawn and found Lincoln sitting in his nightshirt on the edge of the bed, brooding, dejected, mumbling to himself, lost in unseeing abstraction. When at last he spoke, the first words were:

"I tell you this nation cannot endure permanently half slave and half free."

Shortly after this a colored woman in Springfield came to Lincoln with a pitiful story. Her son had gone to St. Louis and taken a job on a Mississippi steamboat. When he arrived in New Orleans he was thrown into jail. He had been born free, but he had no papers to prove it. So he was kept in prison until his boat left. Now he was going to be sold as a slave to pay the prison expenses.

Lincoln took the case to the Governor of Illinois. The governor replied that he had no right or power to interfere. In response to a letter, the Governor of Louisiana replied that he couldn't do anything, either. So Lincoln went back to see the Governor of Illinois a second time, urging him to act, but the governor shook his head.

Lincoln rose from his chair, exclaiming with unusual emphasis: "By God, Governor, you may not have the legal power to secure the release of this poor boy, but I intend to make the ground in this country too hot for the foot of a slave-owner."

The next year Lincoln was forty-six, and he confided to his friend Whitney that he "kinder needed" glasses; so he stopped at a jewelry store and bought his first pair—for thirty-seven and a half cents.

★ ★ ★

14

★ ★ ★

We have now come to the summer of 1858, and we are about to watch Abraham Lincoln making the first great fight of his life. We shall see him emerge from his provincial obscurity and engage in one of the most famous political battles in United States history.

He is forty-nine now—and where has he arrived after all his years of struggle?

In business, he has been a failure.

In marriage, he has found stark, bleak unhappiness.

In law, he is fairly successful, with an income of three thousand a year; but in politics and the cherished desires of his heart, he has met with frustration and defeat.

"With me," he confessed, "the race of ambition has been a failure, a flat failure."

But from now on events move with a strange and dizzying swiftness. In seven more years he will be dead. But in those seven years he will have achieved a fame and luster that will endure to the remotest generations.

His antagonist in the contest we are to watch is Stephen A. Douglas. Douglas is now a national idol. In fact, he is world-renowned.

In the four years that had elapsed since the repeal of the Missouri Compromise, Douglas had made one of the most amazing recoveries in history. He had redeemed himself by a dramatic and spectacular political battle. It came about in this way:

99

Kansas knocked at the door of the Union, asking to be admitted as a slave State. But should she be so admitted? Douglas said "no," because the legislature that had framed her constitution was not a real legislature. Its members had been elected by chicanery and shot-guns. Half the settlers in Kansas—men who had a right to vote—were never registered, and so couldn't vote. But five thousand pro-slavery Democrats who lived in western Missouri and had not the shadow of a legal right to cast ballots in Kansas went to a United States arsenal, armed themselves, and, on election day, marched over into Kansas with flags flying and bands playing—and voted for slavery. The whole thing was a farce, a travesty on justice.

And what did the free-State men do? They prepared for action. They cleaned up their shot-guns, oiled their rifles, and began banging away at signs on trees and knot-holes in barn doors, to improve their marksmanship. They were soon marching and drilling and drinking. They dug trenches, threw up breastworks, and turned hotels into forts. If they couldn't win justice with ballots, they would win it with bullets!

In almost every town and village throughout the North, professional orators harangued the citizenry, passed hats, and collected money to buy arms for Kansas. Henry Ward Beecher, pounding his pulpit in Brooklyn, cried that guns would do more for the salvation of Kansas than Bibles. From that time on, Sharp's rifles were known as "Beecher's Bibles." They were shipped from the East in boxes and barrels labeled as "Bibles," as "Crockery," as "Revised Statutes."

After five free-State settlers had been murdered, an old sheep-raiser, a religious fanatic who cultivated grapes and made wine on the side, rose up on the plains of Kansas and said: "I have no choice. It has been decreed by Almighty God that I should make an example of these pro-slavery men."

His name was John Brown, and he lived at Osawatomie.

One night in May he opened the Bible, read the Psalms of David to his family, and they knelt in prayer. Then after the singing of a few hymns, he and his four sons and a son-in-law mounted their horses and rode across the prairie to a pro-slavery man's cabin, dragged the man and his two boys out of bed, chopped off their arms, and split their heads open with an ax. It rained before morning, and the water washed some of the brains out of the dead men's skulls.

From that time on, both sides slew and stabbed and shot.

The term "Bleeding Kansas" was written on the pages of history.

Now, Stephen A. Douglas knew that a constitution framed by a bogus legislature in the midst of all that fraud and treachery was not worth the blotting-paper that it took to dry it.

So Douglas demanded that the people of Kansas be permitted to vote at an honest and peaceful election on the question of whether Kansas should be admitted as a slave or a free State.

His demand was altogether right and proper. But the President of the United States, James Buchanan, and the haughty pro-slavery politicians in Washington wouldn't tolerate such an arrangement.

So Buchanan and Douglas quarreled.

The President threatened to send Douglas to the political shambles, and Douglas retaliated: "By God, sir, I made James Buchanan; and by God, sir, I'll unmake him."

As Douglas said that, he not only made a threat, but he made history. In that instant, slavery had reached the apex of its political power and arrogance. From that moment on, its power declined with a swift and dramatic abruptness.

The battle that followed was the beginning of the end, for in that fight Douglas split his own party wide open and prepared the way for Democratic disaster in 1860, and so made the election of Lincoln not only possible but inevitable.

Douglas had staked his own political future on what he believed, and on what almost every one in the North believed, was an unselfish fight for a magnificent principle. And Illinois loved him for it. He had now come back to his home State, the most admired and idolized man in the nation.

The same Chicago that had hooted and lowered the flags to half-mast and tolled the church bells as he entered the city in 1854—that same Chicago now despatched a special train with brass bands and reception committees to escort him home. As he entered the city, one hundred and fifty cannon in Dearborn Park roared a welcome, hundreds of men fought to shake his hand, and thousands of women tossed flowers at his feet. People named their first-born in his honor; and it is probably no exaggeration to say that some of his frenzied followers would actually have died for him on the scaffold. Forty years after his death men still boasted that they were "Douglas Democrats."

A few months after Douglas made his triumphal entry into

Chicago the people of Illinois were scheduled to elect a United States Senator. Naturally the Democrats nominated Douglas. And whom did the Republicans put up to run against him? An obscure man named Lincoln.

During the campaign that followed, Lincoln and Douglas met in a series of fiery debates, and these debates made Lincoln famous. They fought over a question charged with emotional dynamite, public excitement rose to fever heat. Throngs such as had never been known before in the history of the United States rushed to hear them. No halls were large enough to accommodate them; so the meetings were held in the afternoon in groves or out on the prairies. Reporters followed them, newspapers played up the sensational contests, and the speakers soon had a nation for their audience.

Two years later, Lincoln was in the White House.

These debates had advertised him, they had paved the way.

For months before the contest began Lincoln had been preparing; as thoughts and ideas and phrases formed in his mind, he wrote them down on stray scraps of paper—on the backs of envelopes, on the margins of newspapers, on pieces of paper sacks. These he stored in his tall silk hat and carried about wherever he went. Finally he copied them on sheets of paper, speaking each sentence aloud as he wrote it, constantly revising, recasting, improving.

After completing the final draft of his first speech, he invited a few intimate friends to meet him one night in the library of the State House. There, behind locked doors, he read his speech, pausing at the end of each paragraph, asking for comments, inviting criticisms. This address contained the prophetic words that have since become famous:

"A house divided against itself cannot stand."

"I believe this government cannot endure permanently half slave and half free.

"I do not expect the Union to be dissolved—I do not expect the house to fall—but I do expect it will cease to be divided.

"It will become all one thing or all the other."

As he read that, his friends were astonished and alarmed. It was too radical, they said; it was "a damn fool utterance," it would drive voters away.

Finally Lincoln rose slowly and told the group of the intense thought that he had given the subject, and ended the conference by declaring that the statement "A house divided against itself cannot stand" was the truth of all human experience.

"It has been true," said Lincoln, "for six thousand years. And I want some universally known figure, expressed in a simple language, that will arouse men to the peril of the times. The time has come when this truth should be uttered, and I am determined neither to change nor modify my assertion. I am willing, if necessary, to perish with it. If it is decreed that I should go down because of this speech, then let me go down linked to the truth. Let me die in the advocacy of what is just and right."

The first of the great debates was held on the twenty-first day of August in the little farming town of Ottawa, seventy-five miles out of Chicago. Crowds began arriving the night before. Soon the hotels, private houses, and livery-stables were filled to capacity; and for a mile up and down the valley camp-fires blazed on bluffs and bottom-lands as if the town were surrounded by an invading army.

Before daybreak the tide set in again; and the sun rose that morning over the Illinois prairies to look down on country roads filled with buggies and wagons, with pedestrians, and with men and women on horseback. The day was hot, the weather had been dry for weeks. Huge clouds of dust arose and drifted over the corn-fields and meadows.

At noon a special train of seventeen cars arrived from Chicago; seats were packed, aisles jammed, and eager passengers rode on the roofs.

Every town within forty miles had brought its band. Drums rolled, horns tooted, there was the tramp, tramp of parading militia. Quack doctors gave free snake-shows and sold their pain-killers. Jugglers and contortionists performed in front of saloons. Beggars and scarlet women plied their trades. Firecrackers exploded, cannon boomed, horses shied and ran away.

In some towns, the renowned Douglas was driven through the streets in a fine carriage drawn by six white horses. A mighty hurrah arose. The cheering was continuous.

Lincoln's supporters, to show their contempt for this display and elegance, drove their candidate through the street on a decrepit old hay-rack drawn by a team of white mules. Behind him came another hay-rack filled with thirty-two girls. Each girl bore the name of a State, and above them rose a huge motto:

Westward the star of empire takes its way.
The girls link on to Lincoln as their mothers linked to Clay.

The speakers, committees, and reporters wedged and squeezed their way through the dense crowd for half an hour before they could reach the platform.

It was protected from the broiling sun by a lumber awning. A score of men climbed on the awning; it gave way under their weight; boards tumbled down on the Douglas committee.

In almost every way the two speakers differed sharply.

Douglas was five feet four. Lincoln was six feet four.

The big man had a thin tenor voice. The little man had a rich baritone.

Douglas was graceful and suave. Lincoln was ungainly and awkward.

Douglas had the personal charm of a popular idol. Lincoln's sallow wrinkled face was filled with melancholy, and he was entirely lacking in physical magnetism.

Douglas was dressed like a rich Southern planter, in ruffled shirt, dark-blue coat, white trousers, and a white broad-brimmed hat. Lincoln's appearance was uncouth, grotesque: the sleeves of his rusty black coat were too short, his baggy trousers were too short, his high stovepipe hat was weather-beaten and dingy.

Douglas had no flair for humor whatever, but Lincoln was one of the greatest story-tellers that ever lived.

Douglas repeated himself wherever he went. But Lincoln pondered over his subject ceaselessly, until he said he found it easier to make a new speech each day than to repeat an old one.

Douglas was vain, and craved pomp and fanfare. He traveled on a special train draped in flags. On the rear of the train was a brass cannon mounted on a box-car. As he approached a town, his cannon fired time after time, to proclaim to the natives that a mighty man was at their gates.

But Lincoln, detesting what he called "fizzlegigs and fireworks," traveled in day-coaches and freight-trains and carried a battered old carpet-bag, and a green cotton umbrella with the handle gone and a string tied around the middle to keep it from flapping open.

Douglas was an opportunist. He had no "fixed political morals," as Lincoln said. To win—that was his goal. But Lincoln was fighting for a great principle, and it mattered to him very little who won now, if only justice and mercy triumphed in the end.

"Ambition has been ascribed to me," he said. "God knows how sincerely I prayed from the first that this field of ambition might not be opened. I claim no insensibility to political honors; but to-day, could the Missouri Compromise be restored, and the whole slavery question replaced on the old ground of 'toleration' by necessity where it exists, with unyielding hostility to the spread of it, on principle, I would, in consideration, gladly agree that Judge Douglas should never be out, and I never in, an office, so long as we both or either, live.

"It makes little difference, very little difference, whether Judge Douglas or myself is elected to the United States Senate; but the great issue which we have submitted to you to-day is far above and beyond any personal interests or the political fortunes of any man. And that issue will live, and breathe, and burn, when the poor, feeble, stammering tongues of Judge Douglas and myself are silent in the grave."

During these debates Douglas maintained that any State, anywhere, at any time, had a right to have slavery if the majority of its citizens voted for it. And he didn't care whether they voted it up or down. His celebrated slogan was this: "Let each State mind its own business and let its neighbors alone."

Lincoln took directly the opposite stand.

"Judge Douglas's thinking slavery is right," he explained, "and my thinking it wrong, is the precise fact upon which depends the whole controversy.

"He contends that whatever community wants slaves has a right to have them. So they have, if it is not a wrong. But if it is a wrong, he cannot say people have a right to do wrong.

"He cares as little whether a State shall be slave or free as whether his neighbor shall plant his farm with tobacco or stock it with horned cattle. But the great mass of mankind differ with Judge Douglas: they consider slavery a great moral wrong."

Douglas went up and down the State, crying out time after time that Lincoln favored giving Negroes social equality.

"No," retorted Lincoln, "all I ask for the Negro is that, if you do not like him, you let him alone. If God gave him but little, let him enjoy that little. He is not my equal in many respects, but in his right to enjoy 'life, liberty, and the pursuit of happiness,' in his right to put into his mouth the bread that his hands have earned, he is my equal and the equal of Judge Douglas and the equal of every living man."

In debate after debate Douglas accused Lincoln of wanting the whites to "hug and marry the blacks."

And time after time, Lincoln was forced to deny it: "I object to the alternative which says that because I do not want a Negro woman for a slave, I must want her for a wife. I have lived until my fiftieth year, and have never had a Negro woman either for a slave or a wife. There are enough white men to marry all the white women; and enough Negro men to marry all the Negro women; and, for God's sake, let them be so married."

Douglas tried to dodge and befog the issues. His arguments, Lincoln said, had got down to the point where they were as thin as "soup made by boiling the shadow of a pigeon that had starved to death." He was using "specious and fantastic arrangements of words, by which a man can prove a horse-chestnut to be a chestnut horse."

"I can't help feeling foolish," continued Lincoln, "in answering arguments that are no arguments at all."

Douglas said things that weren't true. He knew that they were falsehoods, and so did Lincoln.

"If a man," responded Lincoln, "will stand up and assert, and repeat and reassert, that two and two do not make four, I know nothing that will stop him. I cannot work an argument into the consistency of a mental gag and actually close his mouth with it. I don't like to call Judge Douglas a liar, but when I come square up to him, I don't know what else to call him."

And so the fight raged on, week after week. Day after day Lincoln continued his attacks. Others leaped into the fray. Lyman Trumbull called Douglas a liar, and declared that he had been guilty of "the most damnable effrontery that ever man put on." Frederick Douglas, the famous Negro orator, came to Illinois and joined in the assault. The Buchanan Democrats waxed vicious and ferocious in their denunciation of Douglas. Carl Schurz, the fiery German-American reformer, indicted him before the foreign voters. The Republican press in screaming head-lines branded him as "a forger." With his own party divided, and himself hounded and harassed on every side, Douglas was fighting against tremendous odds. In desperation, he wired his friend Usher F. Linder: "The hell-hounds are on my track. For God's sake, Linder, come and help me fight them."

The operator sold a copy of the telegram to the Republicans, and it was head-lined in a score of papers.

Douglas's enemies screamed with delight, and from that day

on as long as he lived, the recipient of the telegram was called "For God's Sake Linder."

On election night, Lincoln remained in the telegraph office, reading the returns. When he saw that he had lost, he started home. It was dark and rainy and gloomy. The path leading to his house had been worn pig-backed and was slippery. Suddenly, one foot shot from under and hit the other. Quickly he recovered his balance. "It's a slip," he said, "and not a fall."

Shortly after that he read an editorial about himself in an Illinois paper. It said:

> Hon. Abe Lincoln is undoubtedly the most unfortunate politician that has ever attempted to rise in Illinois. In everything he undertakes, politically, he seems doomed to failure. He has been prostrated often enough in his political schemes to have crushed the life out of any ordinary man.

The vast crowds that had rushed to hear him debate with Douglas encouraged Lincoln to believe that he might make a little money now by giving lectures; so he prepared to talk on "Discoveries and Inventions," rented a hall in Bloomington, stationed a young lady at the door to sell tickets—and not one solitary person came to hear him. Not one!

So once more he returned to his dingy office with the ink-stain on the wall and the garden seeds sprouting on top of the bookcase.

It was high time he was getting back, for he had been away from his law practice for six months, earning nothing. Now he was out of funds entirely; he didn't have enough cash on hand even to pay his butcher's and grocer's bills.

So again he hitched up Old Buck to his ramshackle buggy, and again he started driving over the prairie circuit.

It was November, and a cold snap was coming. Across the gray sky above him wild geese flew southward, honking loudly; a rabbit darted across the road; off in the woods somewhere a wolf howled. But the somber man in the buggy neither saw nor heard what was going on about him. Hour after hour, he rode on, his chin on his breast, lost in speculation, submerged in despair.

15

WHEN THE NEWLY FORMED Republican party met in Chicago in the spring of 1860 to nominate a Presidential candidate, few people dreamed that Abraham Lincoln had a chance. A short time before that, he himself had written to a newspaper editor: "I must in all candor say I do not think myself fit for the presidency."

It was generally accepted in 1860 that the nomination honors were going to the handsome William H. Seward of New York. There could hardly be any question about that, for straw ballots were taken on the trains carrying the delegates to Chicago, and they gave Seward twice as many votes as all the other candidates combined. On many of the trains there was not a single ballot cast for Abraham Lincoln. It is possible that some of the delegates did not even know that such a man existed.

The convention met on Seward's fifty-ninth birthday. How fitting! He was positive that he would receive the nomination as a birthday present. He was so confident of it that he said good-by to his colleagues in the United States Senate and invited his intimate friends to attend a great feast of celebration at his home in Auburn, New York; and a cannon was rented, hauled into his front yard, loaded, and cocked up in the air, ready to boom the joyous news to the town.

If the convention had started balloting on Thursday night, that cannon would have been fired, and the story of a nation would have been changed; but the voting could not begin until the printer delivered the papers necessary for keeping the tally. And the printer, on his way to the convention, probably stopped for a glass of beer. At any rate, he was late, and consequently there was nothing for the convention to do that Thursday evening but sit and wait for him.

Mosquitoes were bad in the hall, the place was hot and stuffy, and the delegates hungry and thirsty; so some one stood up and moved that the convention adjourn until ten o'clock the next morning. A motion to adjourn is always in order; it takes precedence over all other motions and it is nearly always popular. This one carried with a rush of enthusiasm.

Seventeen hours elapsed before the convention assembled again. That is not a long time, but it was long enough for Seward's career to be wrecked, and Lincoln's made.

The person largely responsible for the wrecking was Horace Greeley, a grotesque-looking man with a head as round as a cantaloupe; with thin, silky hair as light as an albino's; and with a string necktie that usually worked itself out of place until the bow was approximately under his left ear.

Greeley was not even advocating the nomination of Lincoln, but he was determined with all the bitterness of his soul to even up an old score with William H. Seward and Seward's manager, Thurlow Weed.

The trouble was this: For fourteen years, Greeley had fought side by side with these men; he had helped make Seward Governor of New York and then United States Senator; and he had aided Weed tremendously in his battle to become and remain political boss of the State.

And what had Greeley gotten out of all this struggle and combat? Very little but neglect. He had wanted to be made State printer, and Weed had taken that place for himself. He had longed to be appointed postmaster of New York City, and Weed did not offer to recommend him. He had aspired to be governor, or even lieutenant-governor, and Weed not only said "no," but said it in a way that hurt and rankled.

Finally, when he could stand no more, Greeley sat down and wrote a long, stinging letter to Seward. It would fill seven pages of this book, and every paragraph of it was seared with bitterness.

That fiery message had been written on Saturday night, November 11, 1854. . . . And this was 1860. Greeley had waited six long years for an opportunity to get his revenge, but at last it had arrived, and he made the most of it. He didn't go to bed at all, that fateful Thursday night while the Republican nominating convention was having a recess in Chicago; but from sundown until long after dawn, he hurried from delegation to delegation, reasoning, arguing, pleading. His paper, the "New York Tribune," was read all over the North; and it influenced public opinion as no other paper had ever done. He was a famous man, voices were hushed whenever he appeared, and the delegates listened to him with respect.

He hurled all kinds of arguments against Seward. He pointed out that Seward had repeatedly denounced the Masonic order; that in 1830 he had been elected to the State Senate on the anti-Mason ticket, and, as a consequence had aroused bitter, widespread, and undying resentment.

Later, when he was Governor of New York, Seward had favored the destruction of the common-school fund and the establishment of separate schools for foreigners and Catholics, and thus had stirred up another hornet's nest of fiery hatred.

Greeley pointed out that the men who had made up the once powerful Know Nothing party were violently opposed to Seward and would vote for a hound dog in preference to him.

And that wasn't all. Greeley pointed out that this "arch agitator" had been too radical, that his "bloody program" and talk of a higher law than the Constitution had frightened the border States, and that they would turn against him.

"I will bring you the men who are candidates for governor in these States," Greeley promised, "and they will confirm what I say."

He did, and the excitement was intense.

With clenched fists and blazing eyes, the gubernatorial candidates in Pennsylvania and Indiana declared that Seward's nomination meant inevitable defeat in their States, inevitable disaster.

And the Republicans felt that, to win, they must carry those States.

So, suddenly, the flood-tide that had been running toward Seward began to recede. And Lincoln's friends rushed about from delegation to delegation, trying to persuade those who were opposed to Seward to concentrate on Lincoln. Douglas was sure to be nominated by the Democrats, they said, and no man in the country was better equipped to fight Douglas than Lincoln. To him, it was an old job; he was used to it. Besides, Lincoln was born a Kentuckian, and he could win votes in the doubtful border States. Furthermore, he was the kind of candidate the Northwest wanted—a man who had fought his way up from splitting rails and breaking sod, a man who understood the common people.

When arguments like these didn't succeed, they used others. They won Indiana's delegates by promising Caleb B. Smith a place in the Cabinet, and they won Pennsylvania's fifty-six votes with the assurance that Simeon Cameron would sit at Lincoln's right hand.

On Friday morning the balloting began. Forty thousand people had poured into Chicago, eager for excitement. Ten thousand wedged into the convention hall, and thirty thousand packed the streets outside. The seething mob reached for blocks.

Seward led on the first ballot. On the second, Pennsylvania cast her fifty-two votes for Lincoln, and the break began. On the third, it was all but a stampede.

Inside the hall, ten thousand people, half crazed with excitement, leaped upon the seats, shouting, yelling, smashing their hats on one another's heads. A cannon boomed on the roof—and thirty thousand people in the streets raised a shout.

Men hugged one another and danced about wildly, weeping and laughing and shrieking.

One hundred guns at the Tremont House belched and barked their volleys of fire; a thousand bells joined in the clamor; while whistles on railway engines, on steamboats, on factories, were opened and tied open for the day.

For twenty-hour hours the excitement raged.

"No such uproar," declared the "Chicago Tribune," "has been heard on earth since the walls of Jericho fell down."

In the midst of all this rejoicing, Horace Greeley saw Thurlow Weed, the erstwhile "maker of Presidents," shedding bitter tears. At last, Greeley had his sweet revenge.

In the meantime what was happening down in Springfield? Lincoln had gone to his law office as usual that morning and tried to work on a case. Too restless to concentrate, he soon tossed the legal papers aside and went out and pitched ball for a while back of a store, then played a game or two of billiards, and finally went to the "Springfield Journal" to hear the news. The telegraph office occupied the room above. He was sitting in a big arm-chair, discussing the second ballot, when suddenly the operator burst down the stairway, crying: "Mr. Lincoln, you are nominated! You are nominated!"

Lincoln's lower lip trembled slightly, his face flushed. For a few seconds he stopped breathing.

It was the most dramatic moment of his life.

After nineteen years of desolating defeats, he had been suddenly whirled to the dizzy heights of victory.

Men rushed up and down the streets shouting the news. The mayor ordered the firing of a hundred guns.

Scores of old friends flocked about Lincoln, half laughing, half crying, shaking his hands, tossing their hats into the air, yelling in mad excitement.

"Excuse me, boys," he pleaded; "there is a little woman down on Eighth Street who will want to hear this."

And away he dashed, his coat-tails sailing behind him.

The streets of Springfield were rosy all that night with the light of bonfires fed by tar-barrels and rail fences, and the saloons never closed their doors.

It wasn't long before half of the nation was singing:

"Old Abe Lincoln came out of the wilderness,
  Out of the wilderness, out of the wilderness;
Old Abe Lincoln came out of the wilderness,
  Down in Illinois."

16

Sᴛᴇᴘʜᴇɴ A. Dᴏᴜɢʟᴀs did more than any one else to elevate Lincoln to the White House, for Douglas split the Democratic party and put three candidates in the field against Lincoln instead of one.

With the opposition hopelessly divided, Lincoln realized, early in the contest, that he would be victorious; but, nevertheless, he feared that he would not be able to carry his own precinct or his home town. A committee made a house-to-house canvass in advance, to find out how the people in Springfield were going to ballot. When Lincoln saw the result of this canvass, he was astonished: all except three of the twenty-three ministers and theological students in town were against him, and so were many of their stanchest followers. Lincoln commented bitterly: "They pretend to believe in the Bible and be God-fearing Christians; yet by their ballots they are demonstrating that they don't care whether slavery is voted up or down. But I know God cares and humanity cares, and if they don't, surely they have not read their Bibles aright."

It is surprising to discover that all of Lincoln's relatives on his father's side, and all except one on his mother's side, voted against him. Why? Because they were Democrats.

Lincoln was elected by a minority of the votes of the nation. His opponents had approximately three votes to his two. It was a sectional triumph, for of his two million votes only twenty-four thousand came from the South. A change of only one vote in twenty would have given the Northwest to Douglas and thrown the election into the House of Representatives, where the South would have won.

In nine Southern States no one cast a Republican ballot. Think of it. In all Alabama, Arkansas, Florida, Georgia, Louisiana, Mississippi, North Carolina, Tennessee, and Texas not one man voted for Abraham Lincoln. This was ominous.

To appreciate what happened immediately after Lincoln's election, we must review the story of a movement that had raged over the North like a hurricane. For thirty years a fanatical group, obsessed by a holy zeal for the destruction of slavery, had been preparing the country for war. During all that time an unbroken stream of vitriolic pamphlets and bitter books had flowed from their presses; and paid lecturers had visited every city, town, and hamlet in the North, exhibiting the tattered, filthy garments worn by slaves, displaying their chains and manacles, holding up bloodstained whips and spiked collars and other instruments of torture. Escaped slaves themselves were pressed into service and toured the country, giving inflammatory accounts of brutalities they had seen and atrocities they had endured.

In 1839 the American Anti-Slavery Society issued a booklet entitled "American Slavery As It Is—The Testimony of 1,000 Witnesses." In this pamphlet, eye-witnesses related specific instances of cruelties they had observed: slaves had had their hands plunged into boiling water, they had been branded with red-hot irons, their teeth had been knocked out, they had been stabbed with knives, their flesh had been torn by bloodhounds, they had been whipped until they died, had been burned at the stake. Shrieking mothers had had their children torn from them forever and sold in the slave-pen and on the auction-block. Women were whipped because they did not bear more children, and strong white men with big bones and large muscles were offered twenty-five dollars for cohabiting with black women, since light-colored children sold for more money, especially if they were girls.

The favorite and most flaming indictment of the Abolitionist was miscegenation. Southern men were accused of cherishing negro slavery because of their love of "unbridled licentiousness."

"The South," cried Wendell Phillips, "is one great brothel where half a million women are flogged to prostitution."

Tales of sensuality so revolting that they could not be reprinted now, were broadcast in Abolition pamphlets then. Slave-owners were accused of violating their own mulatto daughters and selling them to be the mistresses of other men.

Stephen S. Foster declared that the Methodist Church in the South had fifty thousand black female members who were forced with whips to lead immoral lives, and he declared that the sole reason why Methodist preachers of that region favored slavery was because they wanted concubines for themselves.

Lincoln himself, during his debates with Douglas, declared that in 1850 there were 405,751 mulattoes in the United States, and that nearly all had sprung from black slaves and white masters.

Because the Constitution protected the rights of slave-owners, the Abolitionists cursed it as "a covenant with death and an agreement with hell."

As a climax to all Abolition literature, the wife of a poverty-stricken professor of theology sat down at her dining-room table and wrote a book which she called "Uncle Tom's Cabin." Sobbing as she wrote, she told her story in a storm of feeling. Finally she said God was writing the story. It dramatized and made real the tragedies of slavery as nothing else had ever done. It stirred the emotions of millions of readers and achieved a greater sale and exerted a more profound influence than any other novel that has ever been written.

When Lincoln was introduced to Harriet Beecher Stowe, the author, he called her the little woman that started the big war.

And what was the result of this well-meant but fanatical campaign of overstatement waged by the Abolitionists of the North? Did it convince the Southerners that they were wrong? Far from it. The effect was such as might have been expected. The hatred stirred up by the Abolitionists did what hatred always does: it bred hatred in return. It made the South wish to part company with its insolent, meddlesome critics. Truth seldom flourishes in an atmosphere of politics or of emotion, and on both sides of the Mason and Dixon's Line tragic error had grown to its bloody blossom time.

When the "black Republicans" elected Lincoln in 1860, the Southerners were firmly convinced that slavery was doomed, and that they had to choose at once between abolition and secession. So why not secede? Didn't they have a right to?

That question had been hotly debated back and forth for half a century, and various States at one time or another had threatened to leave the Union. For example: during the War of 1812 the New England States talked very seriously of forming a separate nation; and the Connecticut Legislature passed a resolution declaring that "the state of Connecticut is a free, sovereign and independent state."

Even Lincoln himself had once believed in the right of secession. He had said during a speech in Congress: "Any people anywhere, being inclined and having the power, have the right to rise up and shake off the existing government, and form a new one that suits them better. That is a most valuable, a most sacred right—a right which we hope and believe is to liberate the world.

"Nor is the right confined to cases in which the whole people of an existing government may choose to exercise it. Any portion of such people that can, may revolutionize and make their own of so much of the territory as they inhabit."

He had said that in 1848. This, however, was 1860, and he no longer believed it. But the South did. Six weeks after Lincoln's election South Carolina passed an Ordinance of Secession. Charleston celebrated the new "Declaration of Independence" with martial music and bonfires and fireworks and dancing in the streets. Six other States followed in rapid succession; and two days before Lincoln left Springfield for Washington, Jefferson Davis was elected President of a new nation, founded upon what was called "the great truth . . . that slavery is the negro's natural and normal condition."

The outgoing administration of Buchanan, honeycombed with disloyalty, did nothing whatever to prevent all this; so Lincoln was obliged to sit helplessly in Springfield for three months, and watch the Union dissolving and the republic tottering on the verge of ruin. He saw the Confederacy buying guns and building forts and drilling soldiers; and he realized that he would have to lead a people through a civil war—bitter and bloody.

He was so distressed that he couldn't sleep at night. He lost forty pounds in weight, from worry.

Lincoln, who was superstitious, believed that coming events cast their shadow through dreams and omens. The day after his election in 1860 he went home in the afternoon and threw himself down on a haircloth sofa. Opposite him was a bureau with a swinging mirror; and, as he looked into the mirror, he saw himself reflected with one body but with two faces—one very pale. He was startled, and he got up, but the illusion vanished. He lay down again, and there was the ghost, plainer than before. The thing worried and haunted him; and he told Mrs. Lincoln about it. She was sure it was a sign that he would be elected to a second term of office, but that the death pallor of one face meant he would not live through the second term.

Lincoln himself soon came to believe very strongly that he was going to Washington to die. He received scores of letters with sketches of gibbets and stilettoes; and almost every mail brought him threats of death.

After the election, Lincoln said to a friend:

"I am worrying to know what to do with my house. I don't want to sell myself out of a home, but if I rent it, it will be pretty well used up by the time I get back."

But finally he found a man who he thought would take care of the place and keep it in repair; so Lincoln rented it to him for ninety dollars a year; and then inserted this notice in the "Springfield Journal":

The furniture consisting of Parlor and Chamber Sets, Carpets, Sofas, Chairs, Wardrobes, Bureaus, Bedsteads, Stoves, China, Queensware, Glass, etc., at the residence on the corner of Eighth and Jackson Street is offered at private sale without reserve. For particulars apply at the premises at once.

The neighbors came and looked things over. One wanted a few chairs and a cook-stove, another asked the price of a bed.

"Take whatever you want," Lincoln probably replied, "and pay me what you think it is worth."

They paid him little enough.

Mr. L. L. Tilton, superintendent of the Great Western Railway, bought most of the furniture; and later took it with him to Chicago, where it was destroyed in the great fire of 1871.

A few pieces remained in Springfield; and years afterward a bookseller purchased as much of it as possible and took it to Washington and installed it in the rooming-house where Lincoln died. That house stands almost directly across the street from Ford's Theater, and is now the property of the United States Government—a national shrine and museum.

The second-hand chairs that Lincoln's neighbors could have bought for a dollar and a half apiece, are to-day worth more than their weight in gold and platinum. Everything that Lincoln touched intimately has now taken on value and glory. The black walnut rocking-chair in which he sat when Booth shot him, sold in 1929 for two thousand five hundred dollars. And a letter that he wrote appointing Major-General Hooker Commander-in-Chief of the Army of the Potomac recently sold at public auction for ten thousand dollars, while a collection of four hundred and eighty-five telegrams that he sent during the war, now owned by Brown University, are valued at a quarter of a million dollars. An unsigned manuscript of one of his unimportant talks was recently purchased for eighteen thousand dollars, and a copy of the Gettysburg address in Lincoln's handwriting brought hundreds of thousands.

The people of Springfield in 1861 little realized what caliber of man Lincoln was, and what he was destined to become.

For years the future great President had been walking down their streets almost every morning with a market-basket over his arm, a shawl about his neck, going to the grocery store and butcher's shop and carrying home his provisions. For years he had been going out each evening to a pasture on the edge of town and cutting out his cow from the rest of the herd and driving her home and milking her, grooming his horse, cleaning the stable, and cutting the firewood and carrying it in for the kitchen stove.

Three weeks before he left for Washington, Lincoln began the preparation of his first inaugural address. Wanting solitude and seclusion, he locked himself in an upstairs room over a general store and set to work. He owned very few books himself; but his law partner had something of a library, and Lincoln asked Herndon to bring him a copy of the Constitution, Andrew Jackson's Proclamation against Nullification, Henry Clay's great speech of 1850, and Webster's Reply to Hayne. And so amidst a lot of plunder in dingy, dusty surroundings, Lincoln wrote the famous speech ending with this beautiful plea to the Southern States:

> I am loath to close. We are not enemies but friends. We must not be enemies. Though passion may have strained, it must not break our bonds of affection. The mystic chords of memory, stretching from every battlefield and patriot's grave to every living heart and hearthstone all over this

broad land, will swell the chorus of the Union when again touched, as surely they will be, by the better angel of our nature.

Before leaving Illinois he traveled seventy miles to Charleston, in that State, to say farewell to his stepmother. He called her "Mamma," as he had always done; and she clung to him, saying between her sobs: "I didn't want you to run for President, Abe, and I didn't want to see you elected. My heart tells me that something will happen to you, and that I'll never see you again till we meet in heaven."

During those last days in Springfield, he thought often of the past and New Salem and Ann Rutledge, dreaming once again the dreams that had proved to be far beyond all earthly realities. A few days before he left for Washington he talked at length about Ann, to a New Salem pioneer who had come to Springfield to reminisce and say farewell. "I loved her deeply," Lincoln confessed, "and I think of her now very, very often."

The night before he left Springfield forever Lincoln visited his dingy law office for the last time and settled a few business details. Herndon tells us:

After these things were all disposed of, he crossed to the opposite side of the room and threw himself down on the old office sofa, which, after many years of service, had been moved against the wall for support. He lay for some moments, his face toward the ceiling, without either of us speaking. Presently he inquired, "Billy, how long have we been together?"

"Over sixteen years," I answered.

"We've never had a cross word during all that time, have we?" to which I returned a vehement, "No, indeed we have not."

He then recalled some incidents of his early practice and took great pleasure in delineating the ludicrous features of many a lawsuit on the circuit. . . . He gathered a bundle of books and papers he wished to take with him and started to go; but before leaving he made the strange request that the sign-board which swung on its rusty hinges at the foot of the stairway should remain. "Let it hang there undisturbed," he said, with a significant lowering of his voice. "Give our clients to understand that the election of a President makes no change in the firm of Lincoln and Herndon.

If I live I'm coming back some time, and then we'll go right on practising law as if nothing had ever happened."

He lingered for a moment as if to take a last look at the old quarters, and then passed through the door into the narrow hallway. I accompanied him downstairs. On the way he spoke of the unpleasant features surrounding the Presidential office. "I am sick of office-holding already," he complained, "and I shudder when I think of the tasks that are still ahead."

Lincoln probably was worth about ten thousand dollars at the time; but he was so short of cash then that he had to borrow money from his friends to pay for his trip to Washington.

The Lincolns spent their last week in Springfield at the Chenery House. The night before they left, their trunks and boxes were brought down to the hotel lobby and Lincoln himself roped them. Then he asked the clerk for some of the hotel cards, turned them over, and wrote on the back: "A. Lincoln, Executive Mansion, Washington, D.C.," and tacked them on his baggage.

The next morning, at half-past seven, the dilapidated old bus backed up to the hotel, and Lincoln and his family got in and jolted away to the Wabash station, where a special train was waiting to take them to Washington.

It was dark and rainy, but the station platform was crowded with a thousand or fifteen hundred of his old neighbors. They formed a line and slowly filed by Lincoln, shaking his great bony hand. Finally the ringing of the engine bell warned him that it was time to go aboard. He entered his private car by the front steps and a minute later appeared on the rear platform.

He had not intended to make a speech. He had told the newspaper reporters that it would not be necessary for them to be at the station, as he would have nothing to say. However, as he looked for the last time into the faces of his old neighbors, he felt he must say something. The words he uttered that morning in the falling rain are not to be compared with those he spoke at Gettysburg, or placed beside the sublime spiritual masterpiece that he pronounced on the occasion of his second inauguration. But this farewell speech is as beautiful as one of the Psalms of David, and it contains perhaps more of personal emotion and pathos than any other of Lincoln's addresses.

There were only two times in his life that Lincoln wept when trying to speak. This morning was one of them:

"My friends: No one, not in my situation, can appreciate my feeling of sadness at this parting. To this place, and the kindness of these people, I owe everything. Here I have lived a quarter of a century, and have passed from a young to an old man. Here my children have been born, and one is buried. I now leave, not knowing when or whether ever I may return, with a task before me greater than that which rested upon Washington. Without the assistance of that Divine Being who ever attended him, I cannot succeed. With that assistance, I cannot fail. Trusting in Him, who can go with me, and remain with you, and be everywhere for good, let us confidently hope that all will yet be well. To His care commending you as I hope in your prayers you will commend me, I bid you an affectionate farewell."

17

WHILE LINCOLN was en route to Washington for his inauguration, both the United States Secret Service and private detectives discovered what they believed was a plot to assassinate him as he passed through Baltimore.

In alarm Lincoln's friends pleaded with him to abandon the schedule that had been announced, and urged him to slip into Washington incognito by night.

That sounded cowardly, and Lincoln knew it would raise a storm of scoffs and sneers. He was decidedly against it. But finally, after hours of pleading, he bowed to the wishes of his trusted advisers, and prepared to make the rest of the trip secretly.

As soon as Mrs. Lincoln heard about the altered arrangements she insisted that she would go with him, and when she was told most emphatically that she must come on a later train she lost her temper and protested so loudly that she all but gave the plan away.

It had been announced that Lincoln would speak in Harrisburg, Pennsylvania, on February 22, spend the night there, and then leave the next morning for Baltimore and Washington.

He made his speech in Harrisburg according to schedule; but, instead of spending the night there, he slipped out of the back door of the hotel that evening at six and, disguised in an old threadbare overcoat and a soft wool hat such as he had never worn before, he was driven to an unlighted railway coach, and a few minutes later an engine was whirling him away to Philadelphia, and the telegraph wires in Harrisburg were cut at once so that the information would not be relayed to the would-be assassins.

At Philadelphia, his party had to wait for an hour to change trains and stations. In order to prevent recognition during that time, Lincoln and Allan Pinkerton, the famous detective, drove about the streets of the city in a darkened cab.

At 10:55, leaning on Pinkerton's arm and stooping so as not to draw attention to his height, Lincoln entered the station by a side door. He carried his head bent forward and had his old traveling shawl drawn close so that it almost covered his face. In that guise, he crossed the waiting-room and made his way to the rear section of the last sleeping-car on the train, which one of Pinkerton's aides, a woman, had had cut off from the rest of the car by a heavy curtain and reserved for her "invalid brother."

Lincoln had received scores of threatening letters, declaring that he would never live to enter the White House, and General Winfield Scott, Commander-in-Chief of the Army, feared that Lincoln would be shot during the inaugural address—and so did thousands of others.

Many people in Washington were afraid to attend the ceremony.

So old General Scott had sixty soldiers stationed under the platform at the east portico of the Capitol from which Lincoln read his inaugural address; and he had soldiers standing on guard in the Capitol behind the President, and soldiers encircling the audience in front of him. And after the ceremony, the new President stepped into a carriage and rode back through Pennsylvania Avenue under the protection of buildings covered with sharpshooters in green coats, and between rows of infantrymen with bristling bayonets.

When he finally reached the White House without a bullet in his heart, many people were surprised.

Others were disappointed.

For several years prior to 1861 the nation had been struggling under a financial depression. Suffering had been so intense that the Government had been compelled to send troops to New York City to prevent hungry mobs from breaking into the sub-Treasury.

Thousands of gaunt, desperate men were still looking for work when Lincoln was inaugurated; and they knew that the Republicans, coming into power for the first time, would dismiss all Democratic office-holders, even down to the ten-dollar-a-week clerks.

Scores of applicants were scrambling for every job; and Lincoln had not been in the White House two hours when he was overwhelmed by them. They rushed through the halls; jammed the corridors; took entire possession of the East Room; and invaded even the private parlors.

Beggars came, importuning him for the price of a lunch. One man wanted Lincoln to give him an old pair of pants.

A widow came, seeking an appointment for a man who had promised to marry her provided she could get him an office that would support a family.

Hundreds came merely to get his autograph. An Irishwoman who kept a boarding-house rushed to the White House to implore Lincoln to help her collect a board bill from a government clerk.

As soon as an office-holder became seriously ill, dozens of applicants flocked to Lincoln, asking for the appointment "in case he should die."

Every one was armed with testimonials, but of course Lincoln couldn't read a tenth of them. One day when two applicants for the same post-office thrust huge bundles of letters into his hands he simplified matters by tossing both packages unopened onto the scales, and appointed the man who had the heavier one.

Scores came to see Lincoln again and again, demanding jobs and abusing him savagely because he refused. Many were loafers without a shred of merit. One woman came asking for an appointment for her husband, admitting he was too drunk to come himself.

Their sordid selfishness, their voracious greed, appalled Lincoln. They intercepted him on his way to lunch. They rushed up to his carriage as he drove through the streets, presenting their credentials, begging for jobs. Even after Lincoln had been President for a year and the nation had been at war for ten months, the milling mob still hounded him.

"Will they never cease?" he exclaimed.

The mad onslaught of office-seekers had killed Zachary Taylor before he had been President a year and a half. The worry of it killed "Tippecanoe" Harrison in four weeks. But Lincoln had to endure the office-seekers and run a war at the same time. Finally, however, even his iron constitution all but broke under the strain. Stricken with an attack of smallpox, he said:

"Tell all the office-seekers to come at once, for now I have something I can give to all of them."

Lincoln hadn't been in the White House twenty-four hours when he was confronted with a grave and momentous problem. The garrison holding Fort Sumter, in the harbor at Charleston, South Carolina, was almost out of food. The President had to decide whether to provision the fort or surrender it to the Confederates.

His army and navy advisers said: "Don't try to send food. If you do, it will mean war."

Six of the seven members of his Cabinet said the same thing. But Lincoln knew that he couldn't evacuate Sumter without virtually recognizing secession and encouraging it, and dissolving the Union.

In his inaugural address he had declared that he had the most solemn oath "registered in heaven" to "preserve, protect, and defend" the Union. He intended to keep his oath.

So he gave the orders, and away sailed the U.S.S. *Powhatan,* carrying bacon and beans and bread for Fort Sumter. But no guns, no men, no ammunition.

When Jefferson Davis heard the news he telegraphed General Beauregard to attack Fort Sumter if he thought it necessary.

Major Anderson, in command of the fortress, sent word to General Beauregard that, if he would wait only four days, the garrison would be compelled to evacuate through starvation, for they were already living on nothing but salt pork.

Why didn't Beauregard wait?

Perhaps it was because a few of his advisers felt that "unless blood were sprinkled in the faces of the people," some of the seceding States might return to the Union.

Shooting a few Yankees would arouse enthusiasm and cement the Confederacy.

So Beauregard issued his tragic orders; and, at half-past four on the morning of April 12, a shell screamed through the air and fell hissing into the sea near the walls of the fort.

For thirty-four hours, the bombardment continued.

The Confederates turned the affair into a social event. Brave young men, gay in their new uniforms, fired their cannon to the applause of fashionable society women promenading the wharves and the Battery.

On Sunday afternoon the Union soldiers surrendered the fort and four barrels of salt pork; and, with the Stars and Stripes flying, and the band playing "Yankee Doodle," they sailed away, bound for New York.

For a week Charleston abandoned itself to joy. A *Te Deum* was sung with great pomp in the cathedral; and crowds paraded the streets, drinking and singing and carousing in tap rooms and taverns.

Judged by the loss of life, the bombardment of Sumter was nothing. Neither side lost a man. But judged by the train of events which it set in motion, few battles have been more momentous. It was the beginning of the bloodiest war the world had ever known up to that time.

*

PART THREE

*

★ ★ ★

18

★ ★ ★

Lincoln issued a call for seventy-five thousand men, and threw the country into a frenzy of patriotic fervor. Mass-meetings were held in thousands of halls and public squares, bands played, flags waved, orators harangued, fireworks were set off; and men, leaving the plow and the pencil, flocked to the flag.

In ten weeks, a hundred and ninety thousand recruits were drilling and marching and singing:

"John Brown's body lies a-mouldering in the grave,
But his soul goes marching on."

But who was to lead these troops to victory? There was one recognized military genius in the army then—and only one. His name was Robert E. Lee. He was a Southerner; but, nevertheless, Lincoln offered him the command of the Union Army. If Lee had accepted, the whole history of the war would have been vastly different. For a time he did think seriously of accepting: thought about it, read his Bible, and got down on his knees and prayed about it, and paced the floor of his bedchamber all night, trying honestly to come to a righteous decision.

He agreed with Lincoln on many things. He hated slavery as Lincoln hated it; Lee had freed his own negroes long ago. He loved the Union almost as Lincoln loved it; he believed that it was "perpetual," that secession was "revolution," that "no greater calamity" could befall the nation.

But—and this was the trouble—he was a Virginian, a proud Virginian, a Virginian who put State above Nation. For two hundred years his forebears had been mighty factors in the destiny, first of the Colony, and then of the State. His father, the famous "Light Horse Harry" Lee, had helped Washington chase the redcoats of King George; after that, he had been Governor of Virginia; and he had taught his son, Robert E., to love the State more than the Union.

So when Virginia cast her lot with the South, Lee quietly announced: "I cannot lead a hostile army against my relatives, my children and my home. I go to share the miseries of my people."

That decision probably lengthened the Civil War by two or three years.

To whom could Lincoln now turn for help and guidance? General Winfield Scott was then in command of the army. Scott was an old man. He had won a notable victory at Lundy's Lane in the War of 1812. And this was 1861. Forty-nine years later. He was weary, now, in body and mind. His youthful initiative and courage had long since perished.

Besides, he was suffering from a spinal affliction. "For more than three years," he wrote, "I have been unable to mount a horse or walk more than a few paces at a time, and that with much pain."

In addition, he now had "other and new infirmities—dropsy and vertigo."

Such was the man to whom Lincoln had to look to lead the nation to victory: a broken old soldier who ought to have been in the hospital, with a nurse and a water mattress.

Lincoln had called in April for seventy-five thousand men to serve for three months. Their enlistments would expire in July; so, in the last part of June, a great hue and cry arose for action! Action! Action!

Day after day Horace Greeley kept "The Nation's War Cry" standing in bold type at the head of the "Tribune's" editorial columns: "Forward to Richmond!"

Business was bad. The banks were afraid to extend credit. Even the Government had to pay twelve per cent for borrowed money. People were disturbed. "Now, look here," they said, "there is no use fooling any longer. Let's strike one sharp blow, capture Lee's army, and have this nasty mess over and done with once and for all."

That sounded attractive, and every one agreed.

Every one except the military authorities: they knew the army wasn't ready. But the President, bowing to public clamor, finally ordered an advance.

So, on a hot, brilliant July day, McDowell, with his "Grand Army," thirty thousand strong, marched away to attack the Confederates at Bull Run, a creek in Virginia. No American general then living had ever before commanded so large a body of men.

What an army it was! Raw. Half trained. Several of the regiments had arrived within the last ten days, and had no idea of discipline.

"With all my personal effort," said Sherman, who commanded a brigade, "I could not prevent the men from straggling for water, blackberries, and anything on the way that they fancied."

The Zouaves and Turcos in those days were regarded as mighty warriors; so many soldiers aspired to dress like them and act like them. Consequently, thousands of the troops marched away to Bull Run, that day, with their heads in scarlet turbans, their legs in red baggy breeches. They looked more like a comic-opera troupe than men marching to death.

Several silk-hatted Congressmen drove out to watch the battle, taking with them their wives and pet dogs, and baskets of sandwiches and bottles of Bordeaux.

Finally, at ten o'clock on a broiling day in late July, the first real battle of the Civil War began.

What happened?

As soon as some of the inexperienced troops saw cannon-balls crashing through the trees, heard men shrieking, and saw them pitching forward on the ground with blood running out of their mouths—as soon as they saw this, the Pennsylvania regiment and the New York Battery happened to recall that their ninety-day term of enlistment had expired; and they insisted on being mustered out of service. Then and there! Quick! And, as McDowell reports, they "moved to the rear to the sound of the enemy's cannon."

The rest of the troops fought surprisingly well until about half-past four in the afternoon. Then suddenly the Confederates, throwing twenty-three hundred fresh men into the assault, took the field by storm.

From mouth to mouth ran the report, "Johnston's army has come."

A panic ensued.

Twenty-five thousand soldiers, refusing to obey orders, broke from the field in mad confusion. McDowell and scores of officers made frantic efforts to stem the rout, but it was useless.

Quickly the Confederate artillery shelled the road, already jammed with fleeing soldiers and commissariat wagons and ambulances and the carriages of silk-hatted, sightseeing Congressmen. Women screamed and fainted. Men shouted and cursed and trampled on one another, A wagon was upset on a bridge. The highway was clogged. Plunging and kicking horses were cut from wagons and ambulances and artillery pieces; and frightened men in red turbans and yellow trousers leaped upon them and dashed away, the traces trailing in the dust, the harness dragging at their heels.

They imagined that the Confederate cavalry was in close pursuit. The cry of "the cavalry! the cavalry!" convulsed them with fear.

The grand debacle had now become a terror-stricken mob.

Nothing like it had ever before been witnessed on any American battle-field.

Maddened men threw away their guns, coats, caps, belts, bayonets, and fled as if driven by some unknown fury. Some sank on the road in utter exhaustion and were crushed beneath the oncoming horses and wagons.

The day was Sunday, and the distant roar of the cannon twenty miles away reached Lincoln's ears as he sat in church. At the close of the services, he rushed to the War Department, to read the telegrams that had already begun to pour in from different parts of the field. Fragmentary and incomplete as they were, Lincoln was eager to discuss them with General Scott; so he hurried to the old general's quarters, and found him taking a nap.

General Scott awoke, yawned, rubbed his eyes; but he was so infirm he couldn't get up without help. "He had some sort of harness with a pulley arrangement attached to the ceiling of the room; and, grasping the strap, he pulled his vast bulk into an upright position and swung his feet off the lounge upon the floor."

"I don't know," he said, "how many men are in the field, where they are, how they are armed, how they are equipped, or what they are capable of doing. Nobody comes to tell me, and I am in ignorance about it."

And he was the head of all the Union armies!

The old general looked at a few telegrams that were coming in from the battle-field, told Lincoln there was nothing to worry about, complained of his aching back, and went to sleep again.

At midnight the broken army, in a riot of disorder, began to stagger across the Long Bridge and pour over the Potomac into Washington.

Tables were quickly set up on the sidewalks, wagon-loads of bread suddenly appeared from somewhere, and society women stood over wash-boilers of steaming soup and coffee, dispensing food.

McDowell, utterly exhausted, had fallen asleep under a tree while writing a despatch, his pencil still in his hand, a sentence half finished. His soldiers were too weary now to care for anything, so they threw themselves on the sidewalks and slept, inert as dead men, in the steadily falling rain—some still clutching their muskets as they slept.

Lincoln sat that night until long after dawn, listening to the stories of the newspaper correspondents and silk-hatted civilians who had witnessed the debacle.

Many public men were thrown into a panic. Horace Greeley wanted to end the war at once, on any terms. He was positive the South could never be conquered.

London bankers were so certain that the Union would be destroyed that their agent in Washington rushed to the Treasury Department on Sunday afternoon, demanding that the United States Government give security immediately for forty thousand dollars that was owing them.

He was told to come back on Monday, that the United States Government would probably still be doing business at the old stand then.

Failure and defeat were not new experiences to Lincoln. He had known them all his life; they did not crush him; his faith in the ultimate triumph of his cause remained firm, his confidence unshaken. He went among the disheartened soldiers, shaking hands with them, and saying over and over: "God bless you. God bless you." He cheered them, sat down and ate beans with them, revived their drooping spirits, and talked of brighter to-morrows.

It was to be a long war. He saw that now. So he asked Congress for a levy of four hundred thousand men. Congress raised him a hundred thousand, and authorized half a million to serve for three years.

But who could lead them? Old Scott, unable to walk, unable to get out of bed without a harness and pulley, and snoring the afternoon away during a battle? Absolutely not. He was slated for the discard.

And there now gallops into the limelight one of the most charming and disappointing generals that ever sat in a saddle.

Lincoln's troubles were not over. They were just beginning.

19

DURING THE first few weeks of the war a handsome young general named McClellan marched into West Virginia with twenty cannon and a portable printing-press, and whipped a few Confederates. His battles didn't amount to much—mere skirmishes. That was all. But they were the first victories of the North, so they seemed important. McClellan saw to that; he dashed off scores of dramatic and bombastic despatches on his portable press, proclaiming his achievements to the nation.

A few years later his absurd antics would have been laughed at; but the war was new then, people were confused and eager for some kind of leader to appear; so they took this boastful young officer at his own valuation. Congress offered him a resolution of thanks, people called him "the Young Napoleon," and after the defeat at Bull Run Lincoln brought him to Washington and made him commander of the Army of the Potomac.

He was a born leader of men. His troops would burst into applause when they saw him galloping toward them on his white charger. Besides, he was a hard and conscientious worker; he took the army that had been crushed at Bull Run, drilled it, renewed its self-confidence, and built up its morale. No one could excel him at that sort of thing; and by the time October came he had one of the largest and best-trained armies that had ever been seen in the Western world. His troops were not only trained to fight; they were eager for the fray.

Every one was crying for action—every one but McClellan.

Lincoln repeatedly urged him to strike a blow. But he wouldn't do it. He held parades and talked a lot about what he was going to do; but that was all it amounted to—talk..

He delayed, he procrastinated, he gave all manner of excuses. But go forward he would not.

Once he said he couldn't advance because the army was resting. Lincoln asked him what it had done to make it tired.

Another time—after the Battle of Antietam—an amazing thing happened. McClellan had far more men than Lee. Lee had been defeated; and had McClellan pursued him, he might have captured his army and ended the war. Lincoln kept urging him for weeks to follow Lee—urging by letter, by telegram, and by special messenger. Finally McClellan said he couldn't move because his horses were fatigued and had sore tongues!

It you ever visit New Salem, you will see a depression about a rod down the hillside from Offut's grocery where Lincoln worked as a clerk. The Clary's Grove Boys used to have their cock-fights there, and Lincoln acted as referee. For weeks Bab McNab had been boasting of a young rooster that could whip anything in Sangamon County. But when this fowl was finally put into the pit, he turned tail and refused to fight. Bab, in disgust, grabbed him and tossed him high into the air. The rooster alighted on a pile of firewood near by, then strutted and ruffled up his feathers and crowed defiantly.

"Yes, damn you!" said McNab. "You're great on dress-parade, but you are not worth a cuss in a fight."

Lincoln said that McClellan reminded him of Bab McNab's rooster.

Once, during the Peninsular Campaign, General Magruder with five thousand men held up McClellan with a hundred thousand. McClellan, afraid to attack, threw up breastworks and kept nagging Lincoln for more men, more men, more men.

"If by magic," said Lincoln, "I could reinforce McClellan with a hundred thousand men, he would go into ecstasy, thank me, and tell me he would go to Richmond to-morrow; but when to-morrow came, he would telegraph that he had certain information that the enemy had four hundred thousand men and that he could not advance without reinforcements."

"If McClellan had a million men," said Stanton, Secretary of War, "he would swear that the enemy had two million, and then sit down in the mud and yell for three million."

"The Young Napoleon" had bounded into fame with one

leap, and it had gone to his head like champagne. His egotism was boundless. He described Lincoln and his Cabinet as "hounds" . . . "wretches" . . . "some of the greatest geese I have ever seen."

He was positively insulting to Lincoln; and when the President came to see him, McClellan kept him waiting for half an hour in the anteroom.

Once the general got home at eleven o'clock at night and his servant informed him that Lincoln had been waiting there for hours to see him. McClellan passed the door of the room where the President sat, ignored him, went on upstairs, and sent down word that he had gone to bed.

The newspapers played up incidents like these, and they became the gossip and scandal of Washington. With tears rolling down her cheeks, Mrs. Lincoln implored the President to remove "that awful wind-bag," as she called him.

"Mother," he replied, "I know he doesn't do right, but I mustn't consider my feelings at a time like this. I am willing to hold McClellan's hat, if he will only bring us victories."

The summer drifted into autumn; autumn passed into winter; spring was almost at hand; and still McClellan did nothing but drill men and have dress-parades, and talk.

The nation was aroused, and Lincoln was being condemned and criticized on all sides for McClellan's inaction.

"Your delay is ruining us," cried Lincoln, as he issued an official order for an advance.

McClellan had to move now or resign. So he rushed to Harper's Ferry, ordering his troops to follow immediately. He planned to invade Virginia from that point, after bridging the Potomac with boats which were to be brought through the Chesapeake and Ohio Canal. But, at the last moment, the whole project had to be abandoned because the boats were six inches too wide to float through the canal locks.

When McClellan told Lincoln of this fiasco and said that the pontoons were not ready, the patient, long-suffering President lost his temper at last; and, lapsing into the phraseology of the hay-fields of Pigeon Creek Valley, Indiana, he demanded, *"Why, in the hell, ain't they ready?"*

The nation was asking the same question in about the same tone.

At last, in April, "the Young Napoleon" made a grand speech

to his soldiers, as the older Napoleon used to do, and then started off with one hundred and twenty thousand men singing "The Girl I Left Behind Me."

The war had been going on for a year. McClellan boasted that he was going to clean up the whole thing now, at once, and let the boys get home in time to plant a little late corn and millet.

Incredible as it seems, Lincoln and Stanton were so optimistic that they wired the governors of the various States to accept no more volunteers, to close the recruiting-places, and to sell the public property belonging to these organizations.

One of the military maxims of Frederick the Great was: "Know the man you are fighting." Lee and Stonewall Jackson appreciated full well the kind of a weak-kneed Napoleon they had to deal with—a timid, cautious, whining Napoleon who was never on the battle-field, because he couldn't endure the sight of blood.

So Lee let him spend three months crawling up to Richmond. McClellan got so close that his men could hear the clocks in the church towers striking the hour.

Then the inspired Lee crashed upon him in a series of terrific onslaughts, and, in seven days, forced him back to the shelter of his gunboats and killed fifteen thousand of his men.

Thus the "en grande affair," as McClellan called it, ended in one of the bloodiest failures of the war.

But, as usual, McClellan blamed it all on "those traitors in Washington." The old story: they hadn't sent him enough men. Their "cowardice and folly" made his "blood boil." He hated Lincoln and the Cabinet, now, more than he despised the Confederates. He denounced their actions as "the most infamous thing history has ever recorded."

McClellan had more troops than his enemies—usually far more. He was never able to use at one time all that he then possessed. But he kept on demanding more. More. He asked for an additional ten thousand, then for fifty thousand, finally for a hundred thousand. They were not to be had. He knew it, and Lincoln knew that he knew it. Lincoln told him his demands were "simply absurd."

McClellan's telegrams to Stanton and the President were fiery and insulting. They sounded like the ravings of a madman. They accused Lincoln and Stanton of doing their best to destroy his army. They made charges so grave that the telegraph operator refused to deliver them.

The nation was appalled, Wall Street was seized with panic, the country was submerged in gloom.

Lincoln grew thin and haggard. "I am as nearly inconsolable," he said, "as one can be and live."

McClellan's father-in-law and chief of staff, P. B. Marcy, said there was nothing to do now but capitulate.

When Lincoln heard this, he flushed with anger, sent for Marcy, and said:

"General, I understand you have used the word 'capitulate.' That is a word not to be used in connection with our army."

★ ★ ★

20

★ ★ ★

Lincoln had learned, back in New Salem, that it was easy to rent a building and stock it with groceries; but to make it pay required qualities which neither he nor his drunken partner possessed.

He was destined to discover, through years of heartbreak and bloodshed, that it was easy to get a half million soldiers who were willing to die, and a hundred million dollars to equip them with rifles and bullets and blankets; but to win victories required a kind of leadership which it was almost impossible to find.

"How much in military matters," exclaimed Lincoln, "depends on one master mind!"

So, time and again, he went down on his knees, asking the Almighty to send him a Robert E. Lee or a Joseph E. Johnston or a Stonewall Jackson.

"Jackson," he said, "is a brave, honest, Presbyterian soldier. If we only had such a man to lead the armies of the North, the country would not be appalled with so many disasters."

But where in all the Union forces was another Stonewall Jackson to be found? Nobody knew. Edmund Clarence Stedman published a famous poem every verse of which ended with the plea, "Abraham Lincoln, give us a Man."

It was more than the refrain of a poem. It was the cry of a bleeding and distraught nation.

The President wept as he read it.

For two years he tried to find the leader for whom the

nation was crying. He would give the army to one general who would lead it to futile slaughter, and set ten or thirty or forty thousand widows and orphans weeping and wailing throughout the land. Then this discredited commander would be relieved; and another, equally inept, would try his hand and get ten thousand more slaughtered; and Lincoln, clad in dressing-gown and carpet-slippers, would pace the floor all night as the reports came in, crying over and over:

"My God! What will the country say? My God! What will the country say?"

Then another general would assume command, and the futile slaughter would go on.

Some military critics now hold that McClellan, with all his astounding faults and amazing incapacity, was probably the best commander the Army of the Potomac ever had. So imagine, if you can, what the others must have been!

After McClellan's failure, Lincoln tried John Pope. Pope had done splendid work out in Missouri, had captured an island in the Mississippi and several thousand men.

He was like McClellan in two ways: he was handsome, and he was boastful. He declared that his headquarters was "in the saddle"; and he issued so many bombastic announcements that he was soon called "Proclamation Pope."

"I have come to you from the West, where we have always seen the backs of our enemies." With that blunt, tactless sentence, he opened his first address to the army. He then proceeded to rebuke the troops for their inaction in the East, and insinuated that they were infernal cowards; and ended by boasting of the military miracles he would perform.

This proclamation made the new commander about as popular as a diamond-backed rattlesnake in dog-days: officers and men alike detested him.

McClellan's hatred for him was intense. Pope had come to take his place. Nobody realized that better than did McClellan —he was already writing for a position in New York—and he was consumed with jealousy, was bitter with envy and resentment.

Pope led the army into Virginia; a great battle was imminent; he needed every man he could get; so Lincoln showered McClellan with telegrams, ordering him to rush his men to Pope's aid with all possible celerity.

But did McClellan obey? He did not. He argued, he delayed,

he protested, he telegraphed excuses, he recalled corps that he had sent ahead, and he "exhausted all the resources of a diabolical ingenuity in order to keep Pope from receiving reinforcements." "Let Mr. Pope," said he, contemptuously, "get out of his own scrape."

Even after he heard the roar of the Confederate artillery, he still managed to keep thirty thousand of his troops from going to the aid of his obnoxious rival.

So Lee overwhelmed Pope's army on the old battle-field of Bull Run. The slaughter was terrible. The Federal soldiers again fled in a panic.

It was the story of the first Bull Run over again: once more a bloody and beaten mob poured into Washington.

Lee pursued them with his victorious troops. And even Lincoln believed the capital was lost. Gunboats were ordered up the river, and all the clerks in Washington—civilian and government alike—were called to arms to defend the city.

Stanton, Secretary of War, in a wild panic, telegraphed the governors of half a dozen States, imploring them to send all their militia and volunteer forces by special trains.

Saloons were closed, church bells tolled; men fell on their knees, beseeching Almighty God to save the city.

The old people and the women and children fled in terror. The streets resounded with the hoofs of hurrying horses, with the rattle of carriages dashing away to Maryland.

Stanton, preparing to transfer the Government to New York, ordered the arsenal stripped and all its supplies shipped North.

Chase, Secretary of the Treasury, ordered the nation's silver and gold transferred in feverish haste to the sub-Treasury in Wall Street.

Lincoln, weary and discouraged, exclaimed with a mingled groan and sigh:

"What shall I do? . . . What shall I do? . . . The bottom is out of the tub, the bottom is out of the tub."

People believed that McClellan, in order to get revenge, had longed to see "Mr. Pope" defeated and his army crushed.

Even Lincoln had already called him to the White House and told him that people were accusing him of being a traitor, of wanting to see Washington captured and the South triumphant.

Stanton stormed about in a rage, his face fiery with indignation and hatred. Those who saw him said that if McClellan had walked into the war-office then, Stanton would have rushed at him and knocked him down.

Chase was even more bitter. He didn't want to hit McClellan. He said the man ought to be shot.

And the pious Chase wasn't speaking figuratively. Neither was he exaggerating. He literally wanted McClellan blindfolded, backed up against a stone wall, and a dozen bullets sent crashing through his heart.

But Lincoln, with his understanding nature and Christ-like spirit, condemned no one. True, Pope had failed, but hadn't he done his best? Lincoln, himself, had met defeat too often to blame any one else for failure.

So he sent Pope out to the Northwest to subdue an uprising of Sioux Indians, and gave the army back to McClellan. Why? Because, Lincoln said: "There is no man in the army who can lick these troops of ours into shape half as well as he. . . . If he can't fight, himself, he excels in making others ready to fight." The President knew that he would be condemned for restoring "little Mac" to command. And he was—bitterly. Even by his Cabinet. Stanton and Chase actually declared that they would rather have Washington captured by Lee than to see the traitorous and contemptible McClellan given command of the army again.

Lincoln was so hurt at their violent opposition that he said he would resign if the Cabinet wished it.

A few months later, after the Battle of Antietam, McClellan absolutely refused to obey Lincoln's orders to follow Lee and attack him, so the army was taken away from him again; and his military career was ended forever.

The Army of the Potomac must have another leader. But who was he? Where was he? No one knew.

In desperation, Lincoln offered the command to Burnside. He wasn't fit for it, and he knew it. He refused it twice; and, when it was forced upon him, he wept. Then he took the army and made a rash attack on Lee's fortifications at Fredericksburg, and lost thirteen thousand men. Men uselessly butchered, for there wasn't the faintest hope of success.

Officers as well as privates began to desert in large numbers.

So Burnside, in turn, was relieved, and the army given to another braggart, "Fighting Joe" Hooker.

"May God have mercy on Lee," he vaunted, "for I shall not."

He led what he called "the finest army on the planet" against Lee. He had twice as many men as the Confederates, but Lee hurled him back across the river at Chancellorsville and destroyed seventeen thousand of his troops.

It was one of the most disastrous defeats of the war.

It occurred in May, 1863; and the President's secretary records that he heard the tramp of Lincoln's feet during all the terrible hours of sleepless nights as he paced up and down his room, crying, "Lost! Lost! All is lost!" Finally, however, he went down to Fredericksburg to cheer up "Fighting Joe" and encourage the army.

Lincoln was denounced bitterly for all this futile slaughter; and gloom and discouragement settled over the nation.

And quickly on top of these military sorrows, came a domestic tragedy. Lincoln was inordinately fond of his two little sons, Tad and Willie. He often stole away, on a summer evening, to play "town ball" with them, his coat-tails flying out behind him as he ran from base to base. Sometimes, he would shoot marbles with them all the way from the White House to the war-office. At night he loved to get down on the floor and roll and romp with them. On bright, warm days he would sometimes go out back of the White House and play with the boys and their two goats.

Tad and Willie kept the White House in an uproar, organizing minstrel shows, putting the servants through military drill, running in and out among the office-seekers. If they took a fancy to a certain applicant, they would see that he got in to see "Old Abe" immediately. If they couldn't get him in the front way, they knew of back entrances.

With as little respect for ceremony and precedent as their father had, they dashed in and interrupted a Cabinet meeting once to inform the President that the cat in the basement had just had kittens.

On another occasion the stern Salmon P. Chase was irritated and disgusted because Tad climbed all over his father and finally perched on his shoulder and sat astride of his neck while Chase was discussing the grave financial situation that confronted the country.

Some one gave Willie a pony. He insisted on riding it in all kinds of winter weather; so he got wet and chilled and came down with a severe cold. Soon it had become a serious fever. Night after night Lincoln sat for hours by his bedside; and when the little fellow passed away, his father, choking with sobs, cried:

"My poor boy! My poor boy! He was too good for this earth. God has called him home. It is hard, hard to have him die."

Mrs. Keckley, who was in the room at the time, says:

He buried his head in his hands, and his tall frame was convulsed with emotion. . . . The pale face of her dead boy threw Mrs. Lincoln into convulsions. She was so completely overwhelmed with sorrow she did not attend the funeral.

After Willie's death Mrs. Lincoln could not bear to look upon his picture. Mrs. Keckley tells us:

She could not bear the sight of anything he loved, not even a flower. Costly bouquets were presented to her, but she turned from them with a shudder, and either placed them in a room where she could not see them, or threw them out of the window. She gave away all of Willie's toys . . . and, after his death, she never again crossed the threshold of the Guests' Room in which he died or the Green Room in which he was embalmed.

In a frenzy of grief Mrs. Lincoln called in a so-called spiritualist who masqueraded under the title of "Lord Colchester." This unmitigated impostor was exposed later and ordered out of town under a threat of imprisonment. But Mrs. Lincoln, in her distress, received "Lord Colchester" in the White House; and there, in a darkened room, she was persuaded that the scratching on the wainscoting, the tapping on the wall, and the rapping of the table, were loving messages from her lost boy.

She wept as she received them.

Lincoln, prostrate with grief, sank into a listless despair. He could hardly discharge his public duties. Letters, telegrams lay on his desk unanswered. His physician feared that he might never rally, that he might succumb entirely to his desolation.

The President would sometimes sit and read aloud for hours, with only his secretary or his aide for an audience. Generally it was Shakspere he read. One day he was reading "King John" to his aide, and when he came to the passage in which Constance bewails her lost boy, Lincoln closed the book, and repeated these words from memory:

And, father cardinal, I have heard you say
That we shall see and know our friends in heaven:
If that be true, I shall see my boy again.

"Colonel, did you ever dream of a lost friend," the President asked, "and feel that you were holding sweet communion with him, and yet have a sad consciousness that it was not a reality? I often dream of my boy Willie like that." And dropping his head on the table, Lincoln sobbed aloud.

★ ★ ★

21

★ ★ ★

Whisper HEN LINCOLN turned to his Cabinet, he found there the same quarrels and jealousy that existed in the army.

Seward, Secretary of State, regarded himself as the "Premier," snubbed the rest of the Cabinet, meddled in their affairs, and aroused deep resentment.

Chase, Secretary of the Treasury, despised Seward; detested General McClellan; hated Stanton, Secretary of War; and loathed Blair, the Postmaster-General.

Blair, in turn, went around "kicking over beehives," as Lincoln put it, and boasting that when he "went in for a fight" he "went in for a funeral." He denounced Seward as "an unprincipled liar," and refused to have any dealings with him whatever; and as for Stanton and Chase, he wouldn't condescend even to speak to those scoundrels—not even at a Cabinet meeting.

Blair went in for so many fights that finally he went in for his own funeral—as far as politics were concerned. The hatred that he aroused was so fiery and widespread that Lincoln had to ask him to resign.

There was hatred everywhere in the Cabinet.

The Vice-President, Hannibal Hamlin, wouldn't speak to Gideon Welles, Secretary of the Navy; and Welles, topped with an elaborate wig and decorated with a vast growth of white whiskers, kept a diary, and from almost every page of it, he "hurls the shafts of his ridicule and contempt" at well-nigh all his colleagues.

Welles especially detested Grant, Seward, and Stanton.

And as for the violent, insolent Stanton, he was the most prodigious hater of all. He despised Chase, Welles, Blair, Mrs. Lincoln, and apparently almost every one else in creation.

"He cared nothing for the feeling of others," wrote Grant, "and it gave him more pleasure to refuse a request than to grant it."

Sherman's hatred for the man was so fierce that he humiliated Stanton on a reviewing-stand before a vast audience, and rejoiced about it ten years later as he wrote his Memoirs.

"As I approached Mr. Stanton," says Sherman, "he offered me his hand, but I declined it publicly, and the fact was universally noticed."

Few men who ever lived have been more savagely detested than Stanton.

Almost every man in the Cabinet considered himself superior to Lincoln.

After all, who was this crude, awkward, story-telling Westerner they were supposed to serve under?

A political accident, a "dark horse" that had got in by chance and crowded them out.

Bates, the Attorney-General, had entertained high hopes of being nominated for President, himself, in 1860; and he wrote in his diary that the Republicans made a "fatal blunder" in nominating Lincoln, a man who "lacks will and purpose," and "has not the power to command."

Chase, too, had hoped to be nominated instead of Lincoln; and, to the end of his life, he regarded Lincoln with "a sort of benevolent contempt."

Seward also was bitter and resentful. "Disappointment? You speak to me of disappointment," he once exclaimed to a friend as he paced the floor, "to me who was justly entitled to the Republican nomination for the Presidency and who had to stand aside and see it given to a little Illinois lawyer!

"You speak to me of disappointment!"

Seward knew that if it hadn't been for Horace Greeley, he himself would have been President. He knew how to run things, he had had twenty years of experience in handling the vast affairs of state.

But what had Lincoln ever run? Nothing except a log-cabin

grocery store in New Salem, and he had "run that in the ground."

Oh, yes, and he had had a post-office once, which he carried around in his hat.

That was the extent of the executive experience of this "prairie politician."

And now here he sat, blundering and confused, in the White House, letting things drift, doing nothing, while the country was on a greased chute headed straight for disaster.

Seward believed—and thousands of others believed—that he had been made Secretary of State in order to rule the nation, that Lincoln was to be a mere figurehead. People called Seward the Prime Minister. He liked it. He believed that the salvation of the United States rested with him and him alone.

"I will try," he said when accepting his appointment, "to save freedom and my country."

Before Lincoln had been in office five weeks Seward sent him a memorandum that was presumptuous. Amazing. It was more than that. It was positively insulting. Never before in the history of the nation had a Cabinet member sent such an impudent, arrogant document to a President.

"We are at the end of a month's administration," Seward began, "and yet without a policy either domestic or foreign." Then with a calm assumption of superior wisdom, he proceeded to criticize this ex-grocery, store keeper from New Salem and inform him how the Government ought to be run.

He ended by brazenly suggesting that from now on Lincoln ought to sit in the background where he belonged, and let the suave Seward assume control and prevent the country from going to hell.

One of Seward's suggestions was so wild and erratic as to stun Lincoln. Seward didn't like the way France and Spain had been carrying on lately in Mexico. So he proposed to call them to account. Yes, and Great Britain and Russia, too. And if "satisfactory explanations are not received"—what do you suppose he intended to do?

Declare war. Yes. One war wasn't enough for this statesman. He was going to have a nice little assortment of wars going full blast at the same time.

He did prepare an arrogant note which he proposed sending to England—a note bristling with warnings, threats, and insults.

If Lincoln hadn't deleted the worst passages and toned the others down, it might have caused war.

Seward took a pinch of snuff and declared that he would love to see a European power interfere in favor of South Carolina, for then the North would "pitch into that power," and all the Southern States would help fight the foreign foe.

And it very nearly became necessary to fight England. A Northern gunboat held up a British mail-steamer on the high seas, took off two Confederate commissioners destined for England and France, and lodged them behind prison bars in Boston.

England began preparing for war, shipped thousands of troops across the Atlantic, landed them in Canada, and was ready to attack the North.

Although Lincoln admitted it was "the bitterest pill he had ever swallowed," nevertheless he had to surrender the Confederate commissioners and apologize.

Lincoln was utterly astounded by some of Seward's wild ideas. From the outset Lincoln had keenly realized that he, himself, was inexperienced in handling the vast and cruel responsibilities that confronted him. He needed help—and wisdom, and guidance. He had appointed Seward hoping to get just that. And see what had happened!

All Washington was talking about Seward's running the administration. It touched Mrs. Lincoln's pride, and aroused her boiling wrath. With fire in her eye, she urged her humble husband to assert himself.

"I may not rule myself," Lincoln assured her, "but certainly Seward shall not. The only ruler I have is my conscience and my God and these men will have to learn that yet."

The time came when all of them did.

Salmon P. Chase was the Chesterfield of the Cabinet: strikingly handsome, six feet two inches tall, looking the part of a man born to rule, cultured, a classical scholar, master of three languages, and father of one of the most charming and popular hostesses in Washington society. Frankly, he was shocked to see a man in the White House who didn't know how to order a dinner.

Chase was pious, very pious: he attended church three times on Sunday, quoted the Psalms in his bathtub, and put the motto "In God We Trust" on our national coins. Reading his

Bible and a book of sermons every night before retiring, he was utterly unable to comprehend a President who took to bed with him a volume of Artemus Ward or Petroleum Nasby.

Lincoln's flair for humor, at almost all times and under nearly all circumstances, irritated and annoyed Chase.

One day an old crony of Lincoln's from Illinois called at the White House. The doorkeeper, looking him over with a critical eye, announced that the President couldn't be seen, that a Cabinet meeting was in session.

"That don't make no difference," the caller protested. "You just tell Abe that Orlando Kellogg is here and wants to tell him the story of the stuttering justice. He'll see me."

Lincoln ordered him shown in at once, and greeted him with a fervent handshake. Turning to the Cabinet, the President said:

"Gentlemen: This is my old friend, Orlando Kellogg, and he wants to tell us the story of the stuttering justice. It is a very good story, so let's lay all business aside now."

So grave statesmen and the affairs of the nation waited while Orlando told his yarn and Lincoln had his loud guffaw.

Chase was disgusted. He feared for the future of the nation. He complained that Lincoln "was making a joke out of the war," that he was hurrying the country on to "the abyss of bankruptcy and ruin."

Chase was as jealous as a member of a high-school sorority. He had expected to be made Secretary of State. Why hadn't he? Why had he been snubbed? Why had the post of honor gone to the haughty Seward? Why had he been made a mere Secretary of the Treasury? He was bitter and resentful.

He had to play third fiddle now. Yes, but he would show them; 1864 was coming. There would be another election then, and he was determined to occupy the White House himself after that. He thought of little else now. He threw his whole heart and soul into what Lincoln called "Chase's mad hunt for the Presidency."

To Lincoln's face, he pretended to be his friend. But the moment he was out of sight and out of hearing, Chase was the President's ceaseless, bitter, and sneaking foe. Lincoln was frequently compelled to make decisions that offended influential people. When he did, Chase hurried to the disgruntled victim, sympathized with him, assured him that he was right, whipped up his resentment toward Lincoln, and persuaded him that if

Salmon P. Chase had been running things he would have been treated fairly.

"Chase is like the blue-bottle fly," said Lincoln; "he lays his eggs in every rotten place he can find."

For months Lincoln knew all of this; but with a magnanimous disregard of his own rights, he said:

"Chase is a very able man, but on the subject of the Presidency, I think he is a little insane. He has not behaved very well lately, and people say to me, 'Now is the time to crush him out.' Well, I'm not in favor of crushing anybody out. If there is anything that a man can do and do it well, I say, let him do it. So I am determined, so long as he does his duty as head of the Treasury Department, to shut my eyes to his attack of the White House fever."

But the situation grew steadily worse. When things didn't go Chase's way, he sent in his resignation. He did this five times, and Lincoln went to him and praised him and persuaded him to resume his duties. But finally even the long-suffering Lincoln had enough of it. There had now developed such ill feeling between them that it was unpleasant for them to meet each other. So the next time, the President took Chase at his word and accepted his resignation.

Chase was amazed. His bluff had been called.

The Senate Committee on Finance hurried to the White House in a body. They protested. Chase's going would be a misfortune, a calamity. Lincoln listened, and let them talk themselves out. He then related his painful experiences with Chase; said that Chase always wanted to rule, and resented his (Lincoln's) authority.

"He is either determined to annoy me," said Lincoln, "or that I shall pat him on the shoulder and coax him to stay. I don't think I ought to do it. I will take him at his word. His usefulness as a Cabinet officer is at an end. I will no longer continue the association. I am willing, if necessary, to resign the office of President. I would rather go back to a farm in Illinois and earn my bread with a plow and an ox than to endure any longer the state I have been in."

But what was Lincoln's estimate of the man who had humiliated and insulted him? "Of all the great men I have ever known, Chase is equal to about one and a half of the best of them."

Despite all the ill feeling that had been stirred up, Lincoln then performed one of the most beautiful and magnanimous acts of his career. He conferred upon Chase one of the highest honors a President of the United States can bestow: he made him Chief Justice of the United States Supreme Court.

Chase, however, was a docile kitten in comparison with the stormy Stanton. Short, heavy-set, with the build of a bull, Stanton had something of that animal's fierceness and ferocity.

All his life he had been rash and erratic. His father, a physician, hung a human skeleton in the barn where the boy played, hoping that he too would become a doctor. The young Stanton lectured to his playmates about the skeleton, Moses, hell fire, and the flood; and then went off to Columbus, Ohio, and became a clerk in a book-store. He boarded in a private family, and one morning shortly after he left the house, the daughter of the family fell ill with cholera, and was dead and in her grave when Stanton came home for supper that night.

He refused to believe it.

Fearing that she had been buried alive, he hurried to the cemetery, found a spade, and worked furiously for hours, digging up her body.

Years later, driven to despair by the death of his own daughter, Lucy, he had her body exhumed after she had been buried thirteen months, and kept her corpse in his bedroom for more than a year.

When Mrs. Stanton died, he put her nightcap and nightgown beside him in bed each night and wept over them.

He was a strange man. Some people said that he was half crazy.

Lincoln and Stanton had first met during the trial of a patent case in which they, together with George Harding of Philadelphia, had been retained as counsel for the defendant. Lincoln had studied the case minutely, had prepared with extraordinary care and industry, and wanted to speak. But Stanton and Harding were ashamed of him; they brushed him aside with contempt, humiliated him, and refused to let him say a word at the trial.

Lincoln gave them a copy of his speech, but they were sure it was "trash" and didn't bother to look at it.

They wouldn't walk with Lincoln to and from the courthouse; they wouldn't invite him to their rooms; they wouldn't even sit at a table and eat with him. They treated him as a social outcast.

Stanton said—and Lincoln heard him say it:

"I will not associate with such a damned, gawky, long-armed ape as that. If I can't have a man who is a gentleman in appearance with me in the case, I will abandon it."

"I have never before been so brutally treated as by that man Stanton," Lincoln said. He returned home, mortified, sunk once more in terrible melancholy.

When Lincoln became President, Stanton's contempt and disgust for him deepened and increased. He called him "a painful imbecile," declared that he was utterly incapable of running the Government, and that he ought to be ousted by a military dictator. Stanton repeatedly remarked that Du Chaillu was a fool to run off to Africa, looking for a gorilla, when the original gorilla was, at that moment, sitting in the White House scratching himself.

In his letters to Buchanan, Stanton abused the President in language so violent that it can't be put into print.

After Lincoln had been in office ten months, a national scandal reverberated throughout the land. The Government was being robbed! Millions lost! Profiteers! Dishonest war contracts! And so on.

In addition to that, Lincoln and Simon Cameron, Secretary of War, differed sharply on the question of arming slaves.

Lincoln asked Cameron to resign. He must have a new man to run the War Department. Lincoln knew that the future of the nation might depend upon his choice. He also knew precisely the man he needed. So Lincoln said to a friend:

"I have made up my mind to sit down on all my pride—it may be a portion of my self-respect—and appoint Stanton Secretary of War."

That proved to be one of the wisest appointments Lincoln ever made.

Stanton stood at his desk in the war-office, a regular tornado in trousers, surrounded by clerks trembling like Eastern slaves before their pasha. Working day and night, refusing to go home, eating and sleeping in the war-office, he was filled with wrath and indignation by the loafing, swaggering, incompetent officers that infested the army.

And he fired them right and left and backward and forward.

Cursing and swearing, he insulted meddlesome Congressmen. He waged a fierce and relentless war on dishonest contractors; ignored and violated the Constitution; arrested even generals, clapped them into prison and kept them there for months without trial. He lectured McClellan as if he were drilling a regiment, declared that he must fight. He swore that "the champagne and oysters on the Potomac must stop"; seized all the railroads; commandeered all the telegraph lines, made Lincoln send and receive his telegrams through the war-office; assumed command of all the armies, and wouldn't let even an order from Grant pass through the adjutant-general's office without his approval.

For years Stanton had been racked with head pains, had suffered from asthma and indigestion.

However, he was driven like a dynamo by one absorbing passion: to hack and stab and shoot until the South came back into the Union.

Lincoln could endure anything to achieve that goal.

One day a Congressman persuaded the President to give him an order transferring certain regiments. Rushing to the war-office with the order, he put it on Stanton's desk; and Stanton said very sharply that he would do no such thing.

"But," the politician protested, "you forget I have an order here from the President."

"If the President gave you such an order," Stanton retorted, "he is a damned fool."

The Congressman rushed back to Lincoln, expecting to see him rise up in wrath and dismiss the Secretary of War.

But Lincoln listened to the story, and said with a twinkle in his eye: "If Stanton said I was a damned fool, then I must be, for he is nearly always right. I'll just step over and see him myself."

He did, and Stanton convinced him that his order was wrong and Lincoln withdrew it.

Realizing that Stanton bitterly resented interference, Lincoln usually let him have his way.

"I cannot add to Mr. Stanton's troubles," he said. "His position is the most difficult in the world. Thousands in the army blame him because they are not promoted, and other thousands blame him because they are not appointed. The pressure upon him is immeasurable and unending. He is the rock on the beach of our national ocean against which the breakers dash and roar, dash and roar without ceasing. He fights back the angry waters and prevents them from undermining and overwhelming the land. I do not see how he survives, why he is not crushed and torn to pieces. Without him, I should be destroyed."

Occasionally, however, the President "put his foot down," as he called it; and then—look out. If "Old Mars" said then that he wouldn't do a thing, Lincoln would reply very quietly: "I reckon, Mr. Secretary, you'll *have* to do it."

And done it was.

On one occasion he wrote an order saying: "Without an *if* or an *and* or *but,* let Colonel Elliott W. Rice be made Brigadier-General in the United States army—Abraham Lincoln."

On another occasion he wrote Stanton to appoint a certain man "regardless of whether he knows the color of Julius Cæsar's hair or not."

In the end Stanton and Seward and most of those who began by reviling and scorning Abraham Lincoln learned to revere him.

When Lincoln lay dying in a rooming-house across the street from Ford's Theater, the iron Stanton, who had once denounced him as "a painful imbecile," said, "There lies the most perfect ruler of men the world has ever seen."

John Hay, one of Lincoln's secretaries, has graphically described Lincoln's manner of working in the White House:

> He was extremely unmethodical. It was a four years' struggle on Nicolay's part and mine to get him to adopt some systematic rules. He would break through every regulation as fast as it was made. Anything that kept the people themselves away from him, he disapproved, although they nearly annoyed the life out of him by unreasonable complaints and requests.
>
> He wrote very few letters, and did not read one in fifty that he received. At first we tried to bring them to his notice, but at last he gave the whole thing over to me, and signed, without reading them, the letters I wrote in his name.
>
> He wrote perhaps half a dozen a week himself—not more.
>
> When the President had any rather delicate matter to manage at a distance from Washington, he rarely wrote but sent Nicolay or me.
>
> He went to bed ordinarily from ten to eleven o'clock . . .

and rose early. When he lived in the country at the Soldiers' Home, he would be up and dressed, eat his breakfast (which was extremely frugal, an egg, a piece of toast, coffee, etc.) and ride into Washington all before eight o'clock. In the winter, at the White House, he was not quite so early. He did not sleep well, but spent a good while in bed. . . .

At noon he took a biscuit, a glass of milk in winter, some fruit or grapes in summer. . . . He was abstemious—ate less than any man I know.

He drank nothing but water, not from principle, but because he did not like wine or spirits. . . .

Sometimes he would run away to a lecture or concert or theater for the sake of a little rest. . . .

He read very little. He scarcely ever looked into a newspaper unless I called his attention to an article on some special subject. He frequently said, "I know more about it than any of them." It is absurd to call him a modest man. No great man was ever modest.

★ ★ ★

22

★ ★ ★

Ask the average American citizen to-day why the Civil War was fought; and the chances are that he will reply, "To free the slaves."

Was it?

Let's see. Here is a sentence taken from Lincoln's first inaugural address: "I have no purpose, directly or indirectly, to interfere with the institution of slavery in the States where it now exists. I believe I have no lawful right to do so, and I have no inclination to do so."

The fact is that the cannon had been booming and the wounded groaning for almost eighteen months before Lincoln issued the Emancipation Proclamation. During all that time the radicals and the Abolitionists had urged him to act at once, storming at him through the press and denouncing him from the public platform.

Once a delegation of Chicago ministers appeared at the White House with what they declared was a direct command from Almighty God to free the slaves immediately. Lincoln told them that he imagined that if the Almighty had any advice to offer He would come direct to headquarters with it, instead of sending it around via Chicago.

Finally Horace Greeley, irritated by Lincoln's procrastination and inaction, attacked the President in an article entitled, "The Prayer of Twenty Millions." Two columns bristling with bitter complaints.

Lincoln's answer to Greeley is one of the classics of the war —clear, terse, and vigorous. He closed his reply with these memorable words:

My paramount object in this struggle is to save the Union, and is not either to save or destroy slavery. If I could save the Union without freeing any slave, I would do it; and if I could save it by freeing all the slaves, I would do it; and if I could save it by freeing some and leaving others alone, I would also do that. What I do about slavery and the colored race, I do because I believe it helps to save the Union; and what I forbear, I forbear because I do not believe it would help to save the Union. I shall do less whenever I shall believe what I am doing hurts the cause, and I shall do more whenever I shall believe doing more will help the cause. I shall try to correct errors when shown to be errors, and I shall adopt new views so fast as they shall appear to be true views.

I have here stated my purpose according to my view of official duty; and I intend no modification of my oft-expressed personal wish that all men everywhere could be free.

Lincoln believed that if he saved the Union and kept slavery from spreading, slavery would, in due time, die a natural death. But if the Union were destroyed, it might persist for centuries.

Four slave States had remained with the North, and Lincoln realized that if he issued his Emancipation Proclamation too early in the conflict he would drive them into the Confederacy, strengthen the South, and perhaps destroy the Union forever. There was a saying at the time that "Lincoln would like to have God Almighty on his side; but he must have Kentucky."

So he bided his time, and moved cautiously.

He himself had married into a slave-owning, border-State family. Part of the money that his wife received upon the settlement of her father's estate had come from the sale of slaves. And the only really intimate friend that he ever had—Joshua Speed—was a member of a slave-owning family. Lincoln sympathized with the Southern point of view. Besides, he had the attorney's traditional respect for the Constitution and for law and property. He wanted to work no hardships on any one.

He believed that the North was as much to blame for the existence of slavery in the United States as was the South; and that in getting rid of it, both sections should bear the burden equally. So he finally worked out a plan that was very near to his heart. According to this, the slave-owners in the loyal border States were to receive four hundred dollars for each of their negroes. The slaves were to be emancipated gradually, very gradually. The process was not to be entirely completed until January 1, 1900. Calling the representatives of the border States to the White House, he pleaded with them to accept his proposal.

"The change it contemplates," Lincoln argued, "would come gently as the dews of heaven, not rending or wrecking anything. Will you not embrace it? So much good has not been done, by one effort, in all past time, as, in the providence of God, it is now your high privilege to do. May the vast future not have to lament you have neglected it."

But they did neglect it, and rejected the whole scheme. Lincoln was immeasurably disappointed.

"I must save this Government, if possible," he said; "and it may as well be understood, once for all, that I shall not surrender this game, leaving any available card unplayed. . . . I believe that freeing the slaves and arming the blacks has now become an indispensable military necessity. I have been driven to the alternative of either doing that or surrendering the Union."

He had to act at once, for both France and England were on the verge of recognizing the Confederacy. Why? The reasons were very simple.

Take France's case first. Napoleon III had married Marie Eugénie de Montijo, Comtesse de Teba, reputed to be the most beautiful woman in the world, and he wanted to show off a bit. He longed to cover himself with glory, as his renowned uncle, Napoleon Bonaparte, had done. So when he saw the States slashing and shooting at one another, and knew they were much too occupied to bother about enforcing the Monroe Doctrine, he ordered an army to Mexico, shot a few thousand natives, conquered the country, called Mexico a French empire, and put the Archduke Maximilian on the throne.

Napoleon believed, and not without reason, that if the Confederates won they would favor his new empire; but that if the Federals won, the United States would immediately take steps to put the French out of Mexico. It was Napoleon's wish, therefore, that the South would make good its secession, and he wanted to help it as much as he conveniently could.

At the outset of the war, the Northern navy closed all Southern ports, guarded 189 harbors and patrolled 9,614 miles of coast line, sounds, bayous, and rivers.

It was the most gigantic blockade the world had ever seen.

The Confederates were desperate. They couldn't sell their cotton; neither could they buy guns, ammunition, shoes, medical supplies, or food. They boiled chestnuts and cotton-seed to make a substitute for coffee, and brewed a decoction of blackberry leaves and sassafras root to take the place of tea. Newspapers were printed on wall-paper. The earthen floors of smokehouses, saturated with the drippings of bacon, were dug up and boiled to get salt. Church bells were melted and cast into cannon. Street-car rails in Richmond were torn up to be made into gunboat armor.

The Confederates couldn't repair their railroads or buy new equipment, so transportation was almost at a standstill; corn that could be purchased for two dollars a bushel in Georgia, brought fifteen dollars in Richmond. People in Virginia were going hungry.

Something had to be done at once. So the South offered to give Napoleon III twelve million dollars' worth of cotton if he would recognize the Confederacy and use the French fleet to lift the blockade. Besides, they promised to overwhelm him with orders that would start smoke rolling out of every factory chimney in France night and day.

Napoleon therefore urged Russia and England to join him in recognizing the Confederacy. The aristocracy that ruled England adjusted their monocles, poured a few drinks of Johnny Walker, and listened eagerly to Napoleon's overtures. The United States was getting too rich and powerful to please them. They wanted to see the nation divided, the Union broken. Besides, they needed the South's cotton. Scores of England's factories had closed, and a million people were not only idle but destitute and reduced to actual pauperism. Children were crying for food; hundreds of people were dying of starvation. Public subscriptions to buy food for British workmen were taken up in the remotest corners of the earth: even in far-off India and poverty-stricken China.

There was one way, and only one way, that England could get cotton, and that was to join Napoleon III in recognizing the Confederacy and lifting the blockade.

If that were done, what would happen in America? The South

would get guns, powder, credit, food, railroad equipment, and a tremendous lift in confidence and morale.

And what would the North get? Two new and powerful enemies. The situation, bad enough now, would be hopeless then.

Nobody knew this better than Abraham Lincoln. "We have about played our last card," he confessed in 1862. "We must either change our tactics now or lose the game."

As England saw it, all the colonies had originally seceded from her. Now the Southern colonies had, in turn, seceded from the Northern ones; and the North was fighting to coerce and subdue them. What difference did it make to a lord in London or a prince in Paris whether Tennessee and Texas were ruled from Washington or Richmond? None. To them, the fighting was meaningless and fraught with no high purpose.

"No war ever raging in my time," wrote Carlyle, "was to me more profoundly foolish looking."

Lincoln saw that Europe's attitude toward the war must be changed, and he knew how to do it. A million people in Europe had read "Uncle Tom's Cabin"—had read it and wept and learned to abhor the heartaches and injustice of slavery. So Abraham Lincoln knew that if he issued his Proclamation of Emancipation, Europeans would see the war in a different light. It would no longer be a bloody quarrel over the preservation of a Union that meant nothing to them. Instead, it would be exalted into a holy crusade to destroy slavery. European governments would then not dare to recognize the South. Public opinion wouldn't tolerate the aiding of a people supposed to be fighting to perpetuate human bondage.

Finally, therefore, in July, 1862, Lincoln determined to issue his proclamation; but McClellan and Pope had recently led the army to humiliating defeats. Seward told the President that the time was not auspicious, that he ought to wait and launch the proclamation on the crest of a wave of victory.

That sounded sensible. So Lincoln waited; and two months later the victory came. Then Lincoln called his Cabinet together to discuss the issuing of the most famous document in American history since the Declaration of Independence.

It was a momentous occasion—and a grave one. But did Lincoln act gravely and solemnly? He did not. Whenever he came across a good story, he liked to share it. He used to take one of Artemus Ward's books to bed with him; and when he read something humorous, he would get up, and, clad in nothing but his night-shirt, he would make his way through the halls of the White House to the office of his secretaries, and read it to them.

The day before the Cabinet meeting which was to discuss the issuing of the Emancipation Proclamation, Lincoln had gotten hold of Ward's latest volume. There was a story in it that he thought very funny. So he read it to the Cabinet now, before they got down to business. It was entitled, "High-handed Outrage in Utiky."

After Lincoln had had his laugh, he put the book aside and began solemnly: "When the rebel army was at Frederick, I determined, as soon as it should be driven out of Maryland, to issue a proclamation of emancipation. I said nothing to any one, but I made the promise to myself and—to my Maker. The rebel army is now driven out, and I am going to fulfil that promise. I have called you together to hear what I have written down. I do not wish your advice upon the main matter, for that I have determined for myself. What I have written is that which my reflections have determined me to say. But if there is anything in the expressions I use, or in any minor matter, which any of you thinks had best be changed, I shall be glad to receive the suggestions."

Seward suggested one slight change in wording; then, a few minutes later, he proposed another.

Lincoln asked him why he hadn't made both suggestions at the same time. And then Lincoln interrupted the consideration of the Emancipation Proclamation to tell a story. He said a hired man back in Indiana told the farmer who had employed him that one steer in his best yoke of oxen had died. Having waited a while, the hired man said, "The other ox in that team is dead, too."

"Then why didn't you tell me at once," asked the farmer, "that both of them were dead?"

"Well," answered the hired man, "I didn't want to hurt you by telling you too much at the same time."

Lincoln presented the proclamation to his Cabinet in September, 1862; but it was not to take effect until the first day of January, 1863. So when Congress met the following December, Lincoln appealed to that body for support. In making his plea he uttered one of the most magnificent sentences he ever penned —a sentence of unconscious poetry.

Speaking of the Union, he said:

"We shall nobly save or meanly lose
The last, best hope of earth."

On New Year's Day, 1863, Lincoln spent hours shaking hands with the visitors that thronged the White House. In the middle of that afternoon, he retired to his office, dipped his pen in the ink, and prepared to sign his proclamation of freedom. Hesitating, he turned to Seward and said: "If slavery isn't wrong, nothing is wrong, and I have never felt more certain in my life that I was doing right. But I have been receiving calls and shaking hands since nine o'clock this morning, and my arm is stiff and numb. Now this signature is one that will be closely examined, and if they find my hand trembled, they will say, 'He had some compunctions.' "

He rested his arm a moment, then slowly signed the document, and gave freedom to three and a half million slaves.

The proclamation did not meet with popular approval then. "The only effect of it," wrote Orville H. Browning, one of Lincoln's closest friends and strongest supporters, "was to unite and exasperate the South and divide and distract us in the North."

A mutiny broke out in the army. Men who had enlisted to save the Union swore that they wouldn't stand up and be shot down to free niggers and make them their social equals. Thousands of soldiers deserted, and recruiting fell off everywhere.

The plain people upon whom Lincoln had depended for support failed him utterly. The autumn elections went overwhelmingly against him. Even his home state of Illinois repudiated the Republican party.

And quickly, on top of the defeat at the polls, came one of the most disastrous reverses of the war—Burnside's foolhardy attack on Lee at Fredericksburg and the loss of thirteen thousand men. A stupid and futile butchery. This sort of thing had been going on for eighteen months now. Was it never going to stop? The nation was appalled. People were driven to despair. The President was violently denounced everywhere. He had failed. His general had failed. His policies had failed. People wouldn't put up with this any longer. Even the Republican members of the Senate revolted; and, wanting to force Lincoln out of the White House, they called upon him, demanding that he change his policies and dismiss his entire Cabinet.

This was a humiliating blow. Lincoln confessed that it distressed him more than any other one event of his political life.

"They want to get rid of me," he said, "and I am half disposed to gratify them."

Horace Greeley now sharply regretted the fact that he had forced the Republicans to nominate Lincoln in 1860.

"It was a mistake," he confessed, "the biggest mistake of my life."

Greeley and a number of other prominent Republicans organized a movement having these objects in view: to force Lincoln to resign, to put Hamlin, the Vice-President, in the White House, and then to compel Hamlin to give Rosecrans command of all the Union armies.

"We are now on the brink of destruction," Lincoln confessed. "It appears to me that even the Almighty is against us. I can see hardly a ray of hope."

23

In the spring of 1863, Lee, flushed with a phenomenal series of brilliant victories, determined to take the offensive and invade the North. He planned to seize the rich manufacturing centers of Pennsylvania, secure food, medicine, and new clothes for his ragged troops, possibly capture Washington, and compel France and Great Britain to recognize the Confederacy.

A bold, reckless move! True, but the Southern troops were boasting that one Confederate could whip three Yankees, and they believed it; so when their officers told them they could eat beef twice a day when they reached Pennsylvania, they were eager to be off at once.

Before he quit Richmond, Lee received disquieting news from home. A terrible thing had happened! One of his daughters had actually been caught reading a novel. The great general was distressed; so he wrote, pleading with her to devote her leisure to such innocuous classics as Plato and Homer, and Plutarch's Lives. After finishing the letter, Lee read his Bible and knelt in prayer, as was his custom; then he blew out the candle and turned in for the night. . . .

Presently he was off with seventy-five thousand men. His hungry army plunged across the Potomac, throwing the country into a panic. Farmers rushed out of the Cumberland Valley, driving their horses and cattle before them; and negroes, their eyes white with fear, fled in terror, lest they be dragged back to slavery.

Lee's artillery was already thundering before Harrisburg, when he learned that, back in the rear, the Union Army was threatening to break his lines of communication. So he whirled around as an angry ox would to gore a dog snapping at his heels; and, quite by chance, the ox and the dog met at a sleepy little Pennsylvania village with a theological seminary, a place called Gettysburg, and fought there the most famous battle in the history of our country.

During the first two days of the fighting the Union Army lost twenty thousand men; and, on the third day, Lee hoped finally to smash the enemy by a terrific assault of fresh troops under the command of General George Pickett.

These were new tactics for Lee. Up to this time, he had fought with his men behind breastworks or concealed in the woods. Now he planned to make a desperate attack out in the open.

The very contemplation of it staggered Lee's most brilliant assistant, General Longstreet.

"Great God!" Longstreet exclaimed. "Look, General Lee, at the insurmountable difficulties between our line and that of the Yankees—the steep hills, the tiers of artillery, the fences. And then we shall have to fight our infantry against their battery. Look at the ground we shall have to charge over, nearly a mile of it there in the open, under the line of their canister and shrapnel. It is my opinion that no fifteen thousand men ever arrayed for battle could take that position."

But Lee was adamant. "There were never such men in an army before," he replied. "They will go anywhere and do anything if properly led."

So Lee held to his decision, and made the bloodiest blunder of his career.

The Confederates had already massed one hundred and fifty cannon along Seminary Ridge. If you visit Gettysburg, you can see them there to-day, placed precisely as they were on that fateful July afternoon when they laid down a barrage such as, up to that time, had never before been heard on earth.

Longstreet in this instance had keener judgment than Lee. He believed that the charge could result in nothing but pointless butchery; so he bowed his head and wept and declined to issue the order. Consequently, another officer had to give the command for him; and, in obedience to that command, General

George Pickett led his Southern troops in the most dramatic and disastrous charge that ever occurred in the Western world.

Strangely enough, this general who led the assault on the Union lines was an old friend of Lincoln's. In fact, Lincoln had made it possible for him to go to West Point. He was a picturesque character, this man Pickett. He wore his hair so long that his auburn locks almost touched his shoulders; and, like Napoleon in his Italian campaigns, he wrote ardent love-letters almost daily on the battle-field. His devoted troops cheered him that afternoon as he rode off jauntily toward the Union lines, with his cap set at a rakish angle over his right ear. They cheered and they followed him, man touching man, rank pressing rank, with banners flying and bayonets gleaming in the sun. It was picturesque. Daring. Magnificent. A murmur of admiration ran through the Union lines as they beheld it.

Pickett's troops swept forward at an easy trot, through an orchard and corn-field, across a meadow, and over a ravine. All the time, the enemy's cannon were tearing ghastly holes in their ranks. But on they pressed, grim, irresistible.

Suddenly the Union infantry rose from behind the stone wall on Cemetery Ridge where they had been hiding, and fired volley after volley into Pickett's defenseless troops. The crest of the hill was a sheet of flame, a slaughter-house, a blazing volcano. In a few minutes, all of Pickett's brigade commanders, except one, were down, and four fifths of his five thousand men had fallen.

> A thousand fell where Kemper led;
> A thousand died where Garnett bled;
> In blinding flame and strangling smoke
> The remnant through the batteries broke,
> And crossed the line with Armistead.

Armistead, leading the troops in the final plunge, ran forward, vaulted over the stone wall, and, waving his cap on the top of his sword, shouted:

"Give 'em the steel, boys!"

They did. They leaped over the wall, bayoneted their enemies, smashed skulls with clubbed muskets, and planted the battle-flags of the South on Cemetery Ridge.

The banners waved there, however, only for a moment. But that moment, brief as it was, recorded the high-water mark of the Confederacy.

Pickett's charge—brilliant, heroic—was nevertheless the beginning of the end. Lee had failed. He could not penetrate the North. And he knew it.

The South was doomed.

As the remnant of Pickett's bleeding men struggled back from their fatal charge, Lee, entirely alone, rode out to encourage them, and greeted them with a self-condemnation that was little short of sublime.

"All this has been my fault," he confessed. "It is I who have lost this fight."

During the night of July 4 Lee began to retreat. Heavy rains were falling, and by the time he reached the Potomac the water was so high that he couldn't cross.

There Lee was, caught in a trap, an impassable river in front of him, a victorious enemy behind him. Meade, it seemed, had him at his mercy. Lincoln was delighted; he was sure the Federal troops would swoop down upon Lee's flank and rear now, rout and capture his men, and bring the war to an abrupt and triumphant close. And if Grant had been there, that is probably what would have happened.

But the vain and scholarly Meade was not the bulldog Grant. Every day for an entire week Lincoln repeatedly urged and commanded Meade to attack, but he was too cautious, too timid. He did not want to fight; he hesitated, he telegraphed excuses, he called a council of war in direct violation of orders —and did nothing, while the waters receded and Lee escaped.

Lincoln was furious.

"What does this mean?" he cried. "Great God! What does this mean? We had them within our grasp, and had only to stretch forth our hands and they were ours; yet nothing that I could say or do could make the army move. Under the circumstances, almost any general could have defeated Lee. If I had gone up there, I could have whipped him, myself."

In bitter disappointment, Lincoln sat down and wrote Meade a letter, in which he said:

My dear General, I do not believe you appreciate the magnitude of the misfortune involved in Lee's escape. He was within our easy grasp, and to have closed upon him would, in connection with our other late successes, have ended the war. As it is, the war will be prolonged indefinitely. If you could not safely attack Lee last Monday, how can you possibly do so south of the river, when you can take with you very few more than two-thirds of the force you then had in hand? It would be unreasonable to expect and I do not expect that you can now effect much. Your golden opportunity is gone, and I am distressed immeasurably because of it.

Lincoln read this letter, and then stared out the window with unseeing eyes, and did a bit of thinking: "If I had been in Meade's place," he probably mused to himself, "and had had Meade's temperament and the advice of his timid officers, and if I had been awake as many nights as he had, and had seen as much blood, I might have let Lee escape, too."

The letter was never sent. Meade never saw it. It was found among Lincoln's papers after his death.

The Battle of Gettysburg was fought during the first week of July; six thousand dead and twenty-seven thousand wounded were left on the field. Churches, schools, and barns were turned into hospitals; groans of the suffering filled the air. Scores were dying every hour, corpses were decaying rapidly in the intense heat. The burial parties had to work fast. There was little time to dig graves; so, in many instances, a little dirt was scooped over a body where it lay. After a week of hard rains, many of the dead were half exposed. The Union soldiers were gathered from their temporary graves, and buried in one place. The following autumn the Cemetery Commission decided to dedicate the ground, and invited Edward Everett, the most famous orator in the United States, to deliver the address.

Formal invitations to attend the exercises were sent to the President, to the Cabinet, to General Meade, to all members of both houses of Congress, to various distinguished citizens, and to the members of the diplomatic corps. Very few of these people accepted; many didn't acknowledge the invitation.

The committee had not the least idea that the President would come. In fact, they had not even troubled to write him a personal invitation. He got merely a printed one. They imagined that his secretaries might drop it in the waste-basket without even showing it to Lincoln.

So when he wrote saying he would be present, the committee was astonished. And a bit embarrassed. What should they do?

Ask him to speak? Some argued that he was too busy for that, that he couldn't possibly find time to prepare. Others frankly asked, "Well, even if he had the time, has he the ability?" They doubted it.

Oh, yes, he could make a stump speech in Illinois; but speaking at the dedication of a cemetery? No. That was different. That was not Lincoln's style. However, since he was coming anyway, they had to do something. So they finally wrote him, saying that after Mr. Everett had delivered his oration, they would like to have him make "a few appropriate remarks." That was the way they phrased it—"a few appropriate remarks."

The invitation just barely missed being an insult. But the President accepted it. Why? There is an interesting story behind that. The previous autumn Lincoln had visited the battle-field of Antietam; and, one afternoon while he and an old friend from Illinois, Ward Lamon, were out driving, the President turned to Lamon and asked him to sing what Lincoln called his "sad little song." It was one of Lincoln's favorites.

"Many a time, on the Illinois circuit and often at the White House when Lincoln and I were alone," says Lamon, "I have seen him in tears while I was rendering that homely melody."

It went like this:

I've wandered to the village, Tom; I've sat beneath the tree
Upon the schoolhouse play-ground, that sheltered you and me;
But none were left to greet me, Tom, and few were left to know
Who played with us upon the green, some twenty years ago.

Near by the spring, upon the elm you know I cut your name,—
Your sweetheart's just beneath it, Tom; and you did mine the
    same.
Some heartless wretch has peeled the bark—'twas dying sure
    but slow,
Just as she died whose name you cut, some twenty years ago.

My lids have long been dry, Tom, but tears came to my eyes;
I thought of her I loved so well, those early broken ties:
I visited the old churchyard, and took some flowers to strow
Upon the graves of those we loved, some twenty years ago.

As Lamon sang it now, probably Lincoln fell to dreaming of the only woman he had ever loved, Ann Rutledge, and he thought of her lying back there in her neglected grave on the Illinois prairie; and the rush of these poignant memories filled his eyes with tears. So Lamon, to break the spell of Lincoln's melancholy, struck up a humorous negro melody.

That was all there was to the incident. It was perfectly harmless, and very pathetic. But Lincoln's political enemies distorted it and lied about it and tried to make it a national disgrace. They made it appear like a gross indecency. The New York "World" repeated some version of the scandal every day for almost three months. Lincoln was accused of cracking jokes and singing funny songs on the battle-field where "heavy details of men were engaged in burying the dead."

The truth is that he had cracked no jokes at all, that he had sung no songs, that he had been miles away from the battle-field when the incident occurred, that the dead had all been buried before that, and rain had fallen upon their graves. Such were the facts. But his enemies didn't want facts. They were lusting for blood. A bitter cry of savage denunciation swept over the land.

Lincoln was deeply hurt. He was so distressed that he could not bear to read these attacks, yet he didn't feel that he ought to answer them, for that would merely dignify them. So he suffered in silence, and when the invitation came to speak at the dedication of the Gettysburg cemetery, he welcomed it. It was just the opportunity he desired to silence his enemies and pay his humble tribute to the honored dead.

The invitation came late, and he had only a crowded fortnight in which to prepare his speech. He thought it over during his spare moments—while dressing, while being shaved, while eating his lunch, while walking back and forth between Stanton's office and the White House. He mused upon it while stretched out on a leather couch in the war-office, waiting for the late telegraphic reports. He wrote a rough draft of it on a piece of pale-blue foolscap paper, and carried it about in the top of his hat. The Sunday before it was delivered he said: "I have written it over two or three times, but it is not finished. I shall have to give it another lick before I am satisfied."

He arrived in Gettysburg the night before the dedication. The little town was filled to overflowing. Its usual population of thirteen hundred had been swelled to almost thirty thousand. The weather was fine; the night was clear; a bright full moon rode high through the sky. Only a fraction of the crowd could find beds; thousands paraded up and down the village until dawn. The sidewalks soon became clogged, impassable; so hundreds, locked arm in arm, marched in the middle of the dirt streets, singing, "John Brown's body lies a-mouldering in the grave."

Lincoln devoted all that evening to giving his speech "another lick." At eleven o'clock he went to an adjoining house, where Secretary Seward was staying, and read the speech aloud to him, asking for his criticisms. The next morning, after breakfast, Lincoln continued working over it until a rap at the door reminded him that it was time for him to take his place in the procession headed for the cemetery.

As the procession started, he sat erect at first; but presently his body slouched forward in the saddle; his head fell on his chest, and his long arms hung limp at his sides. . . . He was lost in thought, going over his little speech, giving it "another lick." . . .

Edward Everett, the selected orator of the occasion, made two mistakes at Gettysburg. Both bad—and both uncalled for. First, he arrived an hour late; and, secondly, he spoke for two hours.

Lincoln had read Everett's oration and when he saw that the speaker was nearing his close, he knew his time was coming, and he honestly felt that he wasn't adequately prepared; so he grew nervous, twisted in his chair, drew his manuscript from the pocket of his Prince Albert coat, put on his old-fashioned glasses, and quickly refreshed his memory.

Presently he stepped forward, manuscript in hand, and delivered his little address in two minutes.

Did his audience realize, that soft November afternoon, that they were listening to the greatest speech that had ever fallen from human lips up to that time? No, most of his hearers were merely curious: they had never seen nor heard a President of the United States, they strained their necks to look at Lincoln, and were surprised to discover that such a tall man had such a high, thin voice, and that he spoke with a Southern accent. They had forgotten that he was born a Kentuckian and that he had retained the intonation of his native State; and about the time they felt he was getting through with his introduction and ready to launch into his speech—he sat down.

What! Had he forgotten? Or was it really all he had to say? People were too surprised and disappointed to applaud.

Many a spring, back in Indiana, Lincoln had tried to break ground with a rusty plow; but the soil had stuck to its mold-

board, and made a mess. It wouldn't "scour." That was the
term people used. Throughout his life, when Lincoln wanted to
indicate that a thing had failed, he frequently resorted to the
phraseology of the corn-field. Turning now to Ward Lamon,
Lincoln said:

"That speech is a flat failure, Lamon. It won't scour. The
people are disappointed."

He was right. Every one was disappointed, including Edward
Everett and Secretary Seward, who were sitting on the platform
with the President. They both believed he had failed woefully;
and both felt sorry for him.

Lincoln was so distressed that he worried himself into a
severe headache; and on the way back to Washington, he had
to lie down in the drawing-room of the train and have his head
bathed with cold water.

Lincoln went to his grave believing that he had failed utterly
at Gettysburg. And he had, as far as the immediate effect of his
speech was concerned.

With characteristic modesty, he sincerely felt that the world
would "little note nor long remember" what he said there, but
that it would never forget what the brave men who died had
done there. How surprised he would be if he should come back
to life now and realize that the speech of his that most people
remember is the one that didn't "scour" at Gettysburg! How
amazed he would be to discover that the ten immortal sentences
he spoke there will probably be cherished as one of the literary
glories and treasures of earth centuries hence, long after the
Civil War is all but forgotten.

Lincoln's Gettysburg address is more than a speech. It is
the divine expression of a rare soul exalted and made great
by suffering. It is an unconscious prose poem, and has all the
majestic beauty and profound roll of epic lines:

> Four score and seven years ago
> Our fathers brought forth upon this continent,
> A new nation, conceived in Liberty,
> And dedicated to the proposition
> That all men are created equal.
>
> Now we are engaged in a great civil war,
> Testing whether that nation, or any nation
> So conceived and so dedicated,
> Can long endure. We are met

On a great battle-field of that war.
We have come to dedicate a portion of
That field as a final resting-place
For those who here gave their lives
That that nation might live.
It is altogether fitting and proper
That we should do this.

But, in a larger sense,
We can not dedicate—we can not consecrate—
We can not hallow this ground. The brave men,
Living and dead, who struggled here
Have consecrated it far above our poor power
To add or detract. The world will little note,
Nor long remember what we say here,
But it can never forget what they did here.
It is for us the living, rather, to be dedicated here
To the unfinished work which they who fought here
Have thus far so nobly advanced.
It is rather for us to be here dedicated
To the great task remaining before us—
That from these honored dead we take
Increased devotion to that cause for which
They gave the last full measure of devotion—
That we here highly resolve that these dead
Shall not have died in vain—that this nation,
Under God, shall have a new birth of freedom—
And that government of the people,
By the people, for the people,
Shall not perish from the earth.

24

W<small>HEN</small> the war began, in 1861, a shabby and disappointed man was sitting on a packing-case in a leather store in Galena, Illinois, smoking a clay pipe. His job, so far as he had one, was that of bookkeeper and buyer of hogs and hides from farmers.

His two younger brothers who owned the store didn't want him around at any price, but for months he had tramped the streets of St. Louis, looking in vain for some kind of position, until his wife and four children were destitute. Finally, in despair, he had borrowed a few dollars for a railway ticket and gone to see his father in Kentucky, begging for assistance. The old man had considerable cash, but, being loath to part with any of it, he sat down and wrote his two younger sons in Galena, instructing them to give their elder brother a job.

So they put him on the pay-roll at once, more as a matter of family politics and family charity than anything else.

Two dollars a day—that was his wage—and it was probably more than he was worth, for he had no more business ability than a jack-rabbit; he was lazy and slovenly, he loved corn-whisky, and he was eternally in debt. He was always borrowing small sums of money; so when his friends saw him coming, they used to look the other way and cross the street to avoid meeting him.

Everything he had undertaken in life, so far, had ended in failure and frustration.

So far.

But no more.

For good news and astounding good fortune were just around the corner.

In a little while he was to go flaring and flaming like a shooting star across the firmament of fame.

He couldn't command the respect of his home town now; but in three years he would command the most formidable army the world had ever seen.

In four years he would conquer Lee, end the war, and write his name in blazing letters of fire on the pages of history.

In eight years he would be in the White House.

After that he would make a triumphal tour of the world, with the high and mighty of all lands heaping honors, medals, flowers, and after-dinner oratory upon him—whom people back in Galena had crossed the street to avoid.

It is an astonishing tale.

Everything about it is strange. Even the attitude of his mother was abnormal. She never seemed to care much for him. She refused to visit him when he was President, and she didn't trouble even to name him when he was born. Her relatives attended to that, in a sort of lottery. When he was six weeks old, they wrote their favorite names on strips torn from a paper sack, mixed them in a hat, and drew one out. His grandmother Simpson had been reading Homer, and she wrote on her slip: "Hiram Ulysses." It was drawn, and so, by chance, that was the name he bore at home for seventeen years.

But he was bashful and slow-witted, so the village wits called him "Useless" Grant.

At West Point he had still another name. The politician who made out the papers giving him an appointment to the Military Academy imagined that his middle name must be Simpson, his mother's maiden name, so he went as "U. S. Grant." When the cadets learned this, they laughed and tossed their hats in the air, and shouted, "Boys, we've got Uncle Sam with us!" To the end of his life those who had been his classmates there called him Sam Grant.

He didn't mind. He made few friends, and he didn't care what people called him, and he didn't care how he looked. He wouldn't keep his coat buttoned or his gun clean or his shoes shined, and he was often late for roll-call. And, instead of mastering the military principles used by Napoleon and Frederick the Great, he spent much of his time at West Point poring over novels such as "Ivanhoe" and "The Last of the Mohicans."

The incredible fact is that he never read a book on military strategy in his life.

After he had won the war the people of Boston raised money to buy him a library, appointing a committee to find out what books he already possessed. To its amazement, the committee learned that Grant didn't own a single military treatise of any description.

He disliked West Point and the army and everything connected with it; and, after he had become world-famous, he said to Bismarck while reviewing Germany's troops:

"I haven't much interest in military affairs. The truth is, I am more of a farmer than a soldier. Although I have been in two wars, I never entered the army without regret, and never left it without pleasure."

Grant admitted that his besetting sin was laziness, and that he never liked to study. Even after he graduated from West Point he spelled *knocked* without the initial *k* and *safety* without an *e;* yet he was fairly good at figures, and hoped to be a professor of mathematics. But no position was available, so he spent eleven years with the regular army. He had to have something to eat, and that seemed the easiest way to get it.

In 1853 he was stationed at Fort Humboldt in California. In a near-by village there was a curious character named Ryan. Ryan ran a store, operated a sawmill, and did surveying during the week. On Sunday he preached. Whisky was cheap in those days, and Pastor Ryan kept an open barrel of it in the back of his store. A tin cup was hanging on the barrel, so you could go and help yourself whenever you had the urge. Grant had it often. He was lonely and wanted to forget the army life that he despised; as a result he got drunk so many times that he had virtually to be dismissed from the army.

He didn't have a dollar, and he didn't have a job; so he drifted back east to Missouri and spent the next four years plowing corn and slopping hogs on an eighty-acre farm belonging to his father-in-law. In the wintertime he cut cord-wood, hauled it to St. Louis, and sold it to the city people. But every year he got farther and farther behind, had to borrow more and more.

Finally he quit the farm, moved to St. Louis, and sought employment there. He tried to sell real estate, was a total failure at that, and then drifted about the town for weeks, looking for a job—any kind of job. At last he was in such desperate circumstances that he tried to hire out his wife's negroes, in order to get money to pay the grocer's bill.

Here is one of the most surprising facts about the Civil War: Lee believed that slavery was wrong, and had freed his own negroes long before the conflict came; but Grant's wife owned slaves at the very time that her husband was leading the armies of the North to destroy slavery.

When the war began, Grant was sick of his work in the Galena leather store and wanted to get back into the army.

That ought to have been easy for a West Point graduate, when the army had hundreds of thousands of raw recruits to whip into shape. But it wasn't. Galena raised a company of volunteers, and Grant drilled them because he was the only man in town who knew anything at all about drilling, but when they marched away to war with bouquets in their gun-barrels Grant stood on the sidewalk watching them. They had chosen another man as captain.

Then Grant wrote to the War Department, telling of his experience and asking to be appointed colonel of a regiment. His letter was never answered. It was found in the files of the War Department while he was President.

Finally he got a position in the adjutant's office in Springfield, doing clerical work that a fifteen-year-old girl could have done. He worked all day with his hat on, smoking constantly and copying orders on an old broken-down table with three legs, which had been shoved into a corner for support.

Then a wholly unexpected thing happened, an event that set his feet on the road to fame. The 21st Regiment of Illinois Volunteers had degenerated into an armed mob. They ignored orders, cursed their officers, and chased old Colonel Goode out of camp, vowing that if he showed up again they would nail his hide on a sour-apple tree.

Governor Yates was worried.

He didn't think much of Grant, but after all the man had been graduated from West Point, so the governor took a chance. And on a sunny June day in 1861 Grant walked out to the Springfield fair-grounds to take over the command of a regiment that no one else could rule.

A stick that he carried, and a red bandana tied around his waist—these were his only visible signs of authority.

He didn't have a horse or a uniform, or the money to buy either. There were holes in the top of his sweat-stained hat, and his elbows stuck out of his old coat.

His men began making fun of him at once. One chap started sparring at him behind his back, and another fellow rushed up behind the pugilist and shoved him so hard that he stumbled forward and hit Grant between the shoulders.

Grant stopped all their foolishness immediately. If a man disobeyed orders he was tied to a post and left there all day. If he cursed a gag was put into his mouth. If the regiment was late at roll-call—as they all were on one occasion—they got nothing to eat for twenty-four hours. The ex-hide-buyer from Galena tamed their tempestuous spirits and led them away to do battle down in Missouri.

Shortly after that another piece of amazing good fortune came his way. In those days the War Department was making brigadier-generals by the dozens. Northwestern Illinois had sent Elihu B. Washburne to Congress. Washburne, fired with political ambitions, was desperately eager to show the folks back home that he was on the job, so he went to the War Department and demanded that one brigadier-general come from his district. All right. But who? That was easy: there was only one West Point graduate among Washburne's constituents.

So a few days later Grant picked up a St. Louis newspaper, and read the surprising news that he was a brigadier-general.

He was assigned headquarters at Cairo, Illinois, and immediately began to do things. He loaded his soldiers on boats, steamed up the Ohio, occupied Paducah, a strategic point in Kentucky, and proposed marching down into Tennessee to attack Fort Donelson, which commanded the Cumberland River. Military experts like Halleck said: "Nonsense! You are talking foolishly, Grant. It can't be done. It would be suicide to attempt it."

Grant went ahead and tried it, and captured the fort and fifteen thousand prisoners in one afternoon.

While Grant was attacking, the Confederate general sent him a note, begging for a truce, to arrange terms of capitulation, but Grant replied rather tartly:

"My only terms are unconditional and immediate surrender. I propose to move immediately upon your works."

Simon Buckner, the Confederate general to whom this curt message was addressed, had known Sam Grant at West Point and had lent him money to pay his board bill when he was fired from the army. In view of that loan, Buckner felt that Grant ought to have been a trifle more gracious in his phraseology. But Buckner forgave him and surrendered and spent the afternoon smoking and reminiscing with Grant about old times.

The fall of Fort Donelson had far-reaching consequences: it saved Kentucky for the North, enabled the Union troops to advance two hundred miles without opposition, drove the Confederates out of a large part of Tennessee, cut off their supplies, caused the fall of Nashville and of Fort Columbus, the Gibraltar of the Mississippi, spread profound depression throughout the South, and set church bells ringing and bonfires blazing from Maine to the Mississippi.

It was a stupendous victory, and created a tremendous impression even in Europe. It was really one of the turning-points of the war.

From that time on, U. S. Grant was known as "Unconditional Surrender" Grant, and "I propose to move on your works immediately" became the battle-cry of the North.

Here, at last, was the great leader for which the country had been waiting. Congress made him a major-general; he was appointed commander of the Military Department of Western Tennessee, and quickly became the idol of the nation. One newspaper mentioned that he liked to smoke during a battle, and, presto! over ten thousand boxes of cigars were showered upon him.

But in less than three weeks after all this Grant was actually in tears of rage and mortification because of unfair treatment by a jealous superior officer.

His immediate superior in the West was Halleck, a colossal and unmitigated ass. Admiral Foote called Halleck "a military imbecile," and Gideon Welles, Lincoln's Secretary of the Navy, who knew Halleck intimately, sums him up thus:

"Halleck originates nothing, anticipates nothing, suggests nothing, plans nothing, decides nothing, is good for nothing and does nothing except scold, smoke and scratch his elbows."

But Halleck thought very well of himself. He had been an assistant professor at West Point, had written books on military strategy, international law, and mining, had been director of a silver-mine, president of a railway, a successful attorney, had mastered French and translated a tome on Napoleon. In his own opinion, he was the distinguished scholar, *Henry Wager Halleck*.

And who was Grant? A nobody, a drunken and discredited army captain. When Grant came to see him, before attacking Fort Donelson, Halleck was rude, and dismissed his military suggestions with irritation and contempt. Now Grant had won a great victory and had the nation at his feet, while Halleck was still scratching his elbows in St. Louis, unnoticed and ignored. And it galled Halleck.

To make matters worse, he felt that this erstwhile hide-buyer was insulting him. He telegraphed Grant day after day, and Grant brazenly ignored his orders. At least, so Halleck imagined. But he was wrong. Grant had sent report upon report; but, after the fall of Donelson, a break in telegraphic communications had made it impossible for his telegrams to get through. However, Halleck didn't know this, and he was indignant. Victory and public adulation had gone to Grant's head, had they? Well, he would teach this young upstart a lesson. So he wired McClellan repeatedly, denouncing Grant. Grant was this, Grant was that—insolent, drunk, idle, ignoring orders, incompetent. "I'm tired and worn out with this neglect and inefficiency."

McClellan, too, was envious of Grant's popularity; so he sent Halleck what, in the light of history, is the most amazing telegram of the Civil War: "Do not hesitate to arrest him [Grant] at once if the good of the service requires it, and place C. F. Smith in command."

Halleck immediately took Grant's army away from him, virtually placed him under arrest, and then leaned back in his chair and scratched his elbows with savage satisfaction.

The war was almost a year old now, and the only general who had won a considerable victory for the North stood stripped of all power and in public disgrace.

Later Grant was restored to command. Then he blundered woefully at the Battle of Shiloh; if Johnston, the Confederate general, had not bled to death during the fighting, Grant's entire army might have been surrounded and captured. Shiloh was, at that time, the greatest battle that had ever been fought on this continent, and Grant's losses were staggering—thirteen thousand men. He had acted stupidly; he had been taken by surprise. He deserved criticism, and it came roaring down upon him. He was falsely accused of being intoxicated at Shiloh, and millions believed it. A tidal wave of popular indignation swept over the country, and the public clamored for his removal. But Lincoln said:

"I can't spare this man. He fights."

When people told him Grant drank too much whisky, he inquired: "What brand? I want to send a few barrels to some of my other generals."

The following January Grant assumed command of the expedition against Vicksburg. The campaign against this natural fortress, perched on a high bluff two hundred feet above the Mississippi, was long and heartbreaking. The place was heavily fortified, and the gunboats on the river couldn't elevate their cannon high enough to touch it. Grant's problem was to get his army close enough to attack it.

He went back to the heart of Mississippi and tried to march on it from the east. That failed.

Then he cut away the levees of the river, put his army on boats, and tried to float through the swamps and get at the place from the north. That failed.

Then he dug a canal and tried to change the course of the Mississippi. That failed.

It was a trying winter. Rain fell almost continuously, the river flooded the whole valley, and Grant's troops floundered through miles of swamps, ooze, bayous, tangled forests, and trailing vines. Men stood up to their waists in mud, they ate in the mud, they slept in the mud. Malarial fever broke out, and measles and smallpox. Sanitation was well-nigh impossible, and the death-rate was appalling.

The Vicksburg campaign was a failure—that was the cry that went up everywhere. A stupid failure, a tragic failure, a criminal failure.

Grant's own generals—Sherman, McPherson, Logan, Wilson —regarded his plans as absurd, and believed they would end in black ruin. The press throughout the country was vitriolic, and the nation was demanding Grant's removal.

"He has hardly a friend left except myself," Lincoln said.

Despite all opposition, Lincoln clung to Grant; and he had his faith richly rewarded, for, on July 4, the same day that the timid Meade let Lee escape at Gettysburg, Grant rode into Vicksburg on a horse taken from the plantation of Jefferson Davis, and won a greater victory than any American general had achieved since the days of Washington.

After eight months of desolating failure, Grant had captured forty thousand prisoners at Vicksburg, placed the entire Mississippi River in the hands of the North, and split the Confederacy.

The news set the nation aflame with enthusiasm.

Congress passed a special act in order that Grant could be made lieutenant-general—an honor that no man had worn since the death of Washington—and Lincoln, calling him to the White House, made a short address appointing him commander of all the armies of the Union.

Forewarned that he would have to reply with a speech of acceptance, Grant drew out of his pocket a little wrinkled piece of paper containing only three sentences. As he began to read, the paper shook, his face flushed, his knees trembled, and his voice failed. Breaking down completely, he clutched the shaking paper with both hands, shifted his position, took a deep breath, and began all over again.

The hog-and-hide buyer from Galena found it easier to face bullets than to deliver a speech of eighty-four words before an audience of eleven men.

Mrs. Lincoln, eager to make a social event out of Grant's presence in Washington, had already arranged a dinner and a party in the general's honor. But Grant begged to be excused, saying he must hasten back to the front.

"But we can't excuse you," the President insisted. "Mrs. Lincoln's dinner without you would be 'Hamlet' without Hamlet."

"A dinner to me," replied Grant, "means a million dollars a day loss to the country. Besides, I've had about enough of this show business, anyway."

Lincoln loved a man who would talk like that—one who, like himself, despised "fizzlegigs and fireworks," and one who would "take responsibility and act."

Lincoln's hopes rose and towered now. He was sure that, with Grant in command, all would soon be well.

But he was wrong. Within four months the country was plunged into blacker gloom and deeper despair than ever, and once more Lincoln was pacing the floor throughout the night, haggard and worn and desperate.

25

In May 1864, the triumphant Grant plunged across the Rapidan River with 122,000 men. He was going to destroy's Lee's army forthwith and end the war at once.

Lee met him in the "wilderness" of North Virginia. The place was well named. It was a jungle of rolling hills and swampy swales smothered with a dense second growth of pine and oaks and matted with underbrush so thick that a cottontail could hardly crawl through it. And in those gloomy and tangled woods, Grant fought a grim and bloody campaign. The slaughter was appalling. The jungle itself caught on fire and hundreds of the wounded were consumed by the flames.

At the end of the second day even the stolid Grant was so shaken that he retired to his tent and wept.

But after every battle, no matter what the results, he gave the same order: "Advance! Advance!"

At the end of the sixth bloody day he sent the famous telegram: "I propose to fight it out on this line if it takes all summer."

Well, it did take all summer. Moreover, it took all autumn, and all winter, and a part of the next spring.

Grant had twice as many men in the field now as the enemy had, and back of him, in the North, lay a vast reservoir of manpower upon which he could draw, while the South had almost exhausted its recruits and supplies.

"The rebels," said Grant, "have already robbed the cradle and the grave."

185

Grant held that the quick way and the only way to end the war was to keep on killing Lee's men until Lee surrendered.

What if two Northern soldiers were shot for every one the South lost? Grant could make up the wastage, but Lee couldn't. So Grant kept on blasting and shooting and slaying.

In six weeks he lost 54,926 men—as many as Lee had in his entire army.

In one hour at Cold Harbor he lost seven thousand—a thousand more than had been killed on both sides in three days during the Battle of Gettysburg.

And what advantage was achieved by this ghastly loss?

We shall let Grant himself answer the question: "None whatever." That was his estimate.

The attack at Cold Harbor was the most tragic blunder of his career.

Such slaughter was more than human nerves and human bodies could endure. It broke the morale of the troops; the rank and file of the army were on the verge of mutiny, and the officers themselves were ready to rebel.

"For thirty-six days now," said one of Grant's corps commanders, "there has been one unbroken funeral procession past me."

Lincoln, broken-hearted though he was, realized that there was nothing to do but keep on. He telegraphed Grant to "hold on with a bull dog grip and chew and choke." Then he issued a call for half a million more men, to serve from one to three years.

The call staggered the country. The nation was plunged into an abyss of despair.

"Everything now is darkness and doubt and discouragement," one of Lincoln's secretaries recorded in his diary.

On July 2 Congress adopted a resolution that sounded like the lamentations of one of the Hebrew prophets of the Old Testament. It requested the citizens to "confess and repent of their manifold sins, implore the compassion and forgiveness of the Almighty, and beseech him as the Supreme Ruler of the world not to destroy us as a people."

Lincoln was being cursed now almost as violently in the North as in the South. He was denounced as a usurper, a traitor, a tyrant, a fiend, a monster, "a bloody butcher shouting war to the knife and knife to the hilt, and crying for more victims for his slaughter pens."

Some of his most bitter enemies declared that he ought to be killed. And one evening as he was riding out to his summer headquarters at the Soldiers' Home, a would-be assassin fired at him and put a bullet through his tall silk hat.

A few weeks later the proprietor of a hotel in Meadville, Pennsylvania, found this inscription scratched on a window-pane: "Abe Lincoln Departed this Life August 13, 1864, by the effect of poison." The room had been occupied the night before by a popular actor named Booth—John Wilkes Booth.

The preceding June the Republicans had nominated Lincoln for a second term. But they felt now that they had made a mistake, a woeful mistake. Some of the most prominent men in the party urged Lincoln to withdraw. Others demanded it. They wanted to call another convention, admit that Lincoln was a failure, cancel his nomination, and place another candidate at the head of the ticket.

Even Lincoln's close friend Orville Browning recorded in his diary in July, 1864, that the "nation's great need is a competent leader at the head of affairs."

Lincoln himself now believed that his case was hopeless. He abandoned all thought of being elected for a second term. He had failed. His generals had failed. His war policy had failed. The people had lost faith in his leadership, and he feared that the Union itself would be destroyed.

"Even the heavens," he exclaimed, "are hung in black."

Finally a large group of radicals, disgusted with Lincoln, called another convention, nominated the picturesque General John C. Frémont as their candidate, and split the Republican party.

The situation was grave; and there is hardly a doubt that if Frémont hadn't withdrawn from the race later, General Mc-Clellan, the Democratic candidate, would have triumphed over his divided opponents and the history of the nation would have been changed.

Even with Frémont out of the race, Lincoln received only 200,000 more votes than McClellan.

Notwithstanding the vitriolic condemnation poured upon him, Lincoln went calmly on, doing his best and answering no one.

"I desire," he said, "to so conduct the affairs of this administration that if, at the end, when I come to lay down the reins of power, I have lost every other friend on earth, I shall at least have one friend left, and that friend shall be deep down inside of me. . . . I am not bound to win, but I am bound to be true. I am not bound to succeed, but I am bound to live up to the light I have."

Weary and despondent, he often stretched himself out on a sofa, picked up a small Bible, and turned to Job for comfort: "Gird up now thy loins like a man; for I will demand of thee, and answer thou me."

In the summer of 1864, Lincoln was a changed man, changed in mind and body from the physical giant who had come off the prairies of Illinois three years before. Year by year his laughter had grown less frequent; the furrows in his face had deepened; his shoulders had stooped; his cheeks were sunken; he suffered from chronic indigestion; his legs were always cold; he could hardly sleep; he wore habitually an expression of anguish. He said to a friend: "I feel as though I shall never be glad again."

When Augustus Saint-Gaudens saw a life-mask of Lincoln that had been made in the spring of 1865, the famous sculptor thought that it was a death-mask, insisted that it must be, for already the marks of death were upon his face.

Carpenter, the artist who lived at the White House for months while he was painting the scene of the Emancipation Proclamation, wrote:

> During the first week of the battle of the Wilderness, the President scarcely slept at all. Passing through the main hall of the domestic apartment on one of those days, I met him, clad in a long morning wrapper, pacing back and forth, his hands behind him, great black rings under his eyes, his head bent forward upon his breast—the picture of sorrow and care and anxiety. . . . There were whole days when I could scarcely look into his furrowed face without weeping.

Callers found him collapsed in his chair, so exhausted that he did not look up or speak when they first addressed him.

"I sometimes fancy," he declared, "that every one of the throng that comes to see me daily darts at me with thumb and finger and picks out his piece of my vitality and carries it away."

He told Mrs. Stowe, the author of "Uncle Tom's Cabin," that he would never live to see peace.

"This war is killing me," he said.

His friends, alarmed at the change in his appearance, urged him to take a vacation.

"Two or three weeks would do me no good," he replied. "I cannot fly from my thoughts. I hardly know how to rest. What is tired lies within me and can't be got at."

"The cry of the widow and the orphan," said his secretary, "was always in Lincoln's ear."

Mothers and sweethearts and wives, weeping and pleading, rushed to him daily to obtain pardons for men who had been condemned to be shot. No matter how worn he was, how exhausted, Lincoln always heard their stories, and generally granted their requests, for he never could bear to see a woman cry, especially if she had a baby in her arms.

"When I am gone," he moaned, "I hope it can be said of me that I plucked a thistle and planted a flower wherever I thought a flower would grow."

The generals scolded and Stanton stormed: Lincoln's leniency was destroying the discipline of the army, he must keep his hands off. But the truth is he hated the brutal methods of brigadier-generals, and the despotism of the regular army. On the other hand, he loved the volunteers on whom he had to depend for winning the war—men who, like himself, had come from the forest and farm.

Was one of them condemned to be shot for cowardice? Lincoln would pardon him, saying, "I have never been sure but what I might drop my gun and run, myself, if I were in battle."

Had a volunteer become homesick and run away? "Well, I don't see that shooting will do him any good."

Had a tired and exhausted Vermont farm boy been sentenced to death for falling asleep on sentinel duty? "I might have done the same thing, myself," Lincoln would say.

A mere list of his pardons would fill many pages.

He once wired to General Meade, "I am unwilling for any boy under eighteen to be shot." And there were more than a million boys under that age in the Union armies. In fact, there were a fifth of a million under sixteen, and a hundred thousand under fifteen.

Sometimes the President worked a bit of humor into his most serious messages; as, for example, when he wired Colonel Mulligan, "If you haven't shot Barney D. yet, don't."

The anguish of bereaved mothers touched Lincoln very deeply. On November 21, 1864, he wrote the most beautiful and famous letter of his life. Oxford University has a copy of this letter hanging on its wall, "as a model of pure and exquisite diction which has never been excelled."

Although written as prose, it is really unconscious and resonant poetry:

Executive Mansion,
Washington, Nov. 21, 1864.
To Mrs. Bixby, Boston, Mass.
Dear Madame:
I have been shown in the files of the War Department
A statement of the Adjutant General of Massachusetts
That you are the mother of five sons
Who have died gloriously on the field of battle. I feel
How weak and fruitless must be any words of mine
Which would attempt to beguile you from the grief
Of a loss so overwhelming. But I cannot refrain
From tendering to you the consolation that may be found
In the thanks of the Republic they died to save.
I pray that our Heavenly Father may assuage
The anguish of your bereavement, and leave you only
The cherished memory of the loved and lost,
And the solemn pride that must be yours to have laid
So costly a sacrifice upon the altar of freedom.
Yours very sincerely and respectfully,
A. LINCOLN.

One day Noah Brooks gave Lincoln a volume of Oliver Wendell Holmes's verses. Opening the book, Lincoln began reading the poem "Lexington" aloud, but when he came to the stanza beginning:

Green be the grass where her martyrs are lying!
Shroudless and tombless they sunk to their rest,

his voice quavered, he choked, and handing the volume back to Brooks, he whispered: "You read it. I can't."

Months afterward he recited the entire poem to friends in the White House, without missing a word.

On April 5, 1864, Lincoln received a letter from a broken-hearted girl in Washington County, Pennsylvania. "After long hesitation through dread and fear," she began, "I have at last concluded to inform you of my troubles." The man to whom she had been engaged for some years had joined the army, had later been permitted to go home to vote, and they had, as she put it, "very foolishly indulged too freely in matrimonial affairs." And now "the results of our indulgences are going to bring upon us both an unlawful family providing you do not take mercy upon us and grant him a leave of absence in order to ratify past events. . . . I hope and pray to God that you will not cast me aside in scorn and dismay."

Reading the letter, Lincoln was deeply touched. He stared out the window with unseeing eyes in which there were doubtlessly tears. . . .

Picking up his pen, Lincoln wrote the following words to Stanton across the bottom of the girl's letter: "Send him to her by all means."

The terrible summer of 1864 dragged to an end, and the autumn brought good news: Sherman had taken Atlanta and was marching through Georgia. Admiral Farragut, after a dramatic naval battle, had captured Mobile Bay and tightened the blockade in the Gulf of Mexico. Sheridan had won brilliant and spectacular victories in the Shenandoah Valley. And Lee was now afraid to come out in the open; so Grant was laying siege to Petersburg and Richmond. . . .

The Confederacy had almost reached the end.

Lincoln's generals were winning now, his policy had been vindicated, and the spirits of the North rose as on wings; so, in November, he was elected for a second term. But instead of taking it as a personal triumph, he remarked laconically that evidently the people had not thought it wise "to swap horses while crossing a stream."

After four years of fighting, there was no hatred in Lincoln's heart for the people of the South. Time and again he said: " 'Judge not that ye be not judged.' They are just what we would be in their position."

So in February, 1865, while the Confederacy was already crumbling to dust, and Lee's surrender was only two months away, Lincoln proposed that the Federal Government pay the Southern States four hundred million dollars for their slaves; but every member of his Cabinet was unfriendly to the idea and he dropped it.

The following month, on the occasion of his second inauguration, Lincoln delivered a speech that the late Earl Curzon, Chancellor of Oxford University, declared to be "the purest gold of human eloquence, nay of eloquence almost divine."

Stepping forward and kissing a Bible open at the fifth chapter of Isaiah, he began an address that sounded like the speech of some great character in drama.

"It was like a sacred poem," wrote Carl Schurz. "No ruler had ever spoken words like these to his people. America had never before had a president who had found such words in the depths of his heart."

The closing words of this speech are, in the estimation of the writer, the most noble and beautiful utterances ever delivered by the lips of mortal man. He never reads them without thinking somehow of an organ playing in the subdued light of a great cathedral.

Fondly do we hope—fervently do we pray—that this mighty scourge of war may speedily pass away. Yet, if God wills that it continue until all the wealth piled by the bondman's two hundred and fifty years of unrequited toil shall be sunk, and until every drop of blood drawn with the lash shall be paid by another drawn with the sword, as was said three thousand years ago, so still it must be said, "The judgments of the Lord are true and righteous altogether."

With malice toward none; with charity for all; with firmness in the right, as God gives us to see the right, let us strive on to finish the work we are in; to bind up the nation's wounds; to care for him who shall have borne the battle, and for his widow, and his orphan—to do all which may achieve and cherish a just and lasting peace among ourselves, and with all nations.

Two months later, to a day, this speech was read at Lincoln's funeral services in Springfield.

★ ★ ★

26

★ ★ ★

In the latter part of March, 1865, something very significant happened in Richmond, Virginia. Mrs. Jefferson Davis, wife of the President of the Confederacy, disposed of her carriage horses, placed her personal effects on sale at a dry-goods store, packed up the remainder of her belongings, and headed farther south. . . . Something was about to happen.

Grant had been besieging the Confederate capital now for nine months. Lee's troops were ragged and hungry. Money was scarce, and they were rarely paid; and when they were, it was with the paper script of the Confederacy, which was almost worthless now. It took three dollars of it to buy a cup of coffee, five dollars to buy a stick of firewood, and a thousand dollars was demanded for a barrel of flour.

Secession was a lost cause. And so was slavery. Lee knew it. And his men knew it. A hundred thousand of them had already deserted. Whole regiments were packing up now and walking out together. Those that remained were turning to religion for solace and hope. Prayer-meetings were being held in almost every tent; men were shouting and weeping and seeing visions, and entire regiments were kneeling before going into battle.

But notwithstanding all this piety, Richmond was tottering to its fall.

On Sunday, April 2, Lee's army set fire to the cotton and tobacco warehouses in the town, burned the arsenal, destroyed the half-finished ships at the wharves, and fled from the city at night while towering flames were roaring up into the darkness.

They were no sooner out of town than Grant was in hot pursuit with seventy-two thousand men, banging away at the Confederates from both sides and the rear, while Sheridan's cavalry was heading them off in front, tearing up railway lines, and capturing supply-trains.

Sheridan telegraphed to headquarters, "I think if this thing is pushed, Lee will surrender."

Lincoln wired back, "Let the thing be pushed."

It was; and, after a running fight of eighty miles, Grant finally hemmed the Southern troops in on all sides. They were trapped, and Lee realized that further bloodshed would be futile.

In the meantime Grant, half blind with a violent sick headache, had fallen behind his army and halted at a farmhouse on Saturday evening.

"I spent the night," he records in his Memoirs, "in bathing my feet in hot water and mustard, and putting mustard plasters on my wrists and the back part of my neck, hoping to be cured by morning."

The next morning, he was cured instantaneously. And the thing that did it was not a mustard plaster, but a horseman galloping down the road with a letter from Lee, saying he wanted to surrender.

"When the officer [bearing the message] reached me," Grant wrote, "I was still suffering with the sick-headache, but the instant I saw the contents of the note, I was cured."

The two generals met that afternoon in a small bare parlor of a brick dwelling to arrange terms. Grant as usual was slouchily dressed: his shoes were grimy, he had no sword, and he wore the same uniform that every private in the army wore— except that his had three silver stars on the shoulder to show who he was.

What a contrast he made to the aristocratic Lee, wearing beaded gauntlets and a sword studded with jewels! Lee looked like some royal conqueror who had just stepped out of a steel engraving, while Grant looked more like a Missouri farmer who had come to town to sell a load of hogs and a few hides. For once Grant felt ashamed of his frowzy appearance, and he apologized to Lee for not being better dressed for the occasion.

Twenty years before, Grant and Lee had both been officers

in the regular army while the United States was waging a war against Mexico. So they fell to reminiscing now about the days of long ago, about the winter the "regulars" spent on the border of Mexico, about the poker games that used to last all night, about their amateur production of "Othello" when Grant played the sweetly feminine rôle of Desdemona.

"Our conversation grew so pleasant," Grant records, "that I almost forgot the object of our meeting."

Finally, Lee brought the conversation around to the terms of surrender; but Grant replied to that very briefly, and then his mind went rambling on again, back across two decades, to Corpus Christi and the winter in 1845 when the wolves howled on the prairies . . . and the sunlight danced on the waves . . . and wild horses could be bought for three dollars apiece.

Grant might have gone on like that all afternoon if Lee had not interrupted and reminded him, for the second time, that he had come there to surrender his army.

So Grant asked for pen and ink, and scrawled out the terms. There were to be no humiliating ceremonies of capitulation such as Washington had exacted from the British at Yorktown in 1781, with the helpless enemy parading without guns, between long lines of their exultant conquerors. And there was to be no vengeance. For four bloody years the radicals of the North had been demanding that Lee and the other West Point officers who had turned traitor to their flag be hanged for treason. But the terms that Grant wrote out had no sting. Lee's officers were permitted to keep their arms, and his men were to be paroled and sent home; and every soldier who claimed a horse or a mule could crawl on it and ride it back to his farm or cotton-patch and start tilling the soil once more.

Why were the terms of surrender so generous and gentle? Because Abraham Lincoln himself had dictated the terms.

And so the war that had killed half a million men came to a close in a tiny Virginia village called Appomattox Court House. The surrender took place on a peaceful spring afternoon when the scent of lilacs filled the air. It was Palm Sunday.

On that very afternoon Lincoln was sailing back to Washington on the good ship *River Queen*. He spent several hours reading Shakspere aloud to his friends. Presently he came to this passage in "Macbeth":

Duncan is in his grave;
After life's fitful fever he sleeps well;
Treason has done his worst: nor steel, nor poison,
Malice domestic, foreign levy, nothing,
Can touch him further.

These lines made a profound impression on Lincoln. He read them once, then paused, gazing with unseeing eyes through the port-hole of the ship.

Presently he read them aloud again.

Five days later Lincoln himself was dead.

★ ★ ★

27

★ ★ ★

We must retrace our steps now, for I want to tell you of an amazing thing that happened shortly before the fall of Richmond—an incident that gives one a vivid picture of the domestic miseries that Lincoln endured in silence for almost a quarter of a century.

It happened near Grant's headquarters. The general had invited Mr. and Mrs. Lincoln to spend a week with him near the front.

They were glad to come, for the President was almost exhausted. He hadn't had a vacation since he entered the White House, and he was eager to get away from the throng of office-seekers who were harassing him once more at the opening of his second term.

So he and Mrs. Lincoln boarded the *River Queen* and sailed away down the Potomac, through the lower reaches of Chesapeake Bay, past old Point Comfort, and up the James River to City Point. There, high on a bluff, two hundred feet above the water, sat the ex-hide-buyer from Galena, smoking and whittling.

A few days later the President's party was joined by a distinguished group of people from Washington, including M. Geoffroi, the French minister. Naturally the visitors were eager to see the battle lines of the Army of the Potomac, twelve miles away; so the next day they set out upon the excursion—the men on horseback, Mrs. Lincoln and Mrs. Grant following in a half-open carriage.

General Adam Badeau, Grant's military secretary and aide-de-camp and one of the closest friends General Grant ever had, was detailed to escort the ladies that day. He sat on the front seat of the carriage, facing them and with his back to the horses. He was an eye-witness to all that occurred, and I am quoting now from pages 356-362 of his book entitled "Grant in Peace":

In the course of conversation, I chanced to mention that all the wives of officers at the army front had been ordered to the rear—a sure sign that active operations were in contemplation. I said not a lady had been allowed to remain, except Mrs. Griffin, the wife of General Charles Griffin, who had obtained a special permit from the President.

At this Mrs. Lincoln was up in arms. "What do you mean by that, sir?" she exclaimed. "Do you mean to say that she saw the President alone? Do you know that I never allow the President to see any woman alone?"

She was absolutely jealous of poor, ugly Abraham Lincoln.

I tried to pacify her and to palliate my remark, but she was fairly boiling over with rage. "That's a very equivocal smile, sir," she exclaimed: "Let me out of this carriage at once. I will ask the President if he saw that woman alone."

Mrs. Griffin, afterward the Countess Esterhazy, was one of the best known and most elegant women in Washington, a Carroll, and a personal acquaintance of Mrs. Grant, who strove to mollify the excited spouse, but all in vain. Mrs. Lincoln again bade me stop the driver, and when I hesitated to obey, she thrust her arms past me to the front of the carriage and held the driver fast. But Mrs. Grant finally prevailed upon her to wait till the whole party alighted. . . .

At night, when we were back in camp, Mrs. Grant talked over the matter with me, and said the whole affair was so distressing and mortifying that neither of us must ever mention it; at least, I was to be absolutely silent, and she would disclose it only to the General. But the next day I was released from my pledge, for "worse remained behind."

The same party went in the morning to visit the Army of the James on the north side of the river, commanded by General Ord. The arrangements were somewhat similar to those of the day before. We went up the river in a steamer, and then the men again took horses and Mrs. Lincoln and Mrs. Grant proceeded in an ambulance. I was detailed as before to act as escort, but I asked for a companion in the duty; for after my experience, I did not wish to be the only officer in the carriage. So Colonel Horace Porter was ordered to join the party. Mrs. Ord accompanied her husband; as she was the wife of the commander of an army she was not subject to the order for return; though before that day was over she wished herself in Washington or anywhere else away from the army, I am sure. She was mounted, and as the ambulance was full, she remained on her horse and rode for a while by the side of the President, and thus preceded Mrs. Lincoln.

As soon as Mrs. Lincoln discovered this her rage was beyond all bounds. "What does the woman mean," she exclaimed, "by riding by the side of the President? and ahead of me? Does she suppose that he wants her by the side of him?"

She was in a frenzy of excitement, and language and action both became more extravagant every moment.

Mrs. Grant again endeavored to pacify her, but then Mrs. Lincoln got angry with Mrs. Grant; and all that Porter and I could do was to see that nothing worse than words occurred. We feared she might jump out of the vehicle and shout to the cavalcade.

Once she said to Mrs. Grant in her transports: "I suppose you think you'll get to the White House yourself, don't you?" Mrs. Grant was very calm and dignified, and merely replied that she was quite satisfied with her present position; it was far greater than she had ever expected to attain. But Mrs. Lincoln exclaimed; "Oh! you had better take it if you can get it. 'Tis very nice." Then she reverted to Mrs. Ord, while Mrs. Grant defended her friend at the risk of arousing greater vehemence.

When there was a halt, Major Seward, a nephew of the Secretary of State, and an officer of General Ord's staff, rode up, and tried to say something jocular. "The President's horse is very gallant, Mrs. Lincoln," he remarked; "he insists on riding by the side of Mrs. Ord."

This of course added fuel to the flame.

"What do you mean by that, sir?" she cried.

Seward discovered that he had made a huge mistake, and his horse at once developed a peculiarity that compelled him to ride behind, to get out of the way of the storm.

Finally the party arrived at its destination and Mrs. Ord came up to the ambulance. Then Mrs. Lincoln positively insulted her, called her vile names in the presence of a crowd of officers, and asked what she meant by following up the President. The poor woman burst into tears and inquired what she had done, but Mrs. Lincoln refused to be appeased, and stormed till she was tired. Mrs. Grant still tried to stand by her friend, and everybody was shocked and horrified. But all things come to an end, and after a while we returned to City Point.

That night the President and Mrs. Lincoln entertained General and Mrs. Grant and the General's staff at dinner on the steamer, and before us all Mrs. Lincoln berated General Ord to the President, and urged that he should be removed. He was unfit for his place, she said, to say nothing of his wife. General Grant sat next and defended his officer bravely. Of course General Ord was not removed.

During all this visit similar scenes were occurring. Mrs. Lincoln repeatedly attacked her husband in the presence of officers because of Mrs. Griffin and Mrs. Ord, and I never suffered greater humiliation and pain on account of one not a near personal friend than when I saw the Head of the State, the man who carried all the cares of the nation at such a crisis—subjected to this inexpressible public mortification. He bore it as Christ might have done; with an expression of pain and sadness that cut one to the heart, but with supreme calmness and dignity. He called her "mother," with his old-time plainness; he pleaded with eyes and tones, and endeavored to explain or palliate the offenses of others, till she turned on him like a tigress; and then he walked away, hiding that noble, ugly face that we might not catch the full expression of its misery.

General Sherman was a witness of some of these episodes and mentioned them in his memoirs many years ago.

Captain Barnes, of the navy, was a witness and a sufferer too. Barnes had accompanied Mrs. Ord on her unfortunate ride and refused afterward to say that the lady was to blame. Mrs. Lincoln never forgave him. A day or two afterward he went to speak to the President on some official matter when Mrs. Lincoln and several others were present. The President's wife said something to him unusually offensive that all the company could hear. Lincoln was silent, but after a moment he went up to the young officer, and taking him by the arm led him into his own cabin, to show him a map or a paper, he said. He made no remark, Barnes told me, upon what had occurred. He could not rebuke his wife; but he showed his regret, and his regard for the officer, with a touch of what seemed to me the most exquisite breeding imaginable.

Shortly before these occurrences Mrs. Stanton had visited City Point, and I chanced to ask her some question about the President's wife.

"I do not visit Mrs. Lincoln," was the reply.

But I thought I must have been mistaken; the wife of the Secretary of War must visit the wife of the President; and I renewed my inquiry.

"Understand me, sir?" she repeated; "I do not go to the White House; I do not visit Mrs. Lincoln." I was not at all intimate with Mrs. Stanton and this remark was so extraordinary that I never forgot it; but I understood it afterward.

Mrs. Lincoln continued her conduct toward Mrs. Grant, who strove to placate her and then Mrs. Lincoln became more outrageous still. She once rebuked Mrs. Grant for sitting in her presence. "How dare you be seated," she said, "until I invite you?"

Elizabeth Keckley, who accompanied Mrs. Lincoln on this trip to Grant's headquarters, tells of a dinner party that "Mrs. President" gave aboard the *River Queen.*

One of the guests was a young officer attached to the Sanitary Commission. He was seated near Mrs. Lincoln, and, by way of pleasantry, remarked: "Mrs. Lincoln, you should have seen the President the other day, on his triumphal entry into Richmond. He was the cynosure of all eyes. The ladies kissed their hands to him, and greeted him with the waving of handkerchiefs. He is quite a hero when surrounded by pretty young ladies."

The young officer suddenly paused with a look of embarrassment.

Mrs. Lincoln turned to him with flashing eyes, with the remark that his familiarity was offensive to her.

Quite a scene followed, and I do not think that the Captain who incurred Mrs. Lincoln's displeasure will ever forget that memorable evening.

"I never in my life saw a more peculiarly constituted woman," says Mrs. Keckley. "Search the world over and you will not find her counterpart."

"Ask the first American you meet, 'What kind of a woman was Lincoln's wife?' " says Honoré Willsie Morrow in her book "Mary Todd Lincoln," "and the chances are ninety nine to one hundred that he'll reply that she was a shrew, a curse to her husband, a vulgar fool, insane."

The great tragedy of Lincoln's life was not his assassination, but his marriage.

When Booth fired, Lincoln did not know what had hit him, but for twenty-three years he had reaped almost daily what Herndon described as "the bitter harvest of conjugal infelicity."

"Amid storms of party hate and rebellious strife," says General Badeau, "amid agonies . . . like those of the Cross . . . the hyssop of domestic misery was pressed to Lincoln's lips, and he too said: 'Father, forgive: they know not what they do.' "

One of Lincoln's warmest friends during his life as President was Orville H. Browning, Senator from Illinois. These two men had known each other for a quarter of a century, and Browning was frequently a dinner guest in the White House and sometimes spent the night there. He kept a detailed diary, but one can only wonder what he recorded in it about Mrs. Lincoln, for authors have not been permitted to read the manuscript without pledging their honor not to divulge anything derogatory to her character. This manuscript was recently sold for publication with the provision that all shocking statements regarding Mrs. Lincoln should be deleted before it was put into print.

At public receptions in the White House it had always been customary for the President to choose some lady other than his wife to lead the promenade with him.

But custom or no custom, tradition or no tradition, Mrs.

Lincoln wouldn't tolerate it. What? Another woman ahead of her? And on the President's arm? Never!

So she had her way, and Washington society hooted.

She not only refused to let the President walk with another woman, but she eyed him jealously and criticized him severely for even talking to one.

Before going to a public reception Lincoln would come to his jealous wife, asking whom he might talk to. She would mention woman after woman, saying she detested this one and hated that one.

"But Mother," he would remonstrate, "I must talk with somebody. I can't stand around like a simpleton and say nothing. If you will not tell me who I may talk with, please tell me who I may *not* talk with."

She determined to have her own way, cost what it might, and, on one occasion, she threatened to throw herself down in the mud in front of every one unless Lincoln promoted a certain officer.

At another time she dashed into his office during an important interview, pouring out a torrent of words. Without replying to her, Lincoln calmly arose, picked her up, carried her out of the room, set her down, returned, locked the door, and went on with his business as if he had never been interrupted.

She consulted a spiritualist, who told her that all of Lincoln's Cabinet were his enemies.

That didn't surprise her. She had no love for any of them.

She despised Seward, calling him "a hypocrite," "an abolition sneak," saying that he couldn't be trusted, and warning Lincoln to have nothing to do with him.

"Her hostility to Chase," says Mrs. Keckley, "was bitter."

And one of the reasons was this: Chase had a daughter, Kate, who was married to a wealthy man and was one of the most beautiful and charming women in Washington society. Kate would attend the White House receptions; and, to Mrs. Lincoln's immense disgust, she would draw all the men about her and run away with the show.

Mrs. Keckley says that "Mrs. Lincoln, who was jealous of the popularity of others, had no desire to build up the social position of Chase's daughter through political favor to her father."

With heat and temper, she repeatedly urged Lincoln to dismiss Chase from the Cabinet.

She loathed Stanton, and when he criticized her, she "would return the compliment by sending him books and clippings describing him as an irascible and disagreeable personality."

To all these bitter condemnations, Lincoln would say:

"Mother, you are mistaken; your prejudices are so violent you do not stop to reason. If I listened to you, I should soon be without a cabinet."

She disliked Andrew Johnson intensely; she hated McClellan; she despised Grant, calling him "an obstinate fool and a butcher," declaring that she could handle an army better than he could, and frequently vowing that if he were ever made President, she would leave the country and never come back to it as long as he was in the White House.

"Well, Mother," Lincoln would say, "supposing that we give you command of the army. No doubt you would do much better than any general that has been tried."

After Lee surrendered, Mr. and Mrs. Grant came to Washington. The town was a blaze of light: crowds were making merry with songs and bonfires and revelry; so Mrs. Lincoln wrote the general, inviting him to drive about the streets with her and the President "to see the illumination."

But she did not invite Mrs. Grant.

A few nights later, however, she arranged a theater party and invited Mr. and Mrs. Grant and Mr. and Mrs. Stanton to sit in the President's box.

As soon as Mrs. Stanton received the invitation, she hurried over to Mrs. Grant, to inquire if she were going.

"Unless you accept the invitation," said Mrs. Stanton, "I shall refuse. I will not sit in the box with Mrs. Lincoln unless you are there too."

Mrs. Grant was afraid to accept.

She knew that if the general entered the box, the audience would be sure to greet the "hero of Appomattox" with a salvo of applause.

And then what would Mrs. Lincoln do? There was no telling. She might create another disgraceful and mortifying scene.

Mrs. Grant refused the invitation, and so did Mrs. Stanton; and by refusing, they may have saved the lives of their husbands, for that night Booth crept into the President's box and shot Lincoln; and if Stanton and Grant had been there, he might have tried to kill them also.

★ ★ ★

28

★ ★ ★

In 1863 a group of Virginia slave barons formed and financed a secret society the object of which was the assassination of Abraham Lincoln; and in December, 1864, an advertisement appeared in a newspaper published in Selma, Alabama, begging for public subscriptions for a fund to be used for the same purpose, while other Southern journals offered cash rewards for his death.

But the man who finally shot Lincoln was actuated neither by patriotic desires nor commercial motives. John Wilkes Booth did it to win fame.

What manner of man was Booth? He was an actor, and nature had endowed him with an extraordinary amount of charm and personal magnetism. Lincoln's own secretaries described him as "handsome as Endymion on Latmos, the pet of his little world." Francis Wilson, in his biography of Booth, declares that "he was one of the world's successful lovers. . . . Women halted in the streets and instinctively turned to admire him as he passed."

By the time he was twenty-three, Booth had achieved the status of a matinée idol; and, naturally, his most famous rôle was Romeo. Wherever he played, amorous maidens deluged him with saccharine notes. While he was playing in Boston huge crowds of women thronged the streets in front of the Tremont House, eager to catch but one glimpse of their hero as he passed. One night a jealous actress, Henrietta Irving, knifed him in a hotel room, and then tried to commit suicide; and the morning after Booth shot Lincoln, another of his sweethearts, Ella Turner, an inmate of a Washington "parlor house," was so distressed to learn that her lover had turned murderer and fled the city, that she clasped his picture to her heart, took chloroform, and lay down to die.

But did this flood of female adulation bring happiness to Booth? Very little, for his triumphs were confined almost wholly to the less discriminating audiences of the hinterland, while there was gnawing at his heart a passionate ambition to win the plaudits of the metropolitan centers.

But New York critics thought poorly of him, and in Philadelphia he was hooted off the stage.

This was galling, for other members of the Booth family were famous on the stage. For well-nigh a third of a century, his father, Junius Brutus Booth, had been a theatrical star of the first magnitude. His Shakesperian interpretations were the talk of the nation. No one else in the history of the American stage had ever won such extraordinary popularity. And the old man Booth had reared his favorite son, John Wilkes, to believe that he was to be the greatest of the Booths.

But the truth is that John Wilkes Booth possessed very little talent, and he didn't make the most of the trifling amount he did have. He was good-looking and spoiled and lazy, and he refused to bore himself with study. Instead, he spent his youthful days on horseback, dashing through the woods of the Maryland farm, spouting heroic speeches to the trees and squirrels, and jabbing the air with an old army lance that had been used in the Mexican War.

Old Junius Brutus Booth never permitted meat to be served at the family table, and he taught his sons that it was wrong to kill any living thing—even a rattlesnake. But John Wilkes evidently was not seriously restrained by his father's philosophy. He liked to shoot and destroy. Sometimes he banged away with his gun at the cats and hound dogs belonging to the slaves, and once he killed a sow owned by a neighbor.

Later he became an oyster pirate in Chesapeake Bay, then an actor. Now, at twenty-six, he was a favorite of gushing high-school girls, but, in his own eyes, he was a failure. And besides, he was bitterly jealous, for he saw his elder brother, Edwin, achieving the very renown that he himself so passionately desired.

He brooded over this a long time, and finally decided to make himself forever famous in one night.

This was his first plan: He would follow Lincoln to the theater some night; and, while one of his confederates turned off the gas-lights, Booth would dash into the President's box, rope and tie him, toss him onto the stage below, hustle him through a back exit, pitch him into a carriage, and scurry away like mad in the darkness.

By hard driving, he could reach the sleepy old town of Port Tobacco before dawn. Then he would row across the broad Potomac, and gallop on south through Virginia until he had lodged the Commander-in-Chief of the Union Army safely behind the Confederate bayonets in Richmond.

And then what?

Well, then the South could dictate terms and bring the war to an end at once.

And the credit for this brilliant achievement would go to whom? To the dazzling genius John Wilkes Booth. He would become twice as famous, a hundred times as famous as his brother Edwin. He would be crowned in history with the aura of a William Tell. Such were his dreams.

He was making twenty thousand dollars a year then in the theater, but he gave it all up. Money meant little to him now, for he was playing for something far more important than material possessions. So he used his savings to finance a band of Confederates that he fished out of the backwash of Southern sympathizers floating around Baltimore and Washington. Booth promised each one of them that he should be rich and famous.

And what a motley crew they were! There was Spangler, a drunken stage-hand and crab-fisherman; Atzerodt, an ignorant house-painter and blockade-runner with stringy hair and whiskers, a rough, fierce fellow; Arnold, a lazy farm-hand and a deserter from the Confederate Army; O'Laughlin, a livery-stable worker, smelling of horses and whisky; Surratt, a swaggering nincompoop of a clerk; Powell, a gigantic penniless brute, the wild-eyed, half-mad son of a Baptist preacher; Herold, a silly, giggling loafer, lounging about stables, talking horses and women, and living on the dimes and quarters given him by his widowed mother and his seven sisters.

With this supporting cast of tenth-raters, Booth was preparing to play the great rôle of his career. He spared neither time nor money in planning the minutest details. He purchased a pair of handcuffs, arranged for relays of fast horses at the proper places, bought three boats, and had them waiting in Port Tobacco Creek, equipped with oars and rowers ready to man them at a moment's notice.

Finally, in January, 1865, he believed that the great moment had come. Lincoln was to attend Ford's Theater on the eighteenth of that month, to see Edwin Forrest play "Jack Cade." So the rumor ran about town. And Booth heard it. So he was on hand that night with his ropes and hopes—and what happened? Nothing. Lincoln didn't appear.

Two months later it was reported that Lincoln was going to drive out of the city on a certain afternoon to attend a theatrical performance in a near-by soldiers' encampment. So Booth and his accomplices, mounted on horses and armed with bowie-knives and revolvers, hid in a stretch of woods that the President would have to pass. But when the White House carriage rolled by, Lincoln was not in it.

Thwarted again, Booth stormed about, cursing, pulling at his raven-black mustache, and striking his boots with his riding-whip. He had had enough of this. He was not going to be frustrated any longer. If he couldn't capture Lincoln, by God, he could kill him.

A few weeks later Lee surrendered and ended the war, and Booth saw then that there was no longer any point in kidnapping the President; so he determined to shoot Lincoln at once.

Booth did not have to wait long. The following Friday he had a hair-cut, and then went to Ford's Theater to get his mail. There he learned that a box had been reserved for the President for that night's performance.

"What!" Booth exclaimed. "Is that old scoundrel going to be here to-night?"

Stage-hands were already making ready for a gala performance, draping the left-hand box with flags against a background of lace, decorating it with a picture of Washington, removing the partition, doubling the space, lining it with crimson paper and putting in an unusually large walnut rocking-chair to accommodate the President's long legs.

Booth bribed a stage-hand to place the chair in the precise position that he desired; he wanted it in the angle of the box nearest the audience, so that no one would see him enter. Through the inner door, immediately behind the rocker, he bored a small peep-hole; then dug a notch in the plastering behind the door leading from the dress-circle to the boxes, so that he could bar that entrance with a wooden plank. After that Booth went to his hotel and wrote a long letter to the editor of the "National Intelligencer," justifying the plotted assassination in the name of patriotism, and declaring that posterity would honor him. He signed it and gave it to an actor, instructing him to have it published the next day.

Then he went to a livery-stable, hired a small bay mare that he boasted could run "like a cat," and rounded up his assistants and put them on horses; gave Atzerodt a gun, and told him to shoot the Vice-President; and handed a pistol and knife to Powell, ordering him to murder Seward.

It was Good Friday, ordinarily one of the worst nights of the year for the theater, but the town was thronged with officers and enlisted men eager to see the Commander-in-Chief of the Army, and the city was still jubilant, celebrating the end of the war. Triumphal arches still spanned Pennsylvania Avenue, and the streets were gay with dancing torch-light processions, shouting with high elation to the President as he drove by that night to the theater. When he arrived at Ford's the house was packed to capacity and hundreds were being turned away.

The President's party entered during the middle of the first act, at precisely twenty minutes to nine. The players paused and bowed. The brilliantly attired audience roared its welcome. The orchestra crashed into "Hail to the Chief." Lincoln bowed his acknowledgment, parted his coat-tails, and sat down in a walnut rocking-chair upholstered in red.

On Mrs. Lincoln's right sat her guests: Major Rathbone of the Provost-Marshal General's office and his fiancée, Miss Clara H. Harris, the daughter of Senator Ira Harris of New York, blue-bloods high enough in Washington society to meet the fastidious requirements of their Kentucky hostess.

Laura Keene was giving her final performance of the celebrated comedy "Our American Cousin." It was a gay and joyous occasion; and sparkling laughter rippled back and forth across the audience.

Lincoln had taken a long drive in the afternoon, with his wife; she remarked afterward that he had been happier that day than she had seen him in years. Why shouldn't he be? Peace. Victory. Union. Freedom. He had talked to Mary that afternoon about what they would do when they left the White House at the close of his second term. First, they would take a long rest in either Europe or California; and when they returned, he might open a law office in Chicago, or drift back to Springfield and spend his remaining years riding over the prairie circuit that he loved so well. Some old friends that he had known in Illinois had called at the White House, that same afternoon, and he had been so elated telling jokes that Mrs. Lincoln could hardly get him to dinner.

The night before, he had had a strange dream. He had told the members of his Cabinet about it that morning: "I seemed to be in a singular and indescribable vessel," he said, "that was moving with great rapidity toward a dark and indefinite shore. I have had this extraordinary dream before great events, before victories. I had it preceding Antietam, Stone River, Gettysburg, Vicksburg."

He believed that this dream was a good omen, that it foretold good news, that something beautiful was going to happen.

At ten minutes past ten Booth, inflamed with whisky, and dressed in dark riding-breeches, boots, and spurs, entered the theater for the last time in his life—and noted the position of the President. With a black slouch hat in his hand, he mounted the stairs leading to the dress-circle, and edged his way down an aisle choked with chairs, until he came to the corridor leading to the boxes.

Halted by one of the President's guards, Booth handed him his personal card with confidence and bravado, saying that the President wished to see him; and, without waiting for permission, pushed in and closed the corridor door behind him, wedging it shut with a wooden upright from a music-stand.

Peeping through the gimlet-hole that he had bored in the door behind the President, he gaged the distance, and quietly swung the door open. Shoving the muzzle of his high-calibered derringer close to his victim's head, he pulled the trigger and quickly leaped to the stage below.

Lincoln's head fell forward and then sidewise as he slumped in his chair.

He uttered no sound whatever.

For an instant the audience thought that the pistol-shot and the leap to the stage were a part of the play. No one, not even the actors themselves, suspected that the President had been harmed.

Then a woman's shriek pierced the theater and all eyes turned to the draped box. Major Rathbone, blood gushing from one arm, shouted: "Stop that man! Stop him! He has killed the President!"

A moment of silence. A wisp of smoke floating out of the Presidential box. Then the suspense broke. Terror and mad excitement seized the audience. They burst through the seats, wrenching the chairs from the floor, broke over railings, and, trying to clamber upon the stage, tore one another down and trampled upon the old and feeble. Bones were broken in the crush, women screamed and fainted, and shrieks of agony mingled with fierce yells of "Hang him!" . . . "Shoot him!" . . . "Burn the theater!"

Some one shouted that the playhouse itself was to be bombed. The fury of the panic doubled and trebled. A company of frantic soldiers dashed into the theater at double-quick, and charged the audience with muskets and fixed bayonets, shouting: "Get out of here! Damn you, get out!"

Physicians from the audience examined the President's wound; and, knowing it to be fatal, refused to have the dying man jolted over the cobblestones back to the White House. So four soldiers lifted him up—two at his shoulders and two at his feet—and carried his long, sagging body out of the theater and into the street, where blood dripping from his wound reddened the pavement. Men knelt to stain their handkerchiefs with it—handkerchiefs which they would treasure a lifetime, and, dying, bequeath as priceless legacies to their children.

With flashing sabers and rearing horses, the cavalry cleared a space; and loving hands bore the stricken President across the street to a cheap lodging-house owned by a tailor, stretched his long frame diagonally across a sagging bed far too short for him, and pulled the bed over to a dismal gas-jet that flickered yellow light.

It was a hall room nine by seventeen feet in size, with a cheap reproduction of Rosa Bonheur's painting of "The Horse Fair" hanging above the bed.

The news of the tragedy swept over Washington like a tornado; and, racing in its wake, came the impact of another disaster: at the same hour of the attack on Lincoln, Secretary Seward had been stabbed in bed and was not expected to live. Out of these black facts, fearsome rumors shot through the night like chain-lightning: Vice-President Johnson had been slain.

Stanton had been assassinated. Grant shot. So ran the wild tales.

People were sure now that Lee's surrender had been a ruse, that the Confederates had treacherously crept into Washington and were trying to wipe out the Government with one blow, that the Southern legions had sprung to arms again, that the war, bloodier than ever, was starting once more.

Mysterious messengers dashed through the residence districts, striking the pavement two short staccato raps, thrice repeated—the danger-call of a secret society, the Union League. Awakened by the summons, members grasped their rifles and rushed wildly into the street.

Mobs with torches and ropes boiled through the town, howling: "Burn the theater!" . . . "Hang the traitor!" . . . "Kill the rebels!"

It was one of the maddest nights this nation has ever known!

The telegraph flashed the news, setting the nation on fire. Southern sympathizers and copperheads were ridden on rails and tarred and feathered; the skulls of some were crushed with paving-stones. Photograph galleries in Baltimore were stormed and wrecked because they were believed to contain pictures of Booth; and a Maryland editor was shot because he had published some scurrilous abuse of Lincoln.

With the President dying; with Johnson, the Vice-President, sprawled on his bed stone-drunk and his hair matted with mud; with Seward, Secretary of State, stabbed to the verge of death, the reins of power were grasped immediately by Edward M. Stanton, the gruff, erratic, and tempestuous Secretary of War.

Believing that all high officers of the Government were marked for slaughter, Stanton, in wild excitement, dashed off order after order, writing them on the top of his silk hat as he sat by the bedside of his dying chief. He commanded guards to protect his house and the residences of his colleagues; he confiscated Ford's Theater and arrested every one connected with it; he declared Washington to be in a state of siege; he called out the entire military and police force of the District of Columbia, all the soldiers in the surrounding camps, barracks, and fortifications, the Secret Service men of the United States, the spies attached to the Bureau of Military Justice; he threw pickets around the entire city, fifty feet apart; he set a watch at every ferry, and ordered tugs, steamers, and gunboats to patrol the Potomac.

Stanton wired the chief of police in New York to rush him

his best detectives, telegraphed orders to watch the Canadian border, and commanded the President of the Baltimore and Ohio Railway to intercept General Grant in Philadelphia and bring him back to Washington at once, running a pilot locomotive ahead of his train.

He poured a brigade of infantry into lower Maryland, and sent a thousand cavalrymen galloping after the assassin, saying over and over: "He will try to get South. Guard the Potomac from the city down."

The bullet that Booth fired pierced Lincoln's head below the left ear, plowed diagonally through the brain, and lodged within half an inch of the right eye. A man of lesser vitality would have been cut down instantly; but for nine hours Lincoln lived, groaning heavily.

Mrs. Lincoln was kept in an adjoining room; but every hour she would insist on being brought to his bedside, weeping and shrieking, "O my God, have I given my husband to die?"

Once as she was caressing his face and pressing her wet cheek against his, he suddenly began groaning and breathing louder than ever. Screaming, the distraught wife sprang back and fell to the floor in a faint.

Stanton, hearing the commotion, rushed into the room, shouting, "Take that woman away, and don't let her in here again."

Shortly after seven o'clock the groaning ceased and Lincoln's breathing became quiet. "A look of unspeakable peace," wrote one of his secretaries who was there, "came over his worn features."

Sometimes recognition and understanding flash back into the secret chambers of consciousness immediately before dissolution.

In those last peaceful moments broken fragments of happy memories may have floated brightly through the deep hidden caverns of his mind—vanished visions of the long ago: a log fire blazing at night in front of the open shed in the Buckhorn Valley of Indiana; the roar of the Sangamon plunging over the mill-dam at New Salem; Ann Rutledge singing at the spinning-wheel; Old Buck nickering for his corn; Orlando Kellogg telling the story of the stuttering justice; and the law office at Springfield with the ink-stain on the wall and garden seeds sprouting on top of the bookcase. . . .

Throughout the long hours of the death-struggle Dr. Leale,

an army surgeon, sat by the President's bedside holding his hand. At twenty-two minutes past seven the doctor folded Lincoln's pulseless arms, put half-dollars on his eyelids to hold them shut, and tied up his jaw with a pocket handkerchief. A clergyman offered a prayer. Cold rain pattered down on the roof. General Barnes drew a sheet over the face of the dead President; and Stanton, weeping and pulling down the window-shades to shut out the light of the dawn, uttered the only memorable sentence of that night: "Now he belongs to the ages."

The next day little Tad asked a caller at the White House if his father was in heaven.

"I have no doubt of it," came the reply.

"Then I am glad he has gone," said Tad, "for he was never happy after he came here. This was not a good place for him."

★

PART FOUR

★

★ ★ ★
29
★ ★ ★

The FUNERAL TRAIN bearing Lincoln's body back to Illinois crawled through vast crowds of mourning people. The train itself was smothered in crêpe; and the engine, like a hearse-horse, was covered with a huge black blanket trimmed with silver stars.

As it steamed northward faces began to appear beside the track—faces that rapidly multiplied in numbers and increased in sadness.

For miles before the train reached the Philadelphia station it ran between solid walls of humanity, and when it rolled into the city thousands of people were milling and jamming through the streets. Mourners stood in lines three miles long, stretching away from Independence Hall. They edged forward, inch by inch, for ten hours in order to look down at last upon Lincoln's face for but one second. On Saturday at midnight the doors were closed, but the mourners, refusing to be dispersed, kept their places all night long and by three o'clock Sunday morning the crowds were greater than ever and boys were selling their places in line for ten dollars.

Soldiers and mounted police fought to keep traffic lanes open, while hundreds of women fainted, and veterans who had fought at Gettysburg collapsed as they struggled to keep order.

For twenty-four hours before the funeral services were scheduled to take place in New York excursion trains running day and night poured into that city the greatest crowds it had ever known—crowds that filled the hotels and overflowed into private homes and backwashed across the parks and onto steamboat piers.

The next day sixteen white horses, ridden by Negroes, pulled the hearse up Broadway, while women, frantic with grief, tossed flowers in its path. Behind came the tramp, tramp, tramp of marching feet—a hundred and sixty thousand mourners with swaying banners bearing quotations like these: "Ah, the pity of it, Iago—the pity of it!" . . . "Be still, and know that I am God."

Half a million spectators fought and trampled upon one another in an effort to view the long procession. Second-story windows facing Broadway were rented for forty dollars each, and window-panes were removed in order that the openings might accommodate as many heads as possible.

Choirs robed in white sang hymns on street corners, marching bands wailed their dirges, and at intervals of sixty seconds the roar of a hundred cannon reverberated over the town.

As the crowds sobbed by the bier in City Hall, New York, many spoke to the dead man, some tried to touch his face; and, while the guard was not looking, one woman bent over and kissed the corpse.

When the casket was closed in New York, at noon on Tuesday, thousands who had been unable to view the remains hurried to the trains and sped westward to other points where the funeral car was scheduled to stop. From now on until it reached Springfield the funeral train was seldom out of the sound of tolling bells and booming guns. By day it ran under arches of evergreens and flowers and past hillsides covered with children waving flags; by night its passing was illumined by countless torches and flaming bonfires stretching half-way across the continent.

The country was in a frenzy of excitement. No such funeral had ever before been witnessed, in all history. Weak minds here and there snapped under the strain. A young man in New York slashed his throat with a razor, crying, "I am going to join Abraham Lincoln."

Forty-eight hours after the assassination a committee from Springfield had hurried to Washington, pleading with Mrs. Lincoln to have her husband buried in his home town. At first, she was sharply opposed to the suggestion. She had hardly a friend left in Springfield, and she knew it. True, she had three sisters living there, but she thoroughly disliked two of them and despised the third one, and she felt nothing but contempt for the rest of the gossiping little village.

"My God, Elizabeth!" she said to her colored dressmaker, "I can never go back to Springfield."

So she planned to have Lincoln interred in Chicago or placed under the dome of the National Capitol, in the tomb originally constructed for George Washington.

However, after seven days of pleading, she consented to have the body taken back to Springfield. The town raised a public fund, bought a beautiful tract of land consisting of four city blocks—now occupied by the State Capitol—and set men digging day and night.

Finally, on the morning of May 4, the funeral train was in town, the tomb was ready, and thousands of Lincoln's old friends had forgathered for the services, when Mrs. Lincoln, in a sudden rage of erratic temper, countermanded all plans and haughtily decreed that the body must be interred, not where the tomb had been built, but in the Oak Ridge Cemetery, two miles out in the woods.

There were to be no *ifs* or *ands* or *buts* about it. If she did not have her way, she threatened to use "violent" means to carry the remains back to Washington. Why? For a very unlovely reason: the tomb that had been erected in the middle of Springfield stood on what was known as the "Mather block," and Mrs. Lincoln despised the Mather family. Years before, one of the Mathers had, in some way, aroused her fiery wrath; and now, even in the hushed presence of death, she still cherished her bitter resentment, and would not consent to let Lincoln's body lie for one single night on ground that had been contaminated by the Mathers.

For a quarter of a century this woman had lived under the same roof with a husband who had had "malice toward none," and "charity for all." But like the Bourbon kings of France, she had learned nothing, she had forgotten nothing.

Springfield had to bow to the widow's mandate; and so at eleven o'clock the remains were taken out to a public vault in Oak Ridge Cemetery. Fighting Joe Hooker rode ahead of the hearse; and behind it was led Old Buck, covered with a red, white, and blue blanket on which were embroidered the words, "Old Abe's Horse."

By the time Old Buck got back to his stable, there was not a shred of the blanket left; souvenir-hunters had stripped him bare. And, like buzzards, they swooped down upon the empty hearse, snatching at the draperies and fighting over it until soldiers charged them with bayonets.

For five weeks after the assassination Mrs. Lincoln lay weeping in the White House, refusing to leave her chamber night or day.

Elizabeth Keckley, who was at her bedside during all this time, wrote:

> I shall never forget the scene. The wails of a broken heart, the unearthly shrieks, the terrible convulsions, the wild, tempestuous outbursts of grief from the soul. I bathed Mrs. Lincoln's head with cold water, and soothed the terrible tornado as best I could.
>
> Tad's grief at his father's death was as great as the grief of his mother, but her terrible outbursts awed the boy into silence. . . .
>
> Often at night, when Tad would hear her sobbing, he would get up, and come to her bed in his white sleeping-clothes: "Don't cry, Mamma; I can't sleep if you cry! Papa was good, and he has gone to Heaven. He is happy there. He is with God and brother Willie. Don't cry, Mamma, or I will cry too."

30

THE INSTANT that Booth fired at Lincoln, Major Rathbone, who was sitting in the box with the President, leaped up and grabbed the assassin. But he couldn't hold him, for Booth slashed at him desperately with a bowie-knife, cutting deep gashes in the major's arm. Tearing himself from Major Rathbone's grasp, Booth sprang over the railing of the box and leaped to the stage floor, twelve feet below. But, as he jumped, he caught his spur in the folds of the flag that draped the President's box, fell awkwardly, and broke the small bone in his left leg.

A spasm of pain shot through him. He did not wince or hesitate. He was acting now the supreme rôle of his career: this was the scene that was to make his name immortal.

Quickly recovering himself, he brandished his dagger, shouted the motto of Virginia, *Sic semper tyrannis*—"Thus ever to tyrants"—plunged across the stage, knifed a musician who accidentally got in his way, floored an actress, darted out at the back door, jumped upon his waiting horse, raised the butt of his revolver and knocked down the boy, "Peanut John," who was holding the animal, and spurred madly down the street, the steel shoes from his little horse striking fire from the cobblestones in the night.

For two miles he raced on through the city, passing the Capitol grounds. As the moon rose above the tree-tops he galloped on to the Anacostia bridge. There Sergeant Cobb, the Union sentry, dashed out with rifle and bayonet, demanding:

221

"Who are you? And why are you out so late? Don't you know it is against the rules to let any one pass after nine o'clock?"

Booth, strange to relate, confessed his real name, saying that he lived in Charles County, and, being in town on business, he had waited for the moon to come up and light him home.

That sounded plausible enough; and, anyway, the war was over, so why make a fuss? Sergeant Cobb lowered his rifle and let the rider pass.

A few minutes later Davy Herold, one of Booth's confederates, hurried across the Anacostia bridge with a similar explanation, joined Booth at their rendezvous, and the two of them raced on through the shadows of lower Maryland, dreaming of the wild acclaim that was sure to be theirs in Dixie.

At midnight they halted in front of a friendly tavern in Surrattville; watered their panting horses; called for the field-glasses, guns, and ammunition that had been left there that afternoon by Mrs. Surratt; drank a dollar's worth of whisky; then, boasting that they had shot Lincoln, spurred on into the darkness.

Originally they had planned to ride from here straight for the Potomac, expecting to reach the river early the next morning and row across at once to Virginia. That sounded easy, and they might have done it and never have been captured at all, except for one thing. They could not foresee Booth's broken leg.

But, despite the pain, Booth galloped on that night with Spartan fortitude—galloped on, although the broken, jagged bone was, as he recorded in his diary, "tearing the flesh at every jump" of his horse. Finally when he could endure the punishment no longer, he and Herold swung their horses off to the left, and shortly before daybreak on Saturday morning reined up in front of the house of a country physician named Mudd—Dr. Samuel A. Mudd—who lived twenty miles southeast of Washington.

Booth was so weak and he was suffering so intensely that he couldn't dismount alone. He had to be lifted out of his saddle and carried groaning to an unstairs bedroom. There were no telegraph lines or railways in this isolated region; so none of the natives had yet learned of the assassination. Hence, the doctor suspected nothing. How had Booth come to break his leg? That was simple as Booth explained it—his horse had fallen on him. Dr. Mudd did for Booth what he would have done for any other suffering man; he cut away the boot from the left leg, set the fractured bone, tied it up with pasteboard splints made from a hat-box, fashioned a rude crutch for the cripple, and gave him a shoe to travel with.

Booth slept all that day at Dr. Mudd's house, but as twilight drew on he edged out of the bed painfully. Refusing to eat anything, he shaved off his handsome mustache, threw a long gray shawl around his shoulders so that the end of it would cover the telltale initials tattooed upon his right hand, disguised himself with a set of false whiskers, and paid the doctor twenty-five dollars in greenbacks. Then once more he and Herold mounted their horses and headed for the river of their hopes.

But directly across their path lay the great Zekiah Swamp, a huge bog matted with brush and dogwood, oozy with mud and slimy with stagnant pools—the home of lizards and snakes. In the darkness the two riders missed their way and for hours wandered about, lost.

Late in the night they were rescued by a negro, Oswald Swann. The pain in Booth's leg was so excruciating now that he couldn't sit astride his horse; so he gave Swann seven dollars to haul him the rest of the night in his wagon, and as dawn was breaking on Easter Sunday the driver halted his white mules before "Rich Hill," the home of a wealthy, well-known Confederate, Captain Cox.

Thus ended the first lap of Booth's futile race for life.

Booth told Captain Cox who he was and what he had done; and, to prove his identity, he showed his initials tattooed in India ink on his hand.

He implored Captain Cox, in the name of his mother, not to betray him, pleading that he was sick and crippled and suffering, and declaring that he had done what he thought was best for the South.

Booth was in such a condition now that he couldn't travel any farther, either on horseback or by wagon; so Captain Cox hid the two fugitives in a thicket of pines near his house. The place was more than a thicket, it was a veritable jungle densely undergrown with laurel and holly; and there, for the next six days and five nights, the fugitives waited for Booth's wounded leg to improve enough to permit them to continue their flight.

Captain Cox had a foster-brother, Thomas A. Jones. Jones was a slave-owner, and for years he had been an active agent of the Confederate Government, ferrying fugitives and contraband mail across the Potomac. Captain Cox urged Jones to look after Herold and Booth; so every morning he brought them food

in a basket. Knowing that each wood-path was being searched
and that spies were everywhere, he called his hogs as he carried
the basket and pretended to be feeding his live stock.

Booth, hungry as he was for food, was hungrier still for information. He kept begging Jones to tell him the news, to let
him know how the nation was applauding his act.

Jones brought him newspapers, and Booth devoured them
eagerly, searching in vain, however, for the burst of acclaim he
had coveted so passionately. He found in them only disillusion
and heartbreak.

For more than thirty hours he had been racing toward Virginia, braving the tortures of the flesh. But, violent as they had
been, they were easy to endure compared with the mental anguish that he suffered now. The fury of the North—that was
nothing, he had expected that. But when the Virginia papers
showed that the South—*his South*—had turned upon him, con-
demning and disowning him, he was frantic with disappointment
and despair. He, who had dreamed of being honored as a second Brutus and glorified as a modern William Tell, now found
himself denounced as a coward, a fool, a hireling, a cutthroat.

These attacks stung him like the sting of an adder. They
were bitter as death.

But did he blame himself? No. Far from it. He blamed everybody else—everybody except himself and God. He had been
merely an instrument in the hands of the Almighty. That was
his defense. He had been divinely appointed to shoot Abraham
Lincoln, and his only mistake had been in serving a people "too
degenerate" to appreciate him. That was the phrase he set down
in his diary—"too degenerate."

"If the world knew my heart," he wrote, "that one blow
would have made me great, though I did not desire greatness.
. . . I have too great a soul to die like a criminal."

Lying there, shivering under a horse-blanket, on the damp
ground near Zekiah Swamp, he poured out his aching heart in
tragic bombast:

> Wet, cold and starving, with every man's hand against
> me, I am here in despair, and why? For doing what Brutus
> was honored for—for what made Tell a hero. I have
> stricken down a greater tyrant than they ever knew, and
> I am looked upon as a common cut-throat; yet my action
> was purer than either of theirs. . . . I hoped for no gain.

. . . I think I have done well, I do not repent the blow
I struck.

As Booth lay there writing, three thousand detectives and ten
thousand cavalrymen were scouring every nook and corner of
southern Maryland, searching houses, exploring caves, ransack-
ing buildings, and fine-tooth-combing even the slimy bogs of
Zekiah Swamp, determined to hunt Booth down and bring him
in, dead or alive, and claim the various rewards—approximat-
ing a hundred thousand dollars, offered for his capture. Sometimes he could hear the cavalry who were hunting him, galloping
by on a public road only two hundred yards away.

At times he could hear their horses neighing and whinnying
and calling to one another. Suppose his and Herold's horses
should answer them. That would probably mean capture. So
that night Herold led their horses down into Zekiah Swamp and
shot them.

Two days later buzzards appeared! Specks in the sky at first,
they winged closer and closer, finally wheeling and soaring and
soaring and wheeling directly above the dead animals. Booth
was frightened. The buzzards might attract the attention of the
pursuers, who would almost certainly recognize the body of
his bay mare.

Besides, he had decided that he must somehow get to another
doctor.

So the next night, Friday, April 21—one week after the assassination—he was lifted from the ground and put astride a
horse belonging to Thomas A. Jones, and once more he and
Herold set out for the Potomac.

The night was ideal for their purposes: dense with a misty
fog, and so dark that the men literally had to feel for one
another in the inky blackness.

Jones, faithful dog that he was, piloted them from their
hiding-place to the river, stealing through open fields, over a
public highway, and across a farm. Realizing that soldiers and
Secret Service men were swarming everywhere, Jones would
steal ahead fifty yards at a time, stop, listen, and give a low
whistle. Then Booth and Herold would advance to him.

In that way, slowly, startled by the slightest noise, they traveled for hours, reaching at last the steep and crooked path that
led from the bluff down to the river. A stiff wind had been
blowing that day; and, through the darkness, they could hear

the mournful sound of the water pounding on the sand below.

For almost a week the Union soldiers had been riding up and down the Potomac, destroying every boat on the Maryland shore. But Jones had outwitted them: he had had his colored man, Henry Rowland, using the boat to fish for shad every day, and had had it hidden in Dent's meadow every night.

So when the fugitives reached the water's edge this evening everything was in readiness. Booth whispered his thanks to Jones, paid him seventeen dollars for his boat and a bottle of whisky, climbed in, and headed for a spot on the Virginia shore five miles away.

All through the foggy, ink-black night Herold pulled at the oars while Booth sat in the stern, trying to navigate with compass and candle.

But they hadn't gone far when they struck a flood-tide which is very strong at this point, owing to the narrowness of the channel. It swept them up the river for miles, and they lost their bearings in the fog. After dodging the Federal gunboats that were patrolling the Potomac, they found themselves, at dawn, ten miles up the river, but not one foot nearer to the Virginia shore than they had been the night before.

So they hid all that day in the swamps of Nanjemoy Cove; and the next night, wet and hungry, they pulled across the river; and Booth exclaimed: "I am safe at last, thank God, in glorious old Virginia."

Hurrying to the home of Dr. Richard Stewart, who was an agent for the Confederate Government and the richest man in King George County, Virginia, Booth expected to be welcomed as the saviour of the South. But the doctor had already been arrested several times for aiding the Confederacy, and, now that the war was over, he wasn't going to risk his neck by helping the man who had killed Lincoln. He was too shrewd for that. So he wouldn't let Booth even enter his house. He did give the fugitives a little food, grudgingly, but he made them eat it in the barn, and then sent them to sleep that night with a family of negroes.

And even the negroes didn't want Booth. He had to frighten them into letting him stay with them.

And this in Virginia!

In Virginia, mind you, where he had confidently expected the very hills to reverberate with the lusty cheers that would greet the mere mention of his name.

The end was drawing near now. It came three days later. Booth had not gotten far. He had ferried across the Rappahannock at Port Royal, in the company of three Confederate cavalrymen returning from the war, had ridden one of their horses three miles farther South, and, with their help, had then palmed himself off on a farmer, saying that his name was Boyd and that he had been wounded in Lee's army near Richmond.

And so for the next two days, Booth stayed at the Garrett farm-house, sunning himself on the lawn, suffering from his wound, consulting an old map, studying a route to the Rio Grande, and making notes of the road to Mexico.

The first evening he was there, while he sat at the supper table, Garrett's young daughter began babbling about the news of the assassination, which she had just heard through a neighbor. She talked on and on, wondering who had done it and how much the assassin had been paid for it.

"In my opinion," Booth suddenly remarked, "he wasn't paid a cent, but did it for the sake of notoriety."

The next afternoon, April 25, Booth and Herold were stretched out under the locust trees in the Garrett yard, when suddenly Major Ruggles, one of the Confederate cavalrymen who had helped them across the Rappahannock, dashed up and shouted: "The Yanks are crossing the river. Take care of yourself."

They scurried away to the woods, but when darkness fell they stole back to the house.

To Garrett, that looked suspicious. He wanted to get rid of his mysterious "guests" at once. Was it because he suspected that they might have shot Lincoln? No, he never even thought of that. He imagined they were horse-thieves. When they said at the supper table that they wanted to buy two horses, his suspicions grew, and when bedtime came, and the fugitives, thinking of their safety, refused to go upstairs and insisted on sleeping under the porch or in the barn—then all doubt was removed.

Garrett was positive now that they were horse-thieves. So he put them in an old tobacco warehouse that was being used then for storing hay and furniture—put them in and locked them in with a padlock. And finally, as a double precaution, the old farmer sent his two sons, William and Henry, tiptoeing out in the darkness with blankets, to spend the night in an adjoining corn-crib, where they could watch and see that no horses were whisked away during the night.

The Garrett family went to bed, that memorable evening, half expecting a little excitement.

And they got it before morning.

For two days and nights, a troop of Union soldiers had been hot on the trail of Booth and Herold, picking up clue after clue, talking to an old negro who had seen them crossing the Potomac, and finding Rollins, the colored ferryman who had poled them across the Rappahannock in a scow. This ferryman told them that the Confederate soldier who had given Booth a lift on his horse as they rode away from the river was Captain Willie Jett, and that the captain had a sweetheart who lived in Bowling Green, twelve miles away. Perhaps he had gone there.

That sounded likely enough, so the troopers climbed quickly into their saddles and spurred on in the moonlight toward Bowling Green. Arriving there at midnight, they thundered into the house, found Captain Jett, jerked him out of his bed, thrust a revolver against his ribs, and demanded:

"Where is Booth? Damn your soul, where did you hide him? Tell us or we'll blow your heart out."

Jett saddled his pony, and led the Northern men back to the Garrett farm.

The night was black, the moon having gone down, and there were no stars. For nine miles the dust rose in choking clouds under the galloping feet of the horses. Soldiers rode one on each side of Jett, with the reins of his horse tied to their saddles, so that he couldn't escape in the dark.

At half-past three in the morning the troopers arrived in front of the worn old whitewashed Garrett house.

Quickly, quietly, they surrounded the house and trained their guns on every door and window. Their leader banged on the porch with his pistol butt, demanding admittance.

Presently Richard Garrett, candle in hand, unbolted the door, while the dogs barked furiously, and the wind whipped the tail of his night-shirt against his trembling legs.

Quickly Lieutenant Baker grabbed him by the throat, thrusting a pistol to his head and demanding that he hand over Booth.

The old man, tongue-tied with terror, swore that the strangers were not in the house, that they had gone to the woods.

That was a lie, and it sounded like it; so the troopers jerked him out of the doorway, dangled a rope in his face, and threatened to string him up at once to a locust tree in the yard.

At that instant one of the Garrett boys who had been sleeping in the corn-crib ran up to the house and told the truth. With a rush the troopers encircled the tobacco barn.

There was a lot of talk before the shooting started. For fifteen or twenty minutes the Northern officers argued with Booth, urging him to surrender. He shouted back that he was a cripple, and asked them to "give a lame man a show," offering to come out and fight the entire squad one by one, if they would withdraw a hundred yards.

Herold lost his courage and wanted to surrender. Booth was disgusted.

"You damned coward," he shouted, "get out of here. I don't want you to stay."

And out Herold went, his arms in front of him, ready to be handcuffed, while he pleaded for mercy, declaring from time to time that he liked Mr. Lincoln's jokes, and swearing that he had had no part in the asassination.

Colonel Conger tied him to a tree and threatened to gag him unless he ceased his silly whimpering.

But Booth would not surrender. He felt that he was acting for posterity. He shouted to his pursuers that the word "surrender" was not in his vocabulary, and he warned them to prepare a stretcher for him as they put "one more stain on the glorious old banner."

Colonel Conger resolved to smoke him out, and ordered one of the Garrett boys to pile dry brush against the barn. Booth saw the boy doing it, and cursed him and threatened to put a bullet through him if he didn't stop. He did stop, but Colonel Conger slipped around to a corner of the barn in the rear, pulled a wisp of hay through a crack, and lighted it with a match.

The barn had originally been built for tobacco, with spacings four inches wide left to let in the air. Through these spacings the troopers saw Booth pick up a table to fight the mounting fire—an actor in the limelight for the last time, a tragedian playing the closing scene of his farewell performance.

Strict orders had been given to take Booth alive. The Government didn't want him shot. It wanted to have a big trial and then hang him.

And possibly he might have been taken alive had it not been for a half-cracked sergeant—"Boston" Corbett, a religious fanatic.

Every one had been warned repeatedly not to shoot without

orders. Corbett afterward declared that he had had orders—orders direct from God Almighty.

Through the wide cracks of the burning barn, "Boston" saw Booth throw away his crutch, drop his carbine, raise his revolver, and spring for the door.

"Boston" was positive that he would shoot his way out and make a last, desperate dash for liberty, firing as he ran.

So, to prevent any futile bloodshed, Corbett stepped forward, rested his pistol across his arm, took aim through a crack, prayed for Booth's soul, and pulled the trigger.

At the crack of the pistol Booth shouted, leaped a foot in the air, plunged forward, and fell face down on the hay, mortally wounded.

The roaring flames were moving rapidly now across the dry hay. Lieutenant Baker, eager to get the dying wretch out of the place before he was roasted, rushed into the flaming building and leaped upon him, wrenching his revolver from his clenched fist and pinioning his arms to his side for fear that he might merely be feigning death.

Quickly Booth was carried to the porch of the farmhouse, and a soldier mounted a horse and spurred down the dusty road three miles to Port Royal for a physician.

Mrs. Garrett had a sister, Miss Halloway, who was boarding with her and teaching school. When Miss Halloway realized that the dying man there under the honeysuckle vine on the porch was the romantic actor and great lover, John Wilkes Booth, she said he must be cared for tenderly, and she had a mattress hauled out for him to lie upon; and then she brought out her own pillow, put it under his head, and, taking his head upon her lap, offered him wine. But his throat seemed paralyzed, and he couldn't swallow. Then she dipped her handkerchief in water and moistened his lips and tongue time after time, and massaged his temples and forehead.

The dying man struggled on for two and a half hours, suffering intensely; begging to be turned on his face, his side, his back; coughing and urging Colonel Conger to press his hands down hard upon his throat; and crying out in his agony: "Kill me! Kill me!"

Pleading to have a last message sent to his mother, he whispered haltingly:

"Tell her . . . I did . . . what I thought . . . was best . . . and that I died . . . for my country."

As the end drew near, he asked to have his hands raised so he could look at them; but they were totally paralyzed, and he muttered:

"Useless! Useless!"

They were his last words.

He died just as the sun was rising above the tops of the venerable locust trees in the Garrett yard. His "jaw drew spasmodically and obliquely downward, his eyeballs rolled toward his feet and began to swell . . . and with a sort of gurgle, and sudden check, he stretched his feet and threw back his head." It was the end.

It was seven o'clock. He had died within twenty-two minutes of the time of day Lincoln had died; and "Boston" Corbett's bullet had struck Booth in the back of the head, about an inch below the spot where he himself had wounded Lincoln.

The doctor cut off a curl of Booth's hair, and gave it to Miss Halloway. She kept the lock of hair and the bloody pillow-slip on which his head had lain—kept them and cherished them until, finally, in later years, poverty overtook her and she was obliged to trade half of the stained pillow-slip for a barrel of flour.

★ ★ ★

31

★ ★ ★

Booth had hardly ceased breathing before the detectives were kneeling to search him. They found a pipe, a bowie-knife, two revolvers, a diary, a compass greasy with candle drippings, a draft on a Canadian bank for about three hundred dollars, a diamond pin, a nail file, and the photographs of five beautiful women who had adored him. Four were actresses: Effie Germon, Alice Grey, Helen Western, and "Pretty Fay Brown." The fifth was a Washington society woman, whose name has been withheld out of respect for her descendants.

Then Colonel Doherty jerked a saddle-blanket off a horse, borrowed a needle from Mrs. Garrett, sewed the corpse up in the blanket, and gave an old Negro, Ned Freeman, two dollars to haul the body to the Potomac, where a ship was waiting.

On page 505 of his book entitled the "History of the United States Secret Service" Lieutenant La Fayette C. Baker tells the story of that trip to the river:

When the wagon started, Booth's wound, now scarcely dribbling, began to run anew. Blood fell through the crack of the wagon, and fell dripping upon the axle, and spotting the road with terrible wafers. It stained the planks and soaked the blankets . . . and all the way blood dribbled from the corpse in a slow, incessant, sanguine exudation.

In the midst of all this an unexpected thing happened. Ned Freeman's old wagon, according to Baker, was "a very shaky and absurd" contraption "which rattled like approaching dissolution." It not only "rattled like approaching dissolution," but under the strain and speed of the trip, the rickety old wagon actually began to dissolve there on the roadway. A king-bolt snapped, the wagon pulled apart, the front wheels tore away from the hind ones, the front end of the box fell to the ground with a thud, and Booth's body lurched "forward as if in a last effort to escape."

Lieutenant Baker abandoned the rickety old death-car, commandeered another wagon from a neighboring farmer, pitched Booth's body into that, hurried on to the river, and stowed the corpse aboard a government tug, the *John S. Ide,* which chugged away with it to Washington.

At dawn the next morning the news spread through the city: Booth had been shot. His body was lying that very minute on the gunboat *Montauk,* riding at anchor in the Potomac.

The capital was thrilled, and thousands hurried down to the river, staring in grim fascination at the death-ship.

In the middle of the afternoon Colonel Baker, chief of the Secret Service, rushed to Stanton with the news that he had caught a group of civilians on board the *Montauk,* in direct violation of orders, and that one of them, a woman, had cut off a lock of Booth's hair.

Stanton was alarmed. "Every one of Booth's hairs," he cried, "will be cherished as a relic by the rebels."

He feared that they might become far more than mere relics. Stanton firmly believed that the assassination of Lincoln was part of a sinister plot conceived and directed by Jefferson Davis and the leaders of the Confederacy. And he feared that they might capture Booth's body and use it in a crusade to fire the Southern slaveholders to spring to their rifles once more and begin the war all over again.

He decreed that Booth must be buried with all possible haste, and buried secretly; he must be hidden away and blotted out of existence, with no trinket, no shred of his garments, no lock of his hair, nothing left for the Confederates to use in a crusade.

Stanton issued his orders; and that evening, as the sun sank behind a fiery bank of clouds, two men—Colonel Baker and his cousin, Lieutenant Baker—stepped into a skiff, pulled over to the *Montauk,* boarded her, and did three things in plain sight of the gaping throng on the shore:

First, they lowered Booth's body, now incased in a pine gun-box, over the side of the ship and down into the skiff; next, they lowered a huge ball and heavy chain; then they climbed in themselves, shoved off, and drifted downstream.

The curious crowd on the shore did precisely what the detectives had expected them to do: they raced along the bank, shoving, splashing, talking excitedly, determined to watch the funeral ship and see where the body was sunk.

For two miles they kept even with the drifting detectives. Then darkness crept up the river, clouds blotted out the moon and the stars, and even the sharpest eyes could no longer make out the tiny skiff in midstream.

By the time the detectives reached Geeseborough Point, one of the loneliest spots on the Potomac, Colonel Baker was sure that they were completely hidden from view; so he headed the skiff into the great swamp that begins there—a malodorous spot, rank with rushes and slough weeds, a burial-ground where the army cast its condemned horses and dead mules.

Here, in this eerie morass, the two detectives waited for hours, listening to find out if they had been followed; but the only sounds they could hear were the cry of bullfrogs and the ripple of the water among the sedges.

Midnight came; and, with breathless quiet and the utmost caution, the two men rowed stealthily back up-stream, fearing to whisper, and dreading even the lisping of the oars and the lapping of the water at the gunwales.

They finally reached the walls of the old penitentiary, rowed to a spot where a hole had been chopped in the solid masonry near the water's edge to let them in. Giving the countersign to the officer who challenged them, they handed over a white pine casket with the name "John Wilkes Booth" printed on the lid; and, half an hour later, it was buried in a shallow hole in the southwest corner of a large room in the government arsenal where ammunition was stored. The top of the grave was carefully smoothed over, so that it looked like the rest of the dirt floor.

By sunrise the next morning excited men with grappling-hooks were dragging the Potomac, and raking and prodding among the carcasses of dead mules in the great swamp behind Geeseborough Point.

All over the nation millions were asking what had been done with Booth's body. Only eight men knew the answer—eight loyal men who were sworn never to disclose the secret.

In the midst of all this mystery, wild rumors sprang into existence and newspapers broadcast them over the land. Booth's head and heart had been deposited in the Army Medical Museum at Washington—so said the "Boston Advertiser." Other papers stated that the corpse had been buried at sea. Still others declared it had been burned; and a weekly magazine published an "eye-witness" sketch, showing it being sunk in the Potomac at midnight.

Out of the welter of contradiction and confusion another rumor arose: the soldiers had shot the wrong man, and Booth had escaped.

Probably this rumor arose because Booth dead looked so different from Booth alive. One of the men Stanton ordered to go aboard the gunboat *Montauk* on April 27, 1865, and identify the body, was Dr. John Frederick May, an eminent physician of Washington. Dr. May said that when the tarpaulin that covered the remains was removed—

> to my great astonishment, there was revealed a body in whose lineaments there was to me no resemblance to the man I had known in life. My surprise was so great that I at once said to General Barnes: "There is no resemblance in that corpse to Booth, nor can I believe it to be that of him." . . . It being afterwards, by my request, placed in a sitting position, standing and looking down upon it, I was finally enabled to imperfectly recognize the features of Booth. But never in a human being had a greater change taken place, from the man whom I had seen in the vigor of life and health, than in that of the haggard corpse which was before me, with its yellow and discolored skin, its unkempt and matted hair, and its whole facial expression sunken and sharpened by the exposure and starvation it had undergone.

Other men who saw the corpse did not recognize Booth even "imperfectly," and they told their doubts about the city. And the rumor traveled fast.

Matters were not helped by the secrecy with which the Government guarded the body, the speed and mystery of its burial, and Stanton's refusal to give out any information or to deny ugly tales.

The "Constitutional Union," a paper published in the capital, said the entire performance was a hoax. Other papers joined in the cry. "We know Booth escaped," echoed the "Richmond Examiner." The "Louisville Journal" openly contended that there had been something rotten in the whole show, and that "Baker and his associates had wilfully conspired to swindle the United States Treasury."

The battle raged bitterly; and, as usual in such cases, witnesses sprang up by the hundreds, declaring that they had met Booth and talked to him long after the shooting affray at the Garrett barn. He had been seen here, there, and everywhere: fleeing to Canada, dashing into Mexico, traveling on ships bound for South America, hurrying to Europe, preaching in Virginia, hiding on an island in the Orient.

And so was born the most popular and persistent and mysterious myth in American history. It has lived and thrived for almost three quarters of a century; and, to this day, thousands of people believe it—many of them people of unusual intelligence.

There are even some learned men of the colleges who profess to believe the myth. One of the most prominent churchmen in this country has gone up and down the land, declaring in his lectures to hundreds of audiences that Booth escaped. The author, while writing this chapter, was solemnly informed by a scientifically trained man that Booth had gone free.

Of course, Booth was killed. There can be no doubt of it. The man who was shot in Garrett's tobacco barn used every argument he could think of to save his life; and he had a splendid imagination; but, in his most desperate moments, it never occurred to him to deny that he was John Wilkes Booth. That was too absurd, too fantastic, to try even in the face of death.

And to make doubly sure that it was Booth who had been killed, Stanton sent ten men to identify the corpse after it reached Washington. One, as we have already recorded, was Dr. May. He had cut "a large fibroid tumor" from Booth's neck, and the wound in healing had left "a large and ugly scar." Dr. May, who identified him by that scar says:

> From the body which was produced by the captors, nearly every vestige of resemblance of the living man had disappeared. But the mark made by the scalpel during life remained indelible in death, and settled beyond all ques-

tion at the time, and all cavil in the future, the identity of the man who had assassinated the President.

Dr. Merrill, a dentist, identified the body by a filling he had recently put into one of Booth's teeth.

Charles Dawson, a clerk in the National Hotel, where Booth had stopped, identified the dead man by the initials "J. W. B." tattooed on Booth's right hand.

Gardner, the well-known Washington photographer, identified him; and so did Henry Clay Ford, one of Booth's most intimate friends.

When Booth's body was dug up by order of President Andrew Johnson, on February 15, 1869, it was identified again by Booth's close friends.

Then it was taken to Baltimore to be reburied in the Booth family plot in Greenmount Cemetery; but before it was reburied, it was identified again by Booth's brother and mother, and friends who had known him all his life.

It is doubtful whether any other man who ever lived has been as carefully identified in death as Booth was.

And yet the false legend lives on. During the eighties, many people believed that the Rev. J. G. Armstrong of Richmond, Virginia, was Booth in disguise, for Armstrong had coal-black eyes, a lame leg, dramatic ways, and wore his raven hair long to hide a scar on the back of his neck—so people said.

And other "Booths" arose, no less than twenty of them.

In 1872 a "John Wilkes Booth" gave dramatic readings and sleight-of-hand performances before the students of the University of Tennessee; married a widow; tired of her; whispered that he was the real assassin; and, stating that he was going to New Orleans to get a fortune that awaited him, he disappeared, and "Mrs. Booth" never heard of him again.

In the late seventies a drunken saloon-keeper with the asthma, at Granbury, Texas, confessed to a young lawyer named Bates that he was Booth, showed an ugly scar on the back of his neck, and related in detail how Vice-President Johnson had persuaded him to kill Lincoln and promised him a pardon if he should ever be caught.

A quarter of a century passed; and, on January 13, 1903, a drunken house-painter and dope-fiend, David E. George, killed himself with strychnine in the Grand Avenue Hotel in Enid, Oklahoma. But before he destroyed himself, he "confessed" that he was John Wilkes Booth. He declared that after he shot Lincoln, his friends had hidden him in a trunk and got him aboard a ship bound for Europe, where he lived for ten years.

Bates, the lawyer, read about this in the papers, rushed to Oklahoma, looked at the body, and declared that David E. George was none other than the asthmatic saloon-keeper of Granbury, Texas, who had confessed to him twenty-five years before.

Bates had the undertaker comb the corpse's hair just as Booth had worn his; wept over the remains; had the body embalmed; took it back to his home in Memphis, Tennessee, and kept it in his stable for twenty years, while trying to palm it off on the Government and claim the huge reward that had been offered—and paid—for the capture of Booth.

In 1908 Bates wrote a preposterous book entitled: "The Escape and Suicide of John Wilkes Booth, or the First True Account of Lincoln's Assassination, Containing a Complete Confession by Booth, Many Years after His Crime." He sold seventy thousand copies of his sensational paper-back volume; created a considerable stir; offered his mummified "Booth" to Henry Ford for one thousand dollars; and finally began exhibiting it in side-shows throughout the South, at ten cents a look.

Five different skulls are now being exhibited in carnivals and tents as the skull of Booth.

★ ★ ★

32

★ ★ ★

Aꜰᴛᴇʀ ꜱʜᴇ ʟᴇꜰᴛ the White House Mrs. Lincoln got into serious difficulties, and made an exhibition of herself that became national gossip.

In matters of household expense she was excessively penurious. It had long been customary for the Presidents to give a number of state dinners each season. But Mrs. Lincoln argued her husband into breaking the tradition, saying that these dinners were "very costly"; that these were war-times and public receptions would be more "economical."

Lincoln had to remind her once that "we must think of something besides economy."

When it came, however, to buying things that appealed to her vanity—such as dresses and jewelry—she not only forgot economy, but seemed bereft of all reason and indulged in a fantastic orgy of spending.

In 1861 she had come off the prairie, confidently expecting that as "Mrs. President" she would be the center of the glittering constellation of Washington society. But to her amazement and humiliation she found herself snubbed and ostracized by the haughty aristocrats of that Southern city. In their eyes, she, a Kentuckian, had been untrue to the South: she had married a crude, awkward "nigger-lover" who was making war upon them.

Besides, she had almost no likable personal qualities. She was, it must be admitted, a mean, common, envious, affected, mannerless virago.

Unable to attain social popularity herself, she was bitterly jealous of those who had achieved it. The then reigning queen of Washington society was the renowned beauty Adèle Cutts Douglas, the woman who had married Mrs. Lincoln's former sweetheart, Stephen A. Douglas. The glamorous popularity of Mrs. Douglas and Salmon P. Chase's daughter, inflamed Mrs. Lincoln with envy, and she resolved to win social victories with money—money spent on clothes and jewelry for herself.

"To keep up appearances," she told Elizabeth Keckley, "I must have money, more money than Mr. Lincoln can spare me. He is too honest to make a penny outside of his salary; consequently, I had, and still have, no alternative but to run in debt."

In debt she plunged, to the extent of seventy thousand dollars! A staggering sum when we remember that Lincoln's salary as President was only twenty-five thousand, and that it would have taken every penny of his income for over two years and nine months to pay for her finery alone.

I have quoted several times from Elizabeth Keckley. She was an unusually intelligent negro woman who had bought her freedom and come to Washington to set up a dress-making shop. Within a short time she had the patronage of some of the capital's leading social figures.

From 1861 to 1865 she was with Mrs. Lincoln almost daily in the White House, making dresses and serving her as a personal maid. She finally became not only Mrs. Lincoln's confidante and adviser, but her most intimate friend. The night that Lincoln lay dying, the only person Mrs. Lincoln kept calling for was Elizabeth Keckley.

Fortunately for history, Mrs. Keckley wrote a book about her experiences. It has been out of print for half a century, but dilapidated copies can be purchased now and then from rare-book dealers for ten or twenty dollars. The title is rather long: "Behind the Scenes, by Elizabeth Keckley, Formerly a Slave, but More Recently Modiste and Friend to Mrs. Abraham Lincoln: Or Thirty Years a Slave and Four Years in the White House."

Elizabeth Keckley records that in the summer of 1864, when Lincoln was running for a second term, "Mrs. Lincoln was almost crazy with fear and anxiety."

Why? One of her New York creditors had threatened to sue her; and the possibility that Lincoln's political enemies might get wind of her debts and use them as political thunder in the bitter campaign, drove her almost to distraction.

"If he is reëlected, I can keep him in ignorance of my affairs; but if he is defeated, then the bills will be sent in, and he will know all," she sobbed hysterically.

"I could go down on my knees," she cried to Lincoln "and plead for votes for you."

"Mary," he remonstrated, "I am afraid you will be punished for this overwhelming anxiety. If I am to be elected, it will be all right; if not, you must bear the disappointment."

"And does Mr. Lincoln suspect how much you owe?" inquired Mrs. Keckley.

And here was Mrs. Lincoln's answer, as reported on page 150 of "Behind the Scenes":

"God, no!—this was a favorite expression of hers [Mrs. Lincoln's]—and I would not have him suspect. If he knew that his wife was involved to the extent that she is, the knowledge would drive him mad."

"The only happy feature of Lincoln's assassination," says Mrs. Keckley, "was that he died in ignorance of these debts."

He hadn't been in his grave a week before Mrs. Lincoln was trying to sell his shirts with his initials marked on them, offering them at a shop on Pennsylvania Avenue.

Seward, hearing about it, went, with a heavy heart, and bought up the lot himself.

When Mrs. Lincoln left the White House, she took with her a score of trunks and half a hundred packing-boxes.

That created a good deal of nasty talk.

She had already been repeatedly and publicly accused of swindling the United States Treasury by falsifying an expense-account for the entertainment of Prince Napoleon, and her enemies pointed out that though she had come to the Executive Mansion with only a few trunks, she was now leaving it with a whole car-load of stuff. . . . Why? . . . Was she looting the place? Had she stripped it bare of everything she could?

Even as late as October 6, 1867—almost two and a half years after she left Washington—the "Cleveland Herald," speaking of Mrs. Lincoln, said:

"Let the country know that it required one hundred thousand dollars to make good the spoliation at the White House, and let it be proved who had the benefit of such plundering."

True, a great many things were stolen from the White House during the reign of the "rosy empress," but the fault was hardly hers. She made mistakes, of course: one of the first things she did was to discharge the steward and a number of the other employees, saying she was going to superintend the place herself, and put it on an economical basis.

She tried it, and the servants purloined almost everything except the door-knobs and the kitchen stove. The "Washington Star" for March 9, 1861, records that many of the guests who attended the first White House reception lost their overcoats and evening wraps. It wasn't long before even the White House furnishings were being carted away.

Fifty packing-boxes and a score of trunks! What was in them? Trash, for the most part: useless gifts, statuary, worthless pictures and books, wax wreaths, deer-heads, and a lot of old clothes and hats hopelessly outmoded—things she had worn back in Springfield years before.

"She had a passion," says Mrs. Keckley, "for hoarding old things."

While she was packing, her son Robert, recently graduated from Harvard, advised her to put a match to the old trumpery. When she scorned the idea, he said:

"I hope to heaven that the car that carries these boxes to Chicago catches fire and burns up all your old plunder."

The morning Mrs. Lincoln drove away from the White House, "there was scarcely a friend to tell her good-by," records Mrs. Keckley. "The silence was almost painful."

Even Andrew Johnson, the new President, failed to bid her farewell. In fact, he never even wrote her a line of sympathy after the assassination. He knew that she despised him, and he reciprocated her feelings.

Absurd as it seems now in the light of history, Mrs. Lincoln firmly believed then that Andrew Johnson had been back of the plot to assassinate Lincoln.

With her two sons, Tad and Robert, Lincoln's widow traveled to Chicago, stopped for a week at the Tremont House, found it too expensive, and moved to some "small, plainly-furnished" rooms at a summer resort called Hyde Park.

Sobbing because she couldn't afford better living quarters, she refused to see or even correspond with any of her former friends or relatives, and settled down to teaching Tad to spell.

Tad had been his father's favorite. His real name was Thomas, but Lincoln had nicknamed him "Tad" or "Tadpole" because as a baby he had had an abnormally large head.

Tad usually slept with his father. The child would lie around the office in the White House until he fell asleep, and then the President would shoulder him and carry him off to bed. Tad had always suffered from a slight impediment in his speech, and his father humored him; and, so with the ingenuity of a bright boy, he used his handicap as a foil to ward off attempts to educate him. He was now twelve years old, but he could neither read nor write.

Mrs. Keckley records that during his first spelling lesson, Tad spent ten minutes arguing that "a-p-e" spelled *monkey.* The word was illustrated with a small woodcut of what he believed to be a monkey, and it required the combined efforts of three people to convince him that he was wrong.

Mrs. Lincoln used every means in her power to persuade Congress to give her the hundred thousand dollars that Lincoln would have been paid had he lived out his second term. When Congress refused she was vitriolic in her denunciation of the "fiends" who had blocked her plans with "their infamous and villainous falsehoods."

"The father of wickedness and lies," she said, "will get these hoary-headed sinners when they pass away."

Congress did finally give her twenty-two thousand—approximately the amount that would have been due Lincoln had he served the rest of that year. With this she bought and furnished a marble-front house in Chicago.

Two years elapsed, however, before Lincoln's estate was settled; and, during that time, her expenses mounted and her creditors howled. Presently she had to take in roomers; then boarders; and at last she was obliged to give up her home and move into a boarding-house, herself.

Her exchequer became more and more depleted, until, in September, 1867, she was, as she phrased it, "pressed in a most startling manner for means of subsistence."

So she packed up a lot of her old clothes and laces and jewelry, and, with her face hidden under a heavy crêpe veil, she rushed to New York incognita, registered as a "Mrs. Clark," met Mrs. Keckley there, gathered up an armful of worn dresses, got into a carriage, drove over to the second-hand clothing dealers on Seventh Avenue, and tried to sell her wardrobe. But the prices offered were disappointingly low.

She next tried the firm of Brady & Keyes, diamond brokers, at 609 Broadway. Listening with amazement to her story, they said:

"Now listen, put your affairs in our hands, and we will raise a hundred thousand dollars for you in a few weeks."

That sounded rosy; so she wrote, at their request, two or three letters, telling of her dire poverty.

Keyes flaunted these letters in the face of the Republican leaders, threatening to publish them unless he got cash.

But the only thing he got from these men was their opinion of Mrs. Lincoln.

Then she urged Brady & Keyes to mail a hundred and fifty thousand circulars, appealing to the generosity of people everywhere for aid; but it was well-nigh impossible to get prominent men to sign the letter.

Boiling now with wrath at the Republicans, she turned for help to Lincoln's enemies. The New York "World" was a Democratic paper that had once been suspended by government order, and its editor arrested because of its violent attacks on Lincoln. Through its columns Mrs. Lincoln pleaded poverty, admitting that she was trying to sell not only her old clothes, but even such trifles as "a parasol cover" and "two dress patterns."

It was just before a state election; so the Democratic "World" printed a letter from her, fiercely denouncing such Republicans as Thurlow Weed, William H. Seward, and Henry J. Raymond of the "New York Times."

With its tongue in its cheek, "The World" solemnly invited its Democratic readers to send in cash contributions to care for the abandoned and suffering widow of the first Republican President. There were few contributions.

Next she tried to get the colored people to raise money for her, urging Mrs. Keckley to throw her heart and soul into the undertaking, and promising that if the Negroes raised twenty-five thousand dollars Mrs. Keckley would get a "cut" of three hundred dollars a year during Mrs. Lincoln's life, and all of the twenty-five thousand dollars at Mrs. Lincoln's death.

Then Brady & Keyes advertised a sale of her clothes and jewelry. Crowds thronged to their store, handling the dresses, criticizing them, declaring that they were out of style, that they were absurdly high-priced, that they were "worn" and "jagged under the arms and at the bottom of the skirts," and had "stains on the lining."

Brady & Keyes also opened a subscription-book at their store, hoping that if the sightseers would not buy they might donate money for Mrs. Lincoln.

Finally in despair, the merchants took her clothes and jewels to Providence, Rhode Island, intending to set up an exhibition and charge twenty-five cents admission. The city authorities wouldn't hear of it.

Brady & Keyes did finally sell eight hundred and twenty-four dollars' worth of her effects, but they charged eight hundred and twenty dollars for their services and expenses.

Mrs. Lincoln's campaign to raise money for herself not only failed, it also brought upon her a storm of public condemnation. Throughout the campaign she made a disgraceful exhibition of herself—and so did the public.

She "has dishonored herself, her country and the memory of her late lamented husband," cried the Albany "Journal."

She was a liar and a thief—such was the accusation brought against her by Thurlow Weed in a letter to the "Commercial Advertiser."

For years, back in Illinois, she had been "a terror to the village of Springfield," her "eccentricities were common talk," and "the patient Mr. Lincoln was a second Socrates within his own dwelling"—so thundered the "Hartford Evening Press." But the "Journal" of Springfield stated editorially that for years it had been known that she was deranged, and that she should be pitied for all her strange acts.

"That dreadful woman, Mrs. Lincoln," complained the Springfield, Massachusetts, "Republican," "insists on thrusting her repugnant personality before the world to the great mortification of the nation."

Mortified by these attacks, Mrs. Lincoln poured out her broken heart in a letter to Mrs. Keckley:

> Robert came up last evening like a maniac and almost threatening his life, looking like death because the letters of "The World" were published in yesterday's paper. . . .
> I weep whilst I am writing. I pray for death this morning. Only my darling Taddie prevents my taking my life.

Estranged now from her sisters and kindred, she finally broke even with Robert, defying and maligning him so bitterly that certain passages of her letters had to be deleted before publication.

When Mrs. Lincoln was forty-nine years old, she wrote the Negro dressmaker: "I feel as if I had not a friend in the world save yourself."

No other man in United States history has been so respected and loved as Abraham Lincoln; and possibly no other woman in United States history has been so fiercely denounced as his wife.

Less than a month after Mrs. Lincoln had tried to sell her old clothes, Lincoln's estate was settled. It amounted to $110,-295, and was divided equally among Mrs. Lincoln and her two sons, each receiving $36,765.

Mrs. Lincoln now took Tad abroad and lived in solitude, reading French novels and avoiding all Americans.

Soon she was pleading poverty again. She petitioned the United States Senate to grant her a yearly pension of five thousand dollars. The bill was greeted in the Senate with hisses from the gallery and words of abuse from the floor.

"It is a sneaking fraud!" cried Senator Howell of Iowa.

"Mrs. Lincoln was not true to her husband!" shouted Senator Yates of Illinois. "She sympathized with the rebellion. She is not worthy of our charity."

After months of delay and torrents of condemnation she was finally given three thousand a year.

In the summer of 1871 Tad died of typhoid fever, passing away in violent agony. Robert, her only remaining son, was married.

Alone, friendless, and in despair, Mary Lincoln became the prey of obsessions. One day in Jacksonville, Florida, she bought a cup of coffee and then refused to drink it, swearing it was poisoned.

Boarding a train for Chicago, she wired the family physician, imploring him to save Robert's life. But Robert was not ill. He met her at the station and spent a week with her at the Grand Pacific Hotel, hoping to quiet her.

Often in the middle of the night she would rush to his room, declaring that fiends were attempting to murder her, that Indians "were pulling wires out of her brain," that "doctors were taking steel springs out of her head."

In the daytime she visited the stores, making absurd purchases, paying, for example, three hundred dollars for lace curtains when she had no home in which to hang them.

With a heavy heart Robert Lincoln applied to the County Court of Chicago, for a trial of his mother's sanity. A jury of twelve men decided that she was insane, and she was confined in a private asylum at Batavia, Illinois.

At the end of thirteen months she was, unfortunately, released—released, but not cured. Then the poor, ailing woman went abroad to live among strangers, refusing to write Robert or let him know her address.

One day while living alone in Pau, France, she mounted a step-ladder to hang a picture above the fireplace; the ladder broke, and she fell, injuring her spinal cord. For a long time, she was unable even to walk.

Returning to her native land to die, she spent her last days at the home of her sister Mrs. Edwards, in Springfield, saying over and over: "You ought to pray now that I be taken to my husband and children."

Although she then had six thousand dollars in cash and seventy-five thousand in government bonds, nevertheless her mind was constantly racked by absurd fears of poverty, and she was haunted by the fear that Robert, then Secretary of War, would be assassinated like his father.

Longing to escape from the harsh realities that pressed upon her, she shunned every one, closed her doors and windows, pulled down the shades, darkened her room, and lighted a candle even when the sun was shining bright.

"No urging," says her physician, "would induce her to go out into the fresh air."

And there, amidst the solitude and soft quiet of the candle-light, her memory doubtless winged its way back across the cruel years, and, dwelling at last among the cherished thoughts of her young womanhood, she imagined herself waltzing once more with Stephen A. Douglas, charmed by his gracious manner and listening to the rich music of his melodious vowels and clear-cut consonants.

At times she imagined that her other sweetheart, a young man named Lincoln—Abraham Lincoln—was coming to court her that night. True, he was only a poor, homely, struggling lawyer who slept in an attic above Speed's store, but she believed he might be President if she could stimulate him to try hard, and, eager to win his love, she longed to make herself beautiful for him. Although she had worn nothing but the deepest black for fifteen years, she would, at such times, slip down to the stores in Springfield; and, according to her physician, she purchased and piled up "large quantities of silks and dress goods in trunks and by the cart load, which she never used and which accumulated until it was really feared that the floor of the store room would give way."

In 1882, on a peaceful summer evening, the poor, tired, tempestuous soul was given the release for which she had so often prayed. Following a paralytic stroke, she passed quietly away in her sister's house where, forty years before, Abraham Lincoln had put on her finger a ring bearing the words: "Love is eternal."

* * *

33

* * *

IN 1876, a gang of counterfeiters tried to steal Lincoln's body. It is an astonishing story, which few books on Lincoln say anything about.

"Big Jim" Kinealy's gang, one of the cleverest counterfeiting crews that ever vexed and perplexed the United States Secret Service, had its headquarters, during the seventies, in the guileless corn-and-hog town of Lincoln, Illinois.

For years Big Jim's suave and mild-mannered "shovers," as they were called, had been sneaking out across the country and shoving bogus five-dollar bills across the counters of credulous merchants. The profits had been fantastic. But by the spring of 1876, a deadly paralysis was creeping over the gang, for their supply of counterfeit currency was almost exhausted, and Ben Boyd, the master engraver who made their bogus greenbacks, was in prison.

For months Big Jim sniffed vainly about St. Louis and Chicago, trying to get another engraver to make counterfeit bills. Finally he resolved that somehow the invaluable Ben Boyd must be set free.

Big Jim conceived the unholy idea of stealing the body of Abraham Lincoln, and hiding it away. Then, while the whole North was in an uproar, Big Jim would calmly drive a hard and fabulous bargain: he would agree to return the sacred corpse in exchange for Ben Boyd's pardon and a huge pile of gold.

Dangerous? Not at all. For Illinois had upon her statute-book no law against the purloining of bodies.

So in June, 1876, Big Jim set about clearing the decks for action. He despatched five of his conspirators to Springfield, where they opened a saloon and dance-hall, masquerading as bartenders while making their preparations.

Unfortunately for him, one of his "bartenders" drank too much whisky one Saturday night in June, drifted into a red-light house in Springfield, and talked too much. He boasted that he was soon going to have a barrelful of gold.

He whispered the details: on the eve of the next fourth of July, while Springfield was shooting off rockets, he would be out in the Oak Ridge Cemetery, "stealing old Lincoln's bones," as he put it; and late that night he would bury them in a sand-bar under a bridge spanning the Sangamon.

An hour later the parlor-house madam was hurrying to the police, to tell her thrilling news. By morning she had blabbed it to a dozen other men. Soon the whole town had the story, and the masquerading bartenders dropped their towels and fled the city.

But Big Jim was not defeated. He was only delayed. He shifted his headquarters from Springfield to 294 West Madison Street, Chicago. He owned a saloon there. In the front room his man, Terrence Mullen, dispensed liquor to working-men; and in the back he had a sort of club-room, a secret rendezvous for counterfeiters. A bust of Abraham Lincoln stood over the bar.

For months a thief named Lewis G. Swegles had been patronizing this saloon and working himself into the good graces of Big Jim's gang. He admitted that he had served two terms in the penitentiary for stealing horses, and boasted that he was now "the boss body-snatcher of Chicago." He declared he supplied the medical schools of the town with most of their cadavers. That sounded plausible enough then, for grave-robbing was a national horror; medical colleges, in order to obtain bodies for dissection in their class rooms, were forced to buy them from ghouls who sneaked up to the rear door at two o'clock in the morning, with caps pulled low over their eyes and bulging sacks slung across their backs.

Swegles and Kinealy's gang perfected the details of their plan for rifling Lincoln's tomb. They would stuff the body into a long sack, pitch it into the bottom of a spring-wagon, and, with relays of fresh horses, would drive with all possible speed to northern Indiana; and there with only the water-fowl to see them, they would hide the body among the lonely dunes, where the wind from over the lake would soon wipe out all tell-tale tracks in the shifting sands.

Before leaving Chicago, Swegles bought a London news-paper; and, tearing out a piece, he stuffed the rest inside the bust of Lincoln that stood over the bar at 294 West Madison Street. That night, November 6, he and two of Big Jim's gang climbed aboard a Chicago & Alton train headed for Spring-field, taking with them the fragment of torn newspaper, which they proposed to leave beside the empty sarcophagus as they dashed off with the body. The detectives finding the paper would naturally keep it as a clue. Then while the nation was rocking with excitement, one of the gang would approach the governor of the State and offer to return Lincoln's body for two hundred thousand dollars in gold and the freedom of Ben Boyd.

And how would the governor know that the self-styled spokesman was not an impostor? The gangster would carry with him the London newspaper; the detectives, fitting their frag-ment into the torn page, would accept him as the bona-fide representative of the ghouls.

The gang arrived in Springfield, according to schedule. They had chosen what Swegles called "a damned elegant time" for their adventure. November 7 was election day; for months the Democrats had been denouncing the Republicans for the graft and corruption that had besmirched Grant's second administra-tion, while the Republicans had waved the "bloody shirt" of the Civil War in the face of the Democrats. It was one of the most bitter elections in United States history. That night, while ex-cited crowds were milling about the newspaper offices and jam-ming the saloons, Big Jim's men hurried out to Oak Ridge Cemetery—dark now, and deserted—sawed the padlock off the iron door of Lincoln's tomb, stepped inside, pried the marble lid off the sarcophagus, and lifted the wooden casket half out.

One of the gang ordered Swegles to bring up the horses and spring-wagon which he had been delegated to have ready and waiting in a ravine two hundred yards northeast of the monu-ment. Swegles hurried down the steep bluff until he was lost in the darkness.

Swegles was not a grave-robber. He was a reformed criminal

now employed as a stool-pigeon by the Secret Service. He had no team and wagon waiting in the ravine; but he did have eight detectives waiting for him in the memorial room of the tomb. So he raced around there and gave them the signal they had all agreed upon: he struck a match, lighted a cigar, and whispered the password *"Wash."*

The eight Secret Service men, in their stocking-feet, rushed out of their hiding-place, every man with a cocked revolver in each hand. They dashed around the monument with Swegles, stepped into the dark tomb, and ordered the ghouls to surrender.

There was no answer. Tyrrell, the district chief of the Secret Service, lighted a match. There lay the coffin, half out of the sarcophagus. But where were the thieves? The detectives searched the cemetery in all directions. The moon was coming up over the tree-tops. As Tyrrell rushed up onto the terrace of the monument, he could make out the forms of two men, staring at him from behind a group of statuary. In the excitement and confusion, he began firing at them with both pistols, and in an instant they were firing back. But they weren't the thieves. He was shooting at his own men.

In the meantime, the thieves, who had been waiting a hundred feet away in the darkness, for Swegles to return with the horses, dashed off through the woods.

Ten days later they were caught in Chicago, brought to Springfield, thrown into a jail, and surrounded by heavy guards day and night. For a time there was intense public excitement and indignation. Lincoln's son Robert, who had married into the wealthy Pullman family, employed the best lawyers in Chicago to prosecute the gang. They did what they could, but they had a hard time. There was no law in Illinois, then, against stealing a body. If the thieves had actually stolen the coffin, they might have been prosecuted for that, but they hadn't stolen it; they had not taken it out of the tomb. So the best the high-priced attorneys from Chicago could do was to prosecute the ghouls for having *conspired* to steal a coffin worth seventy-five dollars, the maximum penalty for which offense was five years. But the case did not come to trial for eight months; public indignation had died down by that time, and politics were at work; and, on the first ballot, four jurors actually voted for acquittal. After a few more ballots the twelve men compromised and sent the ghouls to the Joliet prison for one year.

Since Lincoln's friends were afraid that other thieves might steal the body, the Lincoln Monument Association hid it away for two years in an iron coffin under a heap of loose boards lying in a damp, dark passageway behind the catacombs—a sort of cellar. During that time thousands of pilgrims paid their respects to an empty sarcophagus.

For various reasons Lincoln's remains have been moved seventeen times. But they will be moved no more. The coffin is now imbedded in a great ball of steel and solid concrete, six feet beneath the floor of the tomb. It was placed there on September 26, 1901.

On that day the casket was opened, and human eyes gazed down for the last time upon his face. Those who saw him then remarked how natural he appeared. He had been dead thirty-six years; but the embalmers had done their work well, and he still looked very much as he had looked in life. His face was a trifle darker, and there was a touch of mold on one wing of his black tie.

BIBLIOGRAPHY

Badeau, Adam. *Grant in Peace.* Hartford, 1887.

Baker, Gen. La Fayette C. *History of the United States Secret Service.* L. C. Baker, Philadelphia, 1867.

Barton, William E. *The Life of Abraham Lincoln.* The Bobbs-Merrill Company, Indianapolis, 1925.

Barton, William E. *Lincoln at Gettysburg.* The Bobbs-Merrill Company, Indianapolis, 1930.

Barton, William E. *The Women Lincoln Loved.* The Bobbs-Merrill Company, Indianapolis, 1927.

Battles and Leaders of the Civil War. The Century Co., New York, 1887; 4 vols.

Beveridge, Albert J. *Abraham Lincoln.* Houghton Mifflin Company, Boston and New York, 1928.

Browne, Francis F. *The Every-day Life of Abraham Lincoln.* Brown & Howell Company, Chicago, 1913.

Carpenter, F. B. *Six Months at the White House with Abraham Lincoln.* Hurd & Houghton, New York, 1867.

Charnwood, Lord. *Abraham Lincoln.* Henry Holt & Company, New York, 1917.

Coggeshall, E. W. *The Assassination of Abraham Lincoln.* W. M. Hill, Chicago, 1920.

Columbia Historical Society Records.

Dewitt, D. M. *The Assassination of Abraham Lincoln and Its Expiation.* The Macmillan Company, New York, 1909.

Garland, Hamlin. *Ulysses S. Grant, His Life and Character.* The Macmillan Company, New York, 1898, 1920.

Grant, U. S. *Personal Memoirs.* The Century Co., New York, 1885, 1895; 2 vols.

Herndon, William H., and Weik, Jesse W. *The History and Personal Recollections of Abraham Lincoln.* The Herndon's Lincoln Publishing Company, Springfield, Illinois, 1888; 3 vols.

Keckley, Elizabeth. *Behind the Scenes, or Thirty Years a Slave and Four Years in the White House.* G. W. Carleton & Co., New York, 1868.

Lamon, Ward H. *Life of Abraham Lincoln.* Boston, 1872.

Lamon, Ward H. *Recollections of Abraham Lincoln, 1847–1865.* Edited by Dorothy Lamon Teillard. Teillard, Washington, D. C., 1911.

Lewis, Lloyd. *Myths after Lincoln.* Harcourt, Brace and Company, New York, 1929.

Macartney, Clarence E. *Lincoln and His Cabinet.* Charles Scribner's Sons, New York, 1931.

Macartney, Clarence E. *Lincoln and His Generals.* Dorrance and Company, Philadelphia, 1925.

Magazine of History.

Morrow, Honoré Willsie. *Mary Todd Lincoln, an Appreciation of the Wife of Abraham Lincoln.* William Morrow & Company, New York, 1928.

Nicolay, Helen. *Personal Traits of Abraham Lincoln.* The Century Co., New York, 1919.

Nicolay, John G., and Hay, John. *Abraham Lincoln: A History.* The Century Co., New York, 1890; 12 vols.

Oldroyd, Osborn H. *The Assassination of Abraham Lincoln.* Oldroyd, Washington, D. C., 1901.

Power, John C. *History of an Attempt to Steal the Body of Abraham Lincoln.* H. W. Rokker Printing and Publishing House, Springfield, Illinois, 1890.

Rhodes, James Ford. *History of the Civil War, 1861–1865.* The Macmillan Company, New York, 1917.

Rothschild, Alonzo. *Lincoln, Master of Men.* Houghton Mifflin Company, Boston and New York, 1912.

Sandburg, Carl. *Abraham Lincoln, the Prairie Years.* Harcourt, Brace and Company, New York, 1926.

Tarbell, Ida M. *The Life of Abraham Lincoln.* The Macmillan Company, New York, 1917.

Townsend, George A. *The Life, Crime and Capture of John Wilkes Booth.* Dick & Fitzgerald, New York, 1865.

Townsend, William H. *Lincoln and His Wife's Home Town.* The Bobbs-Merrill Company, Indianapolis, 1929.

Weik, Jesse W. *The Real Lincoln.* Houghton Mifflin Company, Boston and New York, 1922.

Wilson, Francis. *John Wilkes Booth; Fact and Fiction of Lincoln's Assassination.* Houghton Mifflin Company, Boston and New York.

Woodward, William E. *Meet General Grant.* Literary Guild of America, New York, 1928.